ELISHA THE PROPHET:

THE LESSONS

OF HIS HISTORY AND TIMES.

BY

ALFRED EDERSHEIM, M.A. (OXON.), D.D.,

VICAR OF LODERS.

New Edition—Revised.

———◆———

WIPF & STOCK · Eugene, Oregon

Wipf and Stock Publishers
199 W 8th Ave, Suite 3
Eugene, OR 97401

Elisha the Prophet
The Lessons of His History and Times
By Edersheim, Alfred
ISBN 13: 978-1-5326-5612-5
Publication date 4/23/2018
Previously published by The Religious Tract Society, 1882

PREFACE.

THIS book, which now appears in a revised form, does not lay claim to be either a Critical or a Historical Commentary, but is intended to follow the Scriptural account of the Life and Work of the Prophet Elisha with the view of pointing out their moral, and learning their lessons, as applicable to all times, and especially to our own. This will explain the absence of exegetical notes, and of all discussion of the points which have been raised, more particularly in connection with this portion of the Old Testament. For the treatment of such questions, as well for the History of that period generally, I must take leave to refer to the corresponding volume of my "Bible-History."

But, still a doctrinal, and, to a certain extent, a critical inference is here forced upon us at the outset. For, a record, so full of the miraculous, which yet can be analysed in all its parts, taken in its literality, and made, portion by portion, the basis of practical lessons, must be capable of rational and scientific defence; a life many centuries ago and under so different circumstances, that speaks to the men of all generations, and more especially to us, the same lessons of God, of His reign and of His grace; of faith, hope, and duty, which it did to them of old, cannot have been legendary, must have been real, God-sent and God-missioned: prophetic. For, this is characteristic of the Prophet: not that he merely foretold the future, nor yet that he admonished as from God in regard to the present, nor even that he combined these two; but that he foretold the future in its bearing on the present, and spake of the present as viewing it in the light of the future, and that he did both as commissioned of God, inspired by God, and working for God. And this, indeed, is the inmost character and the outmost vindication of Revelation itself. Thus, the practical application of the history of Elisha is, in this view of it, also its best critical defence and its historical evidence.

These remarks are, of course, not intended in any wise to keep out of view the strictly miraculous in the record of Elisha's Life. This is not only ever present, but occurs in the history of Elijah and of Elisha, so to speak, in perhaps a more concrete form than in any other portion of the Old Testament. Some of the special reasons for it have been indicated in another place.* But, in general, not to speak of the "need be" of teaching by miracles in the times of old, the miraculous is the necessary light upon what is called the Covenant-History, that is, on the record of God's dealings with His people of old. It both shows these dealings to have been Divine, and it teaches their meaning. It is the revealing of Revelation; the disclosure to them of old, and the evidence to us, that what God had spoken and done, was said and done by God. Without it the path on which God led His people of old, and the voice by which He spake to them, would be undistinguishable. Thus the miraculous is not outside of, forms not an addition to, but is an essential and integral part of the history of the Old Testament and of the people of God.

But we go further. For, to us at least, it is becoming increasingly clear, that the miraculous constitutes one of the necessary conditions of all theistic thinking. The Being and Presence of God *is* the miraculous, and it *implies* the

* See the preface to vol. v. of the "Bible-History."

miraculous: for He is the Living and the True God, and not merely Law or Force; but rather Force and Law are the outcome and the manifestation of God. On any theory therefore, which admits the Being and Presence of God, the miraculous must be the ever present, which, resting on the past, points to the future. Creation is a miracle, equal to, if not greater than any recorded in the Scriptures, and it points to the miracle of Resurrection. The Creation of the present world, out of the elements of a perished world, is as miraculous as the new Creation out of the ruins of the old; and so Creation is not only the *analogon*, but the basis, the symbol, and the type of the Resurrection. As facts they are both equally miraculous: above and beyond the observed laws, order, and succession of natural events, and the operation of what are called Natural Causes, that is, of such as fall within the province of reason and observation. They are miracles, which can neither be explained nor demonstrated, but which necessarily spring from that which implies all Miracles and makes them rational: the Being and the Presence of the Living God, and His purpose of love. And so man, the first Adam, was a miracle; and so the God-man, the second Adam is a miracle, only that, given the first miracle of the Creation, the second miracle of the Resurrection seems almost its sequence; and given the miracle of the first Adam, that of the second, the Lord from heaven, seems not only theologically but almost logically necessary. And all the miraculous in sacred history between these two extreme points, by which, in a sense, all history has become sacred, and attained a meaning, may be described as the links which bind the first and the last, the beginning and the end, into one bright Chain. That Chain is at the same time also the Chain of the Promises, of which in Christ is the Yea and through Him the Amen to the glory of God.

Thus much seemed necessary in the Preface to a volume the object of which is to bring to the men of the present generation the ever-present lessons of a history that is of the past, and yet not of the passing but of the ever present. In conclusion a brief personal explanation may be allowed. Nearly fifteen years have passed since this book first appeared; and almost as many since it has been out of print. It is now republished not only because, from the testimony of many, the Author has reason to believe that the book, in its original form, had proved useful and helpful, but also because he increasingly feels that the lessons of this history are more than ever suitable to the present time. In preparing it once more for the press, nothing had to be altered as regards the subject matter or the substance of the book: for the views of Divine Truth expressed in it at the first are believed to be derived from Holy Scripture, and will, God helping, be set forth and maintained to the end. But as regards the form, and the special mode of expressing these truths, there has been careful revision, the outcome of maturing thought during the years that have intervened— such progress as, in one way or another, will come to us all while under His teaching we are advancing on the road heavenwards. May God in infinite condescension and goodness bless and make use of it as heretofore to the glory of His own Name.

ALFRED EDERSHEIM.

BRIDPORT : *August*, 1882.

CONTENTS.

CHAP.		PAG
I.	THE HUSBANDMAN OF ABEL-MEHOLAH	
II.	THE LONELY WALK	1
III.	DEPARTED, NOT DEAD	2
IV.	ELISHA AND THE FIFTY STRONG MEN	3
V.	THE WATERS OF JERICHO	4
VI.	BETH-EL, OR BETH-AVEN	5
VII.	ELISHA AND THE THREE KINGS	6
VIII.	AN UNEXPECTED ALLY	7
IX.	THE WIDOW'S CRUSE	8
X.	THE GUEST-CHAMBER AT SHUNEM	9
XI.	EFFECTUAL FERVENT PRAYER	10
XII.	AN INTERRUPTED MEAL	11
XIII.	GRACE BEFORE MEAT	12
XIV.	THE CLOUD WITH THE SILVER LINING	13
XV.	THE WASHING OF REGENERATION !	15
XVI.	THE RENEWING OF THE HOLY GHOST	16
XVII.	DANGERS BY THE WAY	17
XVIII.	A VERY PRESENT HELP	18

CONTENTS.

CHAP.		PAGE
XIX.	An Unseen Host	196
XX.	More than Conquerors	208
XXI.	Famine in Samaria	219
XXII.	Unbelief Reproved	230
XXIII.	Strange Tidings	242
XXIV.	Bread Enough and to Spare	253
XXV.	Faith and its Recompense	264
XXVI.	Elisha at Damascus	276
XXVII.	Judgment Commenced	287
XVIII.	Jehu and Jehonadab	298
XXIX.	The Last Interview	309
XXX.	"He, being Dead, yet Speaketh"	318

ELISHA.

CHAPTER I.

THE HUSBANDMAN OF ABEL-MEHOLAH.

> "And the Lord said unto him, Go, return on thy way to the wilderness of Damascus: and when thou comest, anoint Hazael to be king over Syria: and Jehu the son of Nimshi shalt thou anoint to be king over Israel: and Elisha the son of Shaphat of Abel-Meholah shalt thou anoint to be prophet in thy room. And it shall come to pass, that him that escapeth the sword of Hazael shall Jehu slay: and him that escapeth from the sword of Jehu shall Elisha slay. Yet I have left me seven thousand in Israel, all the knees which have not bowed unto Baal, and every mouth which hath not kissed him. So he departed thence, and found Elisha the son of Shaphat, who was ploughing with twelve yoke of oxen before him, and he with the twelfth: and Elijah passed by him, and cast his mantle upon him. And he left the oxen, and ran after Elijah, and said, Let me, I pray thee, kiss my father and my mother, and then I will follow thee. And he said unto him, Go back again: for what have I done to thee? And he returned back from him, and took a yoke of oxen, and slew them, and boiled their flesh with the instruments of the oxen, and gave unto the people, and they did eat. Then he arose, and went after Elijah, and ministered unto him."
> —1 KINGS xix. 15-21.

THEY were dark and troublous days in which Elijah prophesied. The throne was occupied by Israel's weakest and most wicked ruler. King Ahab presented a strange combination of incongruous elements. Undoubtedly he knew, and, in a certain sense, believed the Revelation of Jehovah. Nor was he, despite his daring wickedness, a stranger to religious emotions. Sometimes, indeed, he seemed so entirely under their power as to give hope that

his character and conduct would in future be swayed by
them. Yet he always fell back, first into irresoluteness, and
then into his old sins. Like most weak people, he seemed
lacking in capacity for solid principle and conviction of any
kind. True religion was the only power which, through the
grace of God, would have imparted firmness and purpose to
his character. But true religion he knew not, and alternating
between fear and presumption, he remained all his life long
the ready tool in the hands of his wife Jezebel. Her
character and conduct well accorded with her descent. She
was the daughter of Ethbaal, who had succeeded to the
throne of Sidon by the murder of his predecessor, and who
combined with royalty the chief priesthood of Astarte.
Jezebel possessed, in no small measure, the fanaticism, the
firmness, and the fierceness, for which her race was famous
in history. Never, perhaps, did a single individual exercise
a wider* or more pernicious influence. She flattered the
weakness, and indulged the unrestrained selfishness of Ahab.
In this, however, she only acted consistently with her
Phœnician notions of royalty. The stern independence of
the true Israelite would be not only opposed to all her ideas,
but absolutely hateful to her. It may have been as much
the haughty queen as the fanatical daughter of the chief
priest of Astarte who provided for the maintenance of Baal-
worship. For reasons such as these, Queen Jezebel hated
the religion of Jehovah, and one of the objects of her life
seems to have been to uproot His worship from the land.

In such a time of danger and irreligion, God unexpectedly
sent unexpected help. And this, not by removing the house
of Ahab, nor even by judgment on Jezebel, but by arousing

* It is sufficient to notice that Athaliah, Queen of Judah, was the
daughter of Jezebel. How closely her character resembled that of her
mother, is well known.

His people to the realising conviction that Jehovah was the Living and True God, and that He reigned. Like one of those eastern torrents which bursts with impetuous rush from the mountain-side, carries terror and destruction along its course, and then as suddenly dries up and disappears, Elijah the Tishbite descended from his mountain wilds, discharged his mission, and again disappeared, after laying upon the land and people a three and a half years' curse of utter barrenness and desolation. Equally unexpected was his return at the close of that period. At the gathering on Mount Carmel, the question, as between Jehovah and Baal, was publicly answered by the nation. Evidently the object of Elijah's mission had been to startle by its suddenness, and, by exhibiting the unlimited power of God, to prove that "Jehovah, He is God." And with this corresponds his very name—Elijah, whether we render it "Jehovah is God," or "the strength of Jehovah." Such being its purpose, the mission of Elijah, like that of John the Baptist, though eminently suited to the circumstances and wants of the people, could only be transient and preparatory.

Incredible though it may seem, even the scene on Mount Carmel had made no salutary impression upon Jezebel. Perhaps she regarded the God of Israel as only one of many national deities, and Elijah as a magician more powerful than her priests. The triumph of this God and the ascendency of His prophet only increased the intensity of her hatred. Religion was to her a matter not of absolute truth or the opposite, but a question between national deities, just as in our days many regard all religions as substantially the same; the difference in their opinion lying in the greater or less earnestness, devotedness, and influence of the worshippers. Accordingly, through her influence, Ahab's temporary resolution in favour of Jehovah was soon disposed of, and a vow of revenge, more fierce than any previous, indicated that the long-pending controversy was at last to be brought to the issue of a personal question between the queen and the prophet. And now his life was no longer safe even among the people which had but yesterday owned the Lord. Not one friendly hand was stretched forth from among the thousands who had yesterday witnessed the marvellous display on Mount Carmel. Not a home in Israel could shelter him, on whose head the fierce Phœnician had set such a price. Was this their loudly proclaimed faith in Jehovah—this the only result of his labours? Like John the Baptist's in the mountain-prison of Machærus, the prophet's heart failed. In bitterness and desolateness, he pursued his lonely flight to the ancient Beersheba, the southernmost border of the land, without a sign from God, or a companion among men. But God could not and would not forsake His servant; He assured him of His presence and help by miraculous provision. The Lord will deliver and sustain—but only for further duty; it may be for further trial. Onward must the prophet press by unfrequented paths and lonely by-ways, till he reaches Horeb, the mount of God. There he learns the issue. The signs and seals of his ministry of judgment shall not be wanting; nor yet the comfort of fellowship be withheld. Jezebel and Baal cannot triumph. The storm of wrath shall burst upon an apostate race. Hazael is to be anointed King of Syria, and Jehu King of Israel. This in judgment; but in His kindness has the Lord called Elisha, the son of Shaphat, to be a true yoke-fellow to Elijah. In compassion, only the last of these commissions is to be discharged by the aged prophet himself. As for the mission of Elijah—that of preparation for judgment and mercy—it is drawing to a close. Henceforth another must enter on his labours.

Once more Elijah is directed to turn northwards. But how different does the scene appear! It is as if nature herself sympathised with the visions of comfort and help so lately presented to the soul of the prophet. He now passed through a country, smiling in all the luxuriance of a new spring. The recent plenteous rains had softened the long-parched fields, inviting the labours of the husbandmen by cheerful prospects of plenty. Everywhere the neglected operations were resumed; herds and flocks were browsing in the meadows; busy hands were rapidly putting in the seed. Upwards he travelled along the fertile valley of the Jordan, signs of life and happiness multiplying, till he reached the well-known district of Abel-Meholah. Here the eye of the prophet rested on a busy scene. Twelve yoke of oxen were ploughing up the ground—eleven in charge of hired servants, the twelfth guided by the master's son. Whithersoever he looked, all was the property of one man, and he a true Israelite. These are the fields, and this the cattle of Shaphat; these men are his servants, and this is his son Elisha, whom the prophet had come to call to the service of the Lord.

Better preparation or greater suitableness for the work could scarcely have been found than in Elisha. The son of a godly household, his was the ancient faith of Israel. The times were sadly degenerate, but even in the capital there were uncompromising Naboths, and at court, devout, though perhaps weak Obadiahs. But in the remote country districts, in the peaceful Jordan valley, in places unfrequented by strangers, like Abel-Meholah, there must have been many a home in which the knee had never been bent to Baal. Undoubtedly Shaphat and his son were among the seven thousand faithful witnesses in Israel. The very name Elisha, while unconsciously prophetic of his mission, was also expressive of Shaphat's conviction, that Jehovah was "the

God of salvation," or (otherwise rendered) "my God is salvation." Far from the corruption, the luxury, and the idolatry of the court, Elisha had grown up in the habits of a simple piety. If further evidence of this were required, we should unhesitatingly find it in the reference to the religious feast in the family, which signalised the call of Elisha, and in the ready acquiescence of Shaphat, when his son devoted himself to such a work, and under such circumstances.

A marked characteristic of Elisha was, *contentment with his position and willingness to fulfil its duties, however humble.* It is almost a truism that his whole history shows him to have been distinguished by natural gifts, by strength of character, and by the possession of Divine grace. His outward circumstances were those of wealth and influence. Yet, though, in a manner, born to rule, he was willing to serve, that so he might serve his God. Contentedly he plied his humble avocation, waiting till God, if He pleased, called him to a higher and more prominent place. Men's estimate of themselves is generally in the inverse *ratio* of their qualifications. How few, possessed of gifts, are willing to wait the call of God; how few even without gifts, or else who imagine they have gifts, are willing to wait! It seems to be forgotten that incapacity to serve God in "a few things," is evidence of inability to serve Him in many, and that he who cannot make it possible to be faithful in little, may never be entrusted with that which is great. Besides, the idea seems, at least unconsciously, to obtain, that a certain position or certain circumstances are requisite in order to serve God, that somehow the active service of God must be incompatible with the ordinary duties of daily life, or, at any rate, with such humble avocations as following the plough. The opposite is the case. There is a vast difference between *worship* and *service.*

We *serve* God in *our own* houses, having worshipped Him in *His* house. Service is work, and work for Him where *He* places us, not where we place ourselves. If we cannot or do not serve God in the humble place and in the daily duties which He has assigned to us, assuredly we never can nor will serve Him in any other place or circumstances. That religion must be spurious which leads either to neglect or to a mean estimate of every-day duties—of the duties of home and the home circle—even if it were to exchange them for the excitement of religious meetings. These are, or may be, means of refreshment, of fellowship, and of strengthening, but only to enable us to serve our Lord Jesus Christ in the humbler and more difficult walks of every-day life. But religion consists not in those means, nor in the excitement sometimes connected with them. True religion must act as leaven in every relationship of life. And then, in measure as we are faithful and diligent in whatsoever our hand findeth to do, we may hope to be employed in greater service. Perhaps there would be more religion in the house, if we sought it less out of the house, and rather learned this humbling yet ennobling lesson: in everything to adorn the doctrine of God our Saviour.

Equally marked was Elisha's *readiness to hear the call of God*. It is dangerous either to go before or to lag behind the Providence or the call of God. If the Lord has work for us, He will call us to it. But we must cultivate a spirit of attentive, prayerful readiness. Not that we expect an audible call from heaven, nor trust to an inward voice, but that God will so dispose of all things as to make our duty very plain. For this we must be content to wait; when it comes, we must be willing to obey and to follow. Moses was left for forty years in Midian before he was called to be the leader of Israel; Elisha followed for many years the plough; and we may have before us years of labour and of trial. Yet, when the call came, Elisha immediately recognised that for which he had long been prepared in heart. To many the humble ploughman might have appeared a strange candidate for the prophetic office, very unsuited to the times and the circumstances. And his preparation may seem very different from our conventional ideas of such matters. But let there be no misunderstanding. God forbid that intellect, culture, or education, should be lightly set by. They are good gifts of God, to be consecrated to His service and for His glory. But the call of God consists not in them. They are outward helps for which we should be thankful, and which we are to use as *outward helps*. But if we confound the primary with the secondary, the substance with the accessories, we turn things strangely upside down. There is an outward call, as there is an inward call; an outward preparation, as there is inward preparation. To overlook the *inward* call and preparation were spiritual ignorance and presumption. To ignore the *outward* call and preparation were folly and fanaticism. Nor are the two incompatible. Both are the gifts of God. The one is spiritual, the other external; the one the gift of His Providence, the other that of His grace. But, in His kingdom, providence and grace always work together for His glory.

Another feature in this narrative is *Elisha's personal willingness to follow the call of God to its utmost consequences*. Even less devout husbandmen than Shaphat and his son must, during the three and a half years' barrenness and famine, have learned to know Elijah and his mission. Probably they were among those who, on the summons of the prophet, had hastened to Mount Carmel, and there had witnessed the miraculous interposition of Jehovah. And now the appearance of him, clothed in camel's hair, and girt about the loins with a girdle of skin, was not that of a stranger. The act of Elijah as, in passing by, he unfastened his mantle and threw it over Elisha, was deeply significant. It meant that the one was to appear like the other—that he was to hold the same office, and to discharge the same functions. With the quickness of a ready heart, the son of Shaphat understood the meaning of this action. It was not to a position of wealth, of ease, or of influence that he now felt called. On the contrary, all this had to be relinquished. He, a man of peace, was called from home, friends, and comforts, to endure hardship, to suffer persecution, to bear scorn. Yet he offered not frivolous excuses nor unbelieving objections, but arose and followed the Master. Elijah had passed on, as if unconcerned how Elisha received the call. It had been addressed to him, and it was his part voluntarily to decide for or against its acceptance. This explains what follows in the narrative. Hastening after the prophet, Elisha requested permission to bid farewell to his family and friends; or, as Matthew Henry puts it, he would. "*take* leave, not *ask* leave." The answer of Elijah, "Go back, for what have I done unto thee?" is intended not as a rebuke, but as a trial. It meant, in effect: Unless your heart fully responds; if it fondly lingers on the past, go back to your home. With the call of Christ comes always the decisive question: Are we really willing to follow after Him, not as of necessity, nor from a painful sense of duty, but of a ready mind and joyous heart, choosing Christ as our portion, and deeming His reproach greater riches than the treasures of Egypt? It is as if Elijah had said: Do you ask what future may await you, what work or what trials? I know not. If this call finds an echo in your heart, come; if not, forbear! Come, not because *I* called you; see to it that this be the call of God, to which your heart fully responds; learn for "the excellency of the knowledge of Christ" to count "all things but loss," or else do not regard the call. Only a "*willing* people" can serve Him "in the beauties of holiness." Religion, to be genuine, must be of our own free and joyous, though spiritual, choice. It is not a matter of necessity, the offspring of fear of hell, but the gladsome consent of the heart to the gracious call of the Lord.

And this would remove many difficulties and answer many questions. There are some who argue every point—how much of the world must I give up? what wrong is there in this or that worldly amusement—in the opera, in the theatre, or at the ball? These and similar questions betray only ignorance of the nature of spiritual religion. We refuse to entertain arguments on such points. Who has asked you not to go to the theatre or to the ball-room? Who requires our contributions to the cause of God—or, indeed, that we should take up the cross and follow Him? If our heart cleaves to the world and its pleasures as our god, we are still of the world and in the world. But let us also remember that if our heart *delights* not in the Lord, if His ways are not pleasantness and peace, we still want the first element in genuine religion—a renewed heart.

It is a matter of deep interest to notice, that, contrary to what might have been expected, Elisha met with no difficulty in following the prophet. Like the pilgrim who feared the lion by the way, we too often anticipate imaginary trials and dangers. If we only go forward in simple faith, we shall find that our fears have been groundless. There is not a lion in the way, or else he is chained. Let us not anticipate at all. Assuredly "sufficient unto the day is the evil thereof;" and more than sufficient is He to Whom we have committed both this day, the morrow, and every day.

Elisha immediately began his ministry, and that in his

own house and among his kindred. As in the case of Matthew the publican, the feast of leave-taking, to which the narrative refers, was unquestionably religious—in this instance, most probably sacrificial. In a very marked sense every conversion to God and every service for God must be connected with leave-taking. We must part from friends; we must give up all; we must separate ourselves; we must come out from the world around. And every leave-taking is, in its nature, painful. But how precious to make this leave-taking not needlessly morose, but a religious *festival;* and the first act of our ministry, a joyous testimony to Christ.

The functions which Elisha had at first to perform were of a very humble character. He is described as pouring water on the hands of the prophet, or, in other words, as his personal attendant. There is a voluntary, and therefore false humility, when from choice men leave their proper stations, and the duties which God has assigned to them, for positions and circumstances of their fanciful devising. But humility in the service of our Lord is not produced by outward means, nor is it self-sought. It consists in accepting with a ready heart whatever station God assigns to us. True service lies in setting the Master before us, wherever He may be pleased to place us, and in doing whatsoever our hand findeth to do, with our whole heart, cheerfully, and as unto the Lord. And such humility springs from grace within, not from circumstances without; such service will find its ready opportunities of glorifying the Lord, whether at Abel-Meholah, or in attendance upon Elijah.

CHAPTER II.

THE LONELY WALK.

"And it came to pass, when the Lord would take up Elijah into heaven by a whirlwind, that Elijah went with Elisha from Gilgal. And Elijah said unto Elisha, Tarry here, I pray thee; for the Lord hath sent me to Beth-el. And Elisha said unto him, As the Lord liveth, and as thy soul liveth, I will not leave thee. So they went down to Beth-el. And the sons of the prophets that were at Beth-el came forth to Elisha, and said unto him, Knowest thou that the Lord will take away thy master from thy head to-day? And he said, Yea, I know it; hold ye your peace. And Elijah said unto him, Elisha, tarry here, I pray thee; for the Lord hath sent me to Jericho. And he said, As the Lord liveth, and as thy soul liveth, I will not leave thee. So they came to Jericho. And the sons of the prophets that were at Jericho came to Elisha, and said unto him, Knowest thou that the Lord will take away thy master from thy head to-day? And he answered, Yea, I know it; hold ye your peace. And Elijah said unto him, Tarry, I pray thee, here; for the Lord hath sent me to Jordan. And he said, As the Lord liveth, and as thy soul liveth, I will not leave thee. And they two went on. And fifty men of the sons of the prophets went, and stood to view afar off: and they two stood by Jordan. And Elijah took his mantle, and wrapped it together, and smote the waters, and they were divided hither and thither, so that they two went over on dry ground."—2 KINGS ii. 1-8.

THERE seems no reason to doubt that in the interval between this and the events recorded in a former chapter, Elisha had faithfully followed and humbly served his great master. The silence of Scripture affords no argument to the contrary. For, sacred history is mainly the record of God's covenant-dealings. It chronicles events with the view of illustrating these dealings. Men and their actions are referred to only so far as needful to show what is the working of the Almighty. Keeping this in mind, we may be able in some measure to understand why seemingly trivial circumstances are related, while others of apparently greater importance are omitted from the Old and the New Testament. There was no necessity for detailing much of the private history of patriarchs, prophets, and apostles, however interesting it might have been; there was no need for relating even the events of the infancy and youth of our Blessed Saviour Himself. They might have found a place in a history written from the human point of view; they form the theme of a large portion of the so-called Apocryphal writings; but they are not recorded in the inspired Scriptures. The silence of the Lord, both in His Word and in His Providence, is as solemn and impressive as are His utterances.

Hitherto Elisha had evidently occupied the subordinate position of a witness and a learner. He was now to be called to the forefront of the battle. The time had come when "the Lord would take up Elijah." His work on earth was done, his rest in heaven was to begin. No man is "taken" till his work, whatever it be, is fully done. This is not fatalism, but blessed comfort to the labourers in God's vineyard. "It is vain to rise up early, to sit up late, to eat the bread of sorrow: for so He giveth His beloved sleep." Faith in this respect also knows not fear. Not that such conviction will make us presumptuous, or wanting in that due care which is even implied in the command: "Thou shalt not kill." But it will help to keep us trustful and confident in the work of the Lord. In a certain sense, indeed, the statement just made applies not merely to the children of God. No man is taken till *all* has been finished. There is a ripening either for heaven or for hell, presently going on in the case of every one. The harvest is not gathered till all is fully ripe. The patience and the long-suffering of God waiteth till the measure is accomplished. And there is a measure of wrath to be accomplished, or else a cup of blessing to be filled. *Then* cometh the translation—either upwards to the Father's house or downwards to eternal loss. What a deeply solemn thought that each moment of life, as it imperceptibly passes, is filling up the measure of the one, or finishing the complement of the other. What influence ought this to have on our speaking and hearing, on our reading and praying, on our waiting and working!

"The Lord would take up Elijah into heaven by *a whirlwind*." God has various messengers and various modes of having His commands executed. Sometimes He takes by a whirlwind, at others the "still small voice" summons home His saints. Sometimes His angels seem visibly to bear them on their hands, at others the saints fall asleep in the Lord. Sometimes bystanders are allowed to catch glimpses of the glory which surrounds almost visibly those who are taken into heaven; at others the change is gradual and still. But what matters it, if we but safely reach our home? We may rest assured that God has chosen the mode best suited, alike for those who are taken, and for those who are left behind. Surely, as there are differences in the manner in which God first calls His own, so there are in that in which He at last takes them unto Himself. And Christians should not be unduly concerned about the circumstances which may attend their death-bed. These are among the cares of the morrow, which we ought rather to cast upon Him Who "giveth more grace," satisfied that "the Lord knoweth them that are His," and that "precious in the sight of the Lord is the death of His saints."

It is a curious gloss of some Jewish writers, that Elijah was taken up *to* heaven, but not *into* heaven. The interest which, in our minds, attaches to the event, arises from precisely the opposite of this statement. Not the outward glory, nor the surrounding circumstances, but the fact that the prophet was admitted into the immediate presence of

God, fills us with wonder. In connection with this, it is remarkable that the only two who were thus honoured stood each in special relation to the Lord Jesus. The one, Enoch, prophesied of His second coming; the other, Elijah, was His great forerunner, in the person of John the Baptist. And now that the Lord Himself has ascended up, the first-fruits of them that believe, we await the voice of the Archangel, which shall waken the dead and summon the living "to meet the Lord in the air," that so we may for ever be with Him.

Very significant was the selection of places through which the last lonely walk of Elijah and Elisha must lead them. They passed by Gilgal, where Israel, preceded by the ark of the covenant, had crossed Jordan dry-shod, and where the memorial of God's interposition was still to be seen. The analogy was too striking not to have recalled the event to the two pilgrims. And there was Beth-el, where Jacob in rapt vision had beheld the ladder that connected heaven with earth; and here was Jericho, whose walls had once crumbled into dust before the war-summons of the Lord; and there, again, winding Jordan, which was so soon to part its waters once more.

Thoughts, of which words would have been most inadequate expression, must have filled the hearts of the two prophets. The silence of that walk was only broken by a strange demand, thrice repeated, on the part of Elijah: "Tarry here, I pray thee; for the Lord hath sent me to Bethel," "to Jericho," "to Jordan." What was the meaning of this mysterious request? Was it humility on the part of Elijah, unwillingness to appear before Elisha as more honoured than others had been? Was it a desire to meditate alone on the glory about to be revealed, and to prepare his mind for the solemn event about to take place? But, surely, none of these feelings could at that time have influenced Elijah to make a suggestion, which, if answered otherwise than by Elisha, would have been fraught with such sad consequences, not only to Elisha, but to all Israel. In truth, to understand the narrative, we must try to realise the issue placed before Elisha. He was now to be called to the post of highest honour, but also of greatest responsibility. Was he qualified for it? Had he not deceived himself, and mistaken sincere intentions for a readiness to follow and to obey without reasoning and without questioning? For, this was the first, in one sense the only, qualification for the prophetic office—to obey the Lord literally, to do and to say not less and not more than the Lord directed. It was in this that a prophet of old had failed, when, contrary to the express directions of the Lord, he was persuaded by another prophet to return and to eat bread with him. And to mark for all time the utter disqualification which such divided allegiance implied, terrible judgment had been executed upon him. There really are no cross-providences. Duties can never conflict, and whatsoever is directly pointed out to us by the Word of God can never be set aside, either by what seems a cross-providence or by an advice or command, even though it came from a man of God. In the present instance the grand question was, whether Elisha would obey the plain direction of the Lord, implied in his call to be the minister of Elijah, and continue with him through the approaching death-scene, or else be turned by *any* consideration from the plain path of duty. Under such circumstances it is always dangerous to reason. Satan is a far better logician than we, and good reasons, nay, even prophets' commands, will not be long wanting if a man is desirous of following the bent of his own inclination. Good reasons have always been found for doing that which is wrong.

But, viewing the matter more attentively, the language of

Elijah does not really imply a wish on his part that Elisha should leave him. The prophet states only this as the reason for his demand: "Tarry here, *for* the Lord hath sent me." A long and lonely walk is yet before me, and at the end of it there may await me other and very difficult work. It is better for thee to tarry behind. Similarly, yet from no wish to part from her daughters, Naomi said to them, "Go, return, *for* I am going to my own country." Toil and difficulties await me—turn back; a divided heart is not capable of passing through such trials. There are periods in the history of each among us—sifting, searching, trying times—when our faith and patience will be severely tested. Then, as in the case of Elisha, the question will practically be: Are we prepared to follow, no matter what the difficulties or the trials before us; simply to *follow*, neither questioning the length nor the incidents of the road? Thrice was the suggestion repeated, as when our Lord thrice asked the son of Jonas: "Lovest thou Me?" But there can be no crown without the cross, nor will double portion of the Spirit come without the lonely walk. And so Elisha replied with the strongest possible asseveration, as if it had been wrung out of the inmost soul of that strong man. Come what may, he will cleave to Elijah, even through the waters of Jordan, and through a vision which the heart may tremble to contemplate. He has put his hand to the plough, and he will not look back. And must not this be the experience of every Christian? There are many things around to turn us aside—chief among them, perhaps, when an Elijah himself apparently suggests our going back. It would seem as if we could not do wrong in following his suggestion. Yet it is, after all, but a trial of our faith, such as, in some form or another, will assuredly come to prove, if it were by fire, whether our religion be God-born or man-imparted.

Another incident occurred during this long and lonely walk. At two different places, at Beth-el and Jericho, the "sons of the prophets" came to meet them, influenced by the knowledge that Elijah was to be taken from earth. For the last time they would see the great prophet. Good and questionable motives, religion and religious curiosity, strangely mingled in their conduct. But to Elijah it must have been refreshing to behold in these professed servants of Jehovah a practical reply to his former mournful complaint of being left alone to bear witness to the truth. There were now many, and not only at Ramah and at Kirjath-jearim (1 Sam. x. and xix.), but also at Beth-el and at Jericho, in preparation for the service of the Lord. These schools, from which, as we may infer, many of the prophets proceeded (comp. Amos vii. 14), must have formed a delightful subject of thought for an old prophet about to be removed from his work. The very existence of these schools reminded Israel of better times; their continuance was a germ of hope for the future. There the Word of God would be studied, the dealings of Jehovah traced, and the spiritual meaning of the sacrifices, the services, and the history of Israel considered. Thence, as from a centre, would issue much spiritual knowledge. And surely, if such systematic preparation for the work of the Lord was proper under the Old Testament, it must be so in our days, when there are so many and varied adversaries to meet, and when, if ever, it is needful that the servants of Christ should combine the simplicity of the dove with the wisdom of the serpent. Why should we serve the Lord with that which has cost us neither labour, study, nor preparation? *Beaten* oil was required for the temple-lamp; why then should its quality be now deemed matter of small importance? Most true, it is the grace of God which alone can convert a soul. Most true, the gospel is a simple declaration of the love of God in the gift of our Blessed Saviour, and the more simply and plainly it is presented the better. But is there in all this anything inconsistent with study and preparation? Does learning detract from grace? It is not intended to substitute learning for grace; but may not grace sanctify learning, and so consecrate it unto God? If we are unwilling to entrust our health or outward affairs to those who have not made such matters subject of special study—and this, although we trust for the result, not to the goodness of the means, but to the blessing of God—why should we not similarly act in reference to religious instruction? That highly educated persons may be destitute of religion is surely an argument not against the use, but the abuse of education, and only proves the need of combining grace with learning.

Perhaps no better illustration of these principles could be found than in the state of the schools of the prophets at the time of Elijah. Evidently their influence was little felt for good in the land. And we scarcely wonder at it. For there are times of general lukewarmness and unfaithfulness, when even true Christians, without loosing their personal hold of the truth or of the Lord, decrease in spirituality, and the fine gold seems to become dim. This may specially be the case if a district or place be deprived of sound and faithful religious instruction, or if, in the public services, there is more *about* Christ than *of* Christ. In the days of Jezebel, the prophets of Baal had too long held a prominent position in the land not to exercise an influence for evil, indirectly, even on the schools of the prophets.

It is thus that we regard the attitude, the bearing, and even the question with which they now met Elisha. Their strange forwardness and officiousness, their eagerness to bring bad tidings, and ultimately their intrusive curiosity at the most solemn scene of all, sprang from a sincere but spurious religiousness, which too often finds its counterpart among us. There are morbid dispositions whose eagerness to communicate evil tidings outruns their zeal in any other direction. There is not a scandal in the Church, not a danger in the world, nor a sorrow past, present, or future, which forms not a favourite topic of their conversation. It is a strange manifestation of our love of the Church to be always speaking of her divisions and her weaknesses. If we really feel them, let us make it rather the subject of prayer than of talk. And then how rapidly evils seem to grow as they are repeated! Much of this talk may, no doubt, be due rather to idleness than to evil intention; but we ought to remember that far deeper and more painful wounds have been inflicted, and often far more harm done to the cause of God by an idle, than even by an evil tongue. Against the latter we may be on our guard; the former takes us at unawares. Words are winged messengers of peace or of war, of life or of death; and it is far better, difficult as to some it may seem, to be silent than to speak, when such speaking is in the service of the devil, rather than of God.

The attitude of these fifty men, standing "to view afar off," seems to indicate a mixture of religion and unreligion, similar to that implied in their question to Elisha. They seem rather to have desired the gratification of their religious curiosity than to derive any spiritual lesson. And so it often is in our days. Whenever a great work, such as a revival, is going on, a large number, a mixed multitude, are attracted who really have no spiritual interest at all in the matter, but "come to view afar off." But there is also a lesson for good to be learnt from the distant attitude of these men. One of the most precious qualities even in ordinary life is delicacy. Most painful is the want of it even on the part of those who mean it well. When they touch us, their hand seems rough, and their grasp coarse. And as there is social, so, and much more, is there spiritual delicacy. Some one is convinced of sin and converted unto God. Such cases pre-eminently require much delicacy—we had almost called it shamefacedness. It is impossible to explain, far less to impart, this quality; it must be felt and come spontaneously. But much good has been hindered or retarded by the absence of such delicacy. Let us beware of anything approaching religious platitudes or religious charlatanry. In real religion there is a shrinking from the touch of man and a holy reticence, corresponding to the solemn transaction which has taken place between God and the soul. It is known to God, and will become known to our fellow-men alike by our profession and by the fruits which we bear. For why should we not declare what God has done for our souls? But this does not imply that others should intrude into our innermost sanctuary, and drag into public view that which can only prosper in quiet heart-converse with our God. Against this practice of courting a publicity which too often encourages hypocrisy and destroys all religious modesty, our protest must be emphatic. However we may admit the zeal of such persons, we deprecate their interference. We tell them to let these things alone if they cannot delicately handle them— and if they cannot stand afar off, to remain in Jericho.

And now the two prophets have neared the banks of Jordan. The mantle of Elijah must be baptized in its waters. In the most deeply solemn sense we all must stand by the brink of Jordan. Have we the mantle of Elijah wherewith to divide the waters? Can we pass over dry-shod? Where is now the Lord God of Elijah? In that hour, be it ours to remember that the Lord is nigh unto all such as call upon Him, to such as call upon Him in truth.

CHAPTER III.

DEPARTED, NOT DEAD.

"And it came to pass, when they were gone over, that Elijah said unto Elisha, Ask what I shall do for thee, before I be taken away from thee. And Elisha said, I pray thee, let a double portion of thy spirit be upon me. And he said, Thou hast asked a hard thing: nevertheless, if thou see me when I am taken from thee, it shall be so unto thee; but if not, it shall not be so. And it came to pass, as they still went on, and talked, that, behold, there appeared a chariot of fire, and horses of fire, and parted them both asunder; and Elijah went up by a whirlwind into heaven. And Elisha saw it, and he cried, My father, my father, the chariot of Israel, and the horsemen thereof. And he saw him no more: and he took hold of his own clothes, and rent them in two pieces. He took up also the mantle of Elijah that fell from him, and went back, and stood by the bank of Jordan; and he took the mantle of Elijah that fell from him, and smote the waters, and said, Where is the Lord God of Elijah? And when he also had smitten the waters, they parted hither and thither: and Elisha went over."—2 KINGS ii. 9-14.

WHEN Elijah had smitten the waters with his mantle, a miracle took place far greater than even that which Joshua and Israel had witnessed. The waters of Jordan were divided hither and thither—not now before the ark of Jehovah, but before one who in his day and generation had holpen to bear it. If ever, here was proof offered that not the altar but He to Whom the altar is reared, imparts holiness and power, and that efficacy attaches not to any outward thing, but to the spiritual faith which clings to spiritual realities, and twines around them.

But what strong act of faith this on the part of Elijah! It seemed to show that, with age and trials his faith had not grown weak nor decrepit. As he neared the close of his pilgrimage, he would sum up all his former experience in one grand daring act of faith. He would risk all upon its issue. Such had been the faithfulness and loving-kindness of the Lord to him, such was his present trust in God, that in the most trying hour of all, as he stood by the waters of Jordan, he would stake all on this one act. With his mantle he would smite Jordan. It was as he had expected. They two went over as on dry ground. And is not this true of every Christian? As he nears the close of his pilgrimage, and reaches the Jordan which has yet to be crossed, he must take the distinctive mark of his calling, his mantle, the Righteousness of Christ, and wrapping it up, in one grand act of faith smite with it the waters, even the cold flood of death. Most assuredly they will part. The calmness, and sometimes the triumphant joy with which they who, in anticipation, had perhaps dreaded the last scene, are able to pass through those waters as on dry ground, is surely a miracle infinitely greater than even the literal dividing of the waters of Jordan.

The prophet's mantle, which thus proved superior to the elements of this world, was, as we know, the badge of his office. As so employed and distinguished, not because it belonged to Elijah, had it commanded obedience. Not the individual, but the office, or rather that which constitutes the office, the message of God which he bears, is entitled to respect and attention. "Now, then, we are ambassadors for Christ." But if we have no message from Christ, no special mission from the Lord, we are impotent, no matter what name, honour, or emoluments men may have bestowed upon us. But possession of the prophet's mantle renders us superior to earthly powers and elements. In some respects, indeed, all Christians "have this honour." Spiritually they already have authority, and the nearer they approach glory, the more they rise superior to earthly things. In the "world to come" this rule and superiority will appear in its fullest literality. All things will then be put under their feet and be subject to them. When the waters divided, as Elijah smote them with his mantle, and when St. Peter walked on the Lake of Galilee, may it not have borne symbolic reference to the time when creation, delivered from its curse, shall not, as at present, be in discord with, but in obedience to ransomed man, its God-appointed head and master?

Not with uncertain nor trembling hand, nor with weak and wavering faith had the prophet bent over Jordan. He had *smitten* its waters. The most daring and certain faith is not presumption. It presumes nothing; it only trusts in One Who is tried and precious. The stronger our faith—that is, our trusting in Christ—the more glorifying to God. It is another mark of faith on the part of Elijah that he now invited his successor to ask what he should do for him before he was taken away. The proposal, be it remembered, was made to one who, in that lonely walk, had proved himself prepared for spiritual gifts, and willing to take up the cross and follow the Lord. And already Elisha had passed through Jordan with his master, and made experience of the God of Israel. And yet Elijah himself could scarcely have anticipated the special request. Instead of asking perhaps for some directions to guide him in his future office, or seeking some confirmation of the presence of God to encourage him in entering upon it, Elisha entreats: "Let a double portion of thy spirit rest upon me." Not power, nor zeal, nor eloquence, nor even ability to work miracles; in short, not anything outward constituted in the mind of Elisha the distinctive qualification for, and characteristic of the prophetic office. The Spirit made the prophet. Yet so deep was the sense of his inability and weakness, so high his spiritual ambition to win many souls, that he craved a double portion even of Elijah's spirit. With what godly simplicity and holy sincerity he seemed to concentrate his whole soul into this one request! When all that heaven and earth could afford—all its riches, honours, pleasures—was spread like a scroll before him, and his choice from amongst all was freely offered, he asked for nothing but a double portion of the Holy Spirit. Surely that lonely walk in company with Elijah had been the true expression of his feelings. Elisha was prepared for the prophetic office.

It is, of course, not within reach of any man literally to make his choice from among all that earth or heaven can give. We are all limited and hedged in by circumstances; and yet there is some analogy to this in the experience of all. For as once the Tempter spread in vision before the Master all the kingdoms of the world and their glory, so to our dazzled imagination there seems to lie in the golden sunlight of life's morning all that the boldest ambition of a soul can covet, all that the strongest cravings, affections, desires, or passions of the heart can wish to make their own. Ask what shall be given thee. Young man, what shall it be? Woman, whom seekest thou? Minister of the gospel, what is thy desire at the commencement of thy work? Truthfully speaking, what is the inmost longing of our hearts? If the choice were given, would we ask for success, for prosperity, for what is called happiness—or for a double portion of the Holy Spirit? This is a searching question, and yet one which we should faithfully put to ourselves. Oh that our hearts might be taught to make this answer: "One thing have I desired of the Lord, that will I seek after; that I may dwell in the house of the Lord all the days of my life, to behold the beauty of the Lord, and to inquire in His temple." "Whom have I in heaven but Thee? and there is none upon earth that I desire beside Thee."

But Elisha, although earnestly coveting the best gifts, had yet much to learn concerning their real nature. To address such a request to any man, even to an Elijah, showed how imperfectly the things of the Spirit were understood. Far otherwise is it under the New Dispensation, when we may boldly go to our Master for all that we need. "Ask," says our Lord, "and it shall be given you." "Whatsoever ye shall ask the Father in My name, He will give it you." Two fundamental truths, closely connected, should ever be held firm and fast by the anxious soul. They are: the freeness of the gospel, and, if the expression may be used, the omnipotence of prayer. When driven from refuge to refuge, and at last almost despairing of comfort, two consolations are left us. First, the invitation of Christ is unconditionally addressed to all, whatever their past history or their present state—and hence to each of us individually. Therefore, also, can we further plead this free invitation as our warrant for coming to Christ and asking *all* things—pardon, grace, and whatever we need for time and for eternity. We come and we pray, not on the plea of our faith, but on this, that Jesus died for sinners, and bids sinners as such be reconciled to God. Because of a free gospel we can pray; because of the omnipotence of prayer in the Name of Jesus we can pray at all times and for all things.

The prophet was evidently unprepared for Elisha's request. His reply offered a corrective to his mistake, while it encouraged his hope. "Thou hast asked a hard thing"— one which it is not mine either to give or to refuse. It depends upon Another, and it shall be granted or withheld, according as thou wilt be found capable of taking part in the spiritual transaction about to take place. "If thou see me when I am taken from thee, it shall be so unto thee; but if not, it shall not be so." The reason of this is evident. If the fifty sons of the prophets who viewed afar off had stood quite near, if even they had been side by side with Elisha, they would not have seen the translation of Elijah. It was a spiritual vision, and the manifestation from heaven could only be seen by eyes spiritually opened. The answer of the prophet therefore implied, that if Elisha's request was granted and he received a double portion of the Spirit, then and then only would he see the vision. To behold the translation of Elijah would be evidence to Elisha that his petition had been granted, and that he had received the gift of the Spirit. And so every vision of spiritual glory can only be perceived by a mind that is spiritually enlightened. "The natural man receiveth not the things of the Spirit of God, for they are foolishness unto him; neither can he know them, because they are spiritually discerned." Accordingly, even though we preach the gospel and exhibit Christ, the Holy Spirit alone can open the eyes of the understanding to behold the glory of Jesus, as of the Only-Begotten of the Father, full of grace and truth.

The silent walk along the banks of Jordan had again been resumed, when suddenly a wondrous vision appeared. A chariot of fire—flames not earthly—and horses of fire, parted the two pilgrims, and Elijah wrapt in glory ascended into heaven, as it seemed to the onlooker, in a whirlwind. The heavens had opened, and some rays of the ineffable glory had shone down upon earth. What blessed assurance of their safety, and what anticipation of New Testament glory must this translation of Elijah have conveyed to Old Testament saints! And what confidence in the Lord and blessed hope of His return with all His saints is sealed upon our hearts, when we are allowed in some measure to share Elisha's vision! What passes between the ransomed soul and the ministering angels we know not. Only now and again one and another ray of glory dimly penetrates the denser atmosphere of our earth. Most of us have heard what others have seen, while standing beside those who were ascending to Christ's Father and their Father, how such bright beams of effulgent glory have rested upon and surrounded them in their departing moments, that even the dim vision, permitted to the bystanders, filled them with solemn awe.

And Elisha saw it! Blessed be God, the sun of Israel had not set; the prophet was not dead, though he had departed. The double portion of Elijah's spirit had been granted, and, as pledge of it, Elisha had beheld the vision. Yet, though he had expected this parting, and notwithstanding all the glory around, Elisha at first only realised his own personal loss. Trials are never really expected; the reality always takes us by surprise. "My father, my father!" Spirituality does not uproot, it sanctifies genuine feeling. It is not wrong to mourn; it is only wrong to mourn as those that have no hope. But Elisha soon recovered self-possession, as he recalled the glorious vision which had accompanied the removal of Elijah, and remembered the work now devolving upon himself. "The chariot of Israel and the horsemen thereof!" The prophet was gone, but the prophet's God remained; and the very chariot that had parted them served as assurance to Elisha that his God reigned. Elisha rent his clothes, in token of personal mourning for the removal of his friend and master. Yet personal feeling, whether of sorrow or of joy, must not wholly engross us, nor interfere with earnest activity in the work which God has given us to do. Nor was Elisha to be left to himself. Probably he might now feel the loneliness of his position in proportion to the glory which he had seen surrounding his departing master. But as he looked up towards heaven, behold, the prophet's mantle, which had at first been the symbol of his own prophetic calling, unfastened by a hand not earthly, and flung from Elijah's shoulders, came floating down from heaven to earth. Elijah had no more need of that mantle; his work was done, his joy had begun. But the work of God still remained, and with it was granted grace and power to accomplish it. The mantle which descended had been baptized with fire, as formerly it had been with water. It now came to Elisha directly from heaven. God makes the minister and gives him his work. Ministerial honour comes not from earthly appointments, far less from social position. It depends on our possession of Elijah's mantle, baptized with water and with fire, and come to us from heaven. We are ambassadors for Christ, and in that character alone we claim respect, and that not for ourselves, but for our office and our message.

Elisha took up the mantle thus come down to him. What a contrast between this and the manner in which some seek admission to the ministerial office! Surely the right relations must be fearfully perverted, if worldly motives or ambition are the reason, and trafficking in souls, buying and selling of cures, political reasons or family influence, the means of obtaining our ministry. The common complaint of decrease in the number of candidates for ordination ought to lead us to view the matter in another light. Our first concern should be not as regards the number, but the qualifications of those who are to enter on the holy ministry. And the motives by which we seek to attract them should not be worldly but spiritual. Who will do the Lord's work? Who is filled with zeal for God and love to souls? Who will follow the Master without questioning or doubting? Who is really in earnest, entering the ministry of Christ not as "a profession," but for the "work's sake"? Thus only can we hope to obtain power with God and with man, and to prevail.

And now Elisha stood once more by the bank of Jordan, this time alone, about to make his first trial of the prophet's mantle. Shall it prove in his hands also the means of dividing the waters? There is a time in the history of each of us when we make, as it were, the first trial of our faith; when for the first time we kneel down to plead the promises and to pray, *believing* that all which is written is literally true, that we are accepted in Christ and shall be heard for His sake. Shall the waters divide as we also strike them with the mantle of Elijah? Is He our God, or only the God of the departed prophet? But before we attempt the trial, a most important question has yet to be answered. Have *we* beheld the vision of the Lord, the chariot of Israel and the horsemen thereof? Do we know Him as our God in Christ, reigning, and encompassing His people? Oh that the God of Elijah would open our eyes in faith to behold the spiritual vision of Christ! Then shall we no longer stand "afar off," but "see Him as He is," behold His glory, and receive that double portion of His Spirit, even "grace for grace."

CHAPTER IV.

ELISHA AND THE FIFTY STRONG MEN.

"And he took the mantle of Elijah that fell from him, and smote the waters, and said, Where is the Lord God of Elijah? and when he also had smitten the waters, they parted hither and thither: and Elisha went over. And when the sons of the prophets which were to view at Jericho saw him, they said, The spirit of Elijah doth rest on Elisha. And they came to meet him, and bowed themselves to the ground before him. And they said unto him, Behold now, there be with thy servants fifty strong men; let them go, we pray thee, and seek thy master: lest peradventure the Spirit of the Lord hath taken him up, and cast him upon some mountain, or into some valley. And he said, Ye shall not send. And when they urged him till he was ashamed, he said, Send. They sent therefore fifty men; and they sought three days, but found him not. And when they came again to him (for he tarried at Jericho), he said unto them, Did I not say unto you, Go not?"—2 KINGS ii. 14-18.

THE circumstances in which Elisha was left were, indeed, of peculiar difficulty. Although the vision vouchsafed was pledge of a double portion of Elijah's spirit, and the prophet's mantle had descended to him, yet he was alone, and without any special directions. No audible voice from heaven, no inward communication, indicated his path of duty. He was really cast upon his former general instructions, and his first act must be one of personal decision; or, as in the case of each of us, of personal faith. Perhaps the most trying moments in the life of Elisha were those in which he retraced the short distance from the place of Elijah's ascension till he reached the brink of Jordan. A whole life of faith was again to be summed up in one experiment of God's faithfulness. Once more he stood on the bank of the river. Only a miracle could open a way for him through its waters. He was now to put it to the test, whether by an act of special interposition God would own him as His prophet. He was also to put it to the trial, whether the mantle had divided the waters because it had been Elijah's, or whether its power depended neither on Elijah nor on any other man, however honoured, but on the ever-present help of that God, of Whose commission to His servant this mantle was the symbol. The truth to be exhibited for all time was, that prophetic or apostolic descent depended on the descent of prophetic or apostolic truth and commission. It was not merely as the mantle of Elijah, but as the symbol of God's presence, that it was now to divide the waters. We also must learn to trace our ministerial succession high up, higher even than to the Apostles: we must trace it directly to Christ Himself. "*He gave some Apostles and some prophets, and some evangelists, and some pastors and teachers.*" The true evidence of our ministerial commission lies in the attainment of its object, in "the perfecting of the saints," in "the work of the ministry," and in "the edifying of the body of Christ."

Most fully did Elisha realise this, and most ample evidence did he give that his prayer for a double measure of the Spirit had really been granted, when, in smiting the waters, he exclaimed, "Where is now the Lord God of Elijah?" He looked no longer to Elijah, but to Elijah's God, for help and preparation. He had learned to distinguish between the mere instrument and Him Who is "the same yesterday, and to-day, and for ever." We can almost imagine what feelings would agitate the heart of Elisha, as he was now to learn the reality of his ministry, as of power and of God. Alternately looking up to heaven and down into Jordan, he smote its waters. And, lo, obedient they part, and the prophet passes to the other side. What bearing on all his after-history must this event have had, and what encouragement must it have afforded him in all his labours and trials! He could never forget the assurance conveyed to him at the commencement of his ministry. He could now speak of the power of the Lord, not as of a theory or speculation, but as of experience and personal knowledge. There is a certitude flowing into the hearts of Christians from the experience of answered prayers, a strength derived by the soldier of Christ from a sense of the presence of his Captain, against which no amount of outward difficulties or seeming impossibilities can prevail. Literally, all things are possible to him that believeth. And herein lies the explanation of the *practical* character of the doctrine which we profess. A joyous Christian, or one who has experienced the help of his God, must be an undaunted labourer, and a fearless soldier of the Lord Jesus. But trembling hands can neither guide the plough nor handle the sword.

It has been well remarked that the last work of Elijah was also the first of Elisha, as if to indicate that the one took up the work precisely where the other had left it. Ministers change, but the work remains unchanged. None of us is really needed. Jehovah reigneth, and He will carry on His own work by whom and as He appointeth. We often mourn and fear when some great instrument for good has been removed, or when what we deemed needful for His cause is taken away. Surely the Lord still remaineth, and He is nigh to all that call upon Him.

The prophet has passed through the trial of his faith; he must now pass through that of his patience. Even in ordinary life not unfrequently one of our chief difficulties comes from the presence of unbidden, uncongenial, and unsuitable advisers. It were far better to be left alone than to have the aid obtruded of those who are morally incompetent to the task. This holds specially true in works of a religious character, when intrusive zeal is too often prompted by want of deeper insight or experience. We distrust those who have a ready explanation and a ready remedy in every difficulty. Too often it is only the outcome of spiritual ignorance or of superficiality. Yet in the interest of peace it may be needful to bear with them. All this is painfully illustrated by the history about to follow.

On the other side Jordan, the sons of the prophets who had come "to view afar off" were in waiting for Elisha. No doubt they had most earnestly endeavoured to see what would happen. Yet it is evident that they had perceived but little of what had passed. They had not seen Elijah's ascent; but they had beheld the waters parting at the bidding of Elisha. And, impressed with the obvious meaning of this miracle, they came forward to bow before Elisha. "The spirit of Elijah doth rest on Elisha." They had seen something of the working of Elisha, but nothing of that of Elisha's God; they recognised the spirit of Elijah, but they were ignorant of the Spirit of God. Yet even so it was well that they should have been made to recognise the superiority and the office of Elisha. There is a large class of persons who acknowledge only one claim on their respect: that of *power*. They will own us if we possess, and reject us if we seem to lack it—and this quite irrespective of the source whence our power may be derived. Of this it is well to be aware, since both danger and help may come from it. Danger—since it may tempt to religious (not to say worldly) unscrupulousness in seeking to obtain this power by any means; yet, on the other hand, also help—since it may put at our disposal sources of indirect strength. When Israel goes out of Egypt in *triumph*, a "mixed multitude" will follow their steps. Under one aspect, however, the matter possesses a most serious present interest. Too often good men and really useful "societies" have been led astray by this pursuit after "power," till the all-absorbing interest seemed to be to secure popularity. It is matter for grief and shame to hear good men advocating a good cause, as if the one object in view were to obtain support, as though outward support were synonymous with spiritual success! It is not only that the scorn of the world may be excited, and that not unjustly, by the glaring inconsistency of relying on such means, nor that the noblest cause may be thereby degraded to the level of religious charlatanism, but—and on this all depends—that the blessing of the Lord may be withdrawn on account of it. It cannot be lawful to seek support by any expedient on the plea that the cause is good. The end does not sanctify the means. God can easily, and He will certainly, provide for the carrying on of His own work. We rely on other means than worldly policy or outward support. And surely if there were more of faith, and hence of prayer, the larger blessing would not be withheld.

It is instructive to notice how history repeats itself. The suggestion of those sons of the prophets by the bank of Jordan many centuries ago reminds us of the strange mistakes which men make in our own days in connection with religion. One of these consists in self-confidence. They profess to understand every event, and undertake to meet every eventuality. If they have only sufficient means, in their opinion, the result will be assured. "Behold now, there be with thy servants fifty strong men; let them go, we pray thee, and seek thy master." Fifty strong men with the sons of the prophets—how much could they accomplish! Numbers, capacity, and office were here combined. Such a company seemed to them equal to any emergency. Yet all the time they perceived not the incongruity between the means proposed and the end sought. And this is another characteristic of the carnal mind in religion. But, assuredly, only disappointment and shame will be the outcome of such attempts.

There is no reason to suppose that the proposal of these men was prompted by distrust of Elisha, or indeed by any other motive than love for Elijah, and an honest belief that something had taken place which came within range of their power. They had known that Elijah was to be taken up, and they seemed to have inferred that his removal was effected by the Spirit of the Lord. But, according to their limited knowledge and capacity, they could find no further explanation of it, than the supposition that the Spirit might again cast him on some mountain, or leave him in some lonely valley. But in such case the fifty strong men might come to the rescue; they would go and search for, and deliver him from the perilous position in which he might be.

All this, of course, argued almost incredible misapprehension of the whole, or indeed of any spiritual transaction. Yet, strange as the proposal sounds in our ears, it is, in some aspects of it, not singular to those sons of the prophets. Ignorance of what is really spiritual, joined to mere zeal and earnestness, too often seeks to attain spiritual ends by only outward means. The Apostle admonished his contemporaries that the weapons of their warfare were not carnal. The warning is equally requisite in our days. Attempts to excite the senses by gorgeous ceremonial and other stimulants to the religious imagination, by which, according to some, religious truth is to be conveyed to the uneducated; according to others, the æsthetic feelings of the educated are to be enlisted on behalf of religion—what are they but an attempt to produce a spiritual result by purely outward means? More than that, with deepest reverence for the blessed ordinances of our Lord, is it not possible to pervert even these from their real import and objects? Religion consists not in anything outward, whatever it be, nor in anything that one man can do to, or for another. Religion is in the soul; it is a transaction between God and the human heart; it is a new life imparted and nourished by the Holy Spirit. Its beginning is spiritual union to the Lord Jesus; its growth is in fellowship with Him. Outward means have indeed their important use. They are channels; but the channel is empty, unless the rain from heaven filleth the pools. To outward things by themselves, and irrespective of higher realities, no true and permanent value attaches. It is the grace of God which bringeth salvation; and the kingdom of God consisteth, not in anything outward, however useful or cherished, but in righteousness, and peace, and joy in the Holy Ghost.

Under these circumstances it may appear strange that Elisha had not explained the translation of Elijah to the sons of the prophets, and informed them of the real state of the case. In point of fact, he only told them, "Ye shall not send." But to have said more might, in plain New Testament language, have been to cast pearls before swine. They would not have understood it, and it would not have quenched a zeal which at last forced the prophet into unwilling acquiescence. For, the zeal of those whose religion is not spiritual often exceeds that of the children of God. The sectarian is generally far more zealous for his Shibboleth than the child of God against the common enemies of Israel, or for Israel's God. The reason is, that his party zeal constitutes the sum and substance of his religion. If it be taken from him, nothing else is left. He is not so much a Christian as a member of this or that party, or else he holds certain peculiar views or distinctive points, which to him are all in all. But too often, in measure as we are zealous for little things, we neglect the great, and the tithing of mint, anise, and cummin is, alas, not unfrequently conjoined with neglect of the weightier matters of the law. Truth—*all* truth is, indeed, of the deepest importance. It is the truth of God, and therefore we have no right to part with it, even though it may seem of subordinate importance. But truth is not incompatible with charity. God has many children. Some are young, and others advanced; some are weak, others strong. God knows them all, and cares for them all, and will lead them all. Let *us* seek to hold the truth in love, to be as stringent as we can towards ourselves, and as charitable as we may towards others. Perhaps, in the great day of perfect learning, we all may have to be put right in our understanding of many things, which at present we think we know. Till then, while calmly defending what we believe to be God's truth, yet if the one thing needful be found, peace be on the Israel of God, on all who love the Lord Jesus in sincerity and in truth.

The sons of the prophets had urged " Elisha till he was ashamed." Their zeal and earnestness for the safety of Elijah might have cast suspicion on the continued opposition of the one who should have been the most deeply interested in it. And so Elisha reluctantly yielded. We must take care that our good be not evil spoken of. Yet the line of demarcation is very narrow which separates really lawful compliance, for the sake of peace and charity, from that which is selfish, worldly, and hypocritical, by which the Christian conscience is fatally wounded, and even common self-respect may be lost. Nor are we often more wise than those sons of the prophets in "urging" our requests. The lesson to Israel, when, contrary to Moses' injunction, they would go to battle, and that of Balaam, who would at last go to the camp of Moab, are forgotten when we insist upon our own desires, and while, perhaps, obtaining our object, get with it leanness to our souls. As in so many instances, in this also the root of the evil lies in unbelief. If we raised our minds from things seen, and learned to *trust* where we cannot see; if the horizon of our faith were not so bounded, our hearts would be at peace, nor would we be tempted to think and feel as if, when Elijah is taken from us, Elijah's God were also gone.

The fruitless search continued for three days. Then the sons of the prophets returned to Elisha. Yet their labour had not been quite in vain, if they now learned to understand the lesson conveyed in the reproof of the prophet: "Did I not say unto you, Go not?" Blessed be that grace which brings us back to the Lord, even after a long and fruitless search for that which can never be found on earth! The prodigal's shame and the father's joy mingle, when, feeling that all the past has been only "labour for that which satisfieth not," we return unto Him Who is waiting to welcome us. And in the case of God's own people, much of the painful discipline by which they are ultimately drawn closer to Him seems to consist in this, that God allows His people to go on till at length they find that in their own ways there is only shame and disappointment. Then they return unto the Lord, to receive in a humbled spirit His loving reproof, and henceforth to walk softly with their God.

Perhaps yet another lesson may be derived from this strange mixture of unbelief and superstition in the sons of the prophets. On their supposition, that Elijah might be found on some mountain or in some valley, it was surely superstition to attribute his removal to the agency of the Spirit of the Lord. If Elijah were really hidden in some secluded spot, his removal could not have been the work of the Spirit. On the other hand, if his removal had been effected by heavenly agency, it could not have been to some lonely place upon earth. We frequently meet similar combinations of unbelief and superstition. There are those who reject the Word of God only to become victims of the strangest delusions. A sudden transition from scepticism to abject superstition is by no means uncommon. And how far such folly may be carried, we all know. How many who will not believe the warnings of the Lord, perhaps live in open sin, are a prey to the grossest popular superstitions; almost tremble at signs and tokens of the most trivial kind; and partly credit, partly dread the most irrational prognostications. What is the meaning of this strange inconsistency? It means that the mind of man, created for spiritual realities, can never wholly shake itself free from their consciousness. We dread when we do not know, and we tremble when we do not believe. Alike safety, peace, and calm are only found with the enlightened Christian. He has nothing to fear whose God and Father is the God of Jacob. He is strong and calm whom the truth has made free, and who knoweth in Whom he has believed.

CHAPTER V.

THE WATERS OF JERICHO.

"He tarried at Jericho . . . . . . And the men of the city said unto Elisha, Behold, I pray thee, the situation of this city is pleasant, as my lord seeth: but the water is naught, and the ground barren. And he said, Bring me a new cruse, and put salt therein. And they brought it to him. And he went forth unto the spring of the waters, and cast the salt in there, and said, Thus saith the Lord, I have healed these waters; there shall not be from thence any more death or barren land. So the waters were healed unto this day, according to the saying of Elisha which he spake."
—2 KINGS ii. 18-22.

THE contrast between the mission of Elijah and that of his successor appears from the commencement to the close of their work. The suddenness with which, without previous preparation, the prophet from Gilead had come upon Ahab and his court, was in character with the terrible judgment which formed the burden of his first message. On the other hand, Elisha, the peaceful husbandman of Abel-Meholah, must have been well known to many of his contemporaries. For probably eight or nine years he had occupied the subordinate position of "ministering" to Elijah. Unlike his predecessor, who seems not to have had any fixed abode, Elisha, after his instalment in the prophetic office, settled, at least for a time, at Jericho. And his first public act was one, not of judgment, but of mercy; not of drying up each fountain and spring in the land, till every green spot was shrivelled and licked up by the glare of a continuous sunshine, but of healing the spring at Jericho, and thereby converting the barren landscape into one of luxuriant beauty, and decking it with the constant riches of an eastern clime.

In fact, this difference between the mission of Elijah and that of Elisha had its deeper meaning. Each was symbolical—

the one of the Law, the other of the Gospel; the one of judgment, the other of mercy. Elijah was the precursor of St. John the Baptist; Elisha, that of our Blessed Lord and Saviour Jesus Christ. Nor did this ever appear more clearly than in the first act of his ministry, which may be regarded as the summary of his whole after-life. Elisha remained at Jericho, apparently waiting till the Lord would point out his special work. For, even after we have given ourselves to the service of the Lord, we must wait on Him in a spirit of humble dependence, till He point out the means, and open the way of usefulness to us. Yet the time so spent in Jericho was not lost. Irrespective of the preparation which the prophet underwent during this period of retirement, his presence and character as prophet became known to his fellow-citizens. Perhaps the widest and holiest influence which the Christian can exercise is that which is least observed. It is the influence, felt but not seen, of a life different and distinct from the world around. To be distinct from the world, it is not necessary to be singular. It is possible to be distinct without being singular, as much as to be singular without being distinct from the world. The children of God ought to learn this lesson. We have the light. Let its rays be cast upon the glorious Person of Christ, upon the blessed truths of His Gospel, and not upon the angularities of our own character. Distinctiveness is an attractive, singularity a repelling force. Let us seek to attract men to Christ by the beauties of holiness, instead of deterring them by the rugged outlines of a hard and stern character, too often falsely designating that as principle which is only the outcome of unbending uncharitableness.

The men of Jericho had become aware of the presence of a prophet among them; and, wiser than others in similar circumstances, they availed themselves of the blessing within their reach. It is a great matter to discern our privileges.

The waters of Jericho would not have been healed had the inhabitants ignored the prophet, either from unconcern or prejudice. But, in truth, theirs was a felt urgent need, which human means could not reach. It will be remembered that when Joshua took possession of Jericho, he laid the Lord's curse upon the doomed city. It had been the first to resist Israel, and against its bulwarks not earthly weapons, but the Presence and the Voice of Jehovah had prevailed. To all future generations it was to remain desolate, a monument alike to Israel and to the world of the events there enacted. As if to render it for ever uninhabitable, the very springs of water, on which in the East the life of a district depends, were turned into bitterness, while a cloud of terrible judgment would hang over the household of him whose sacrilegious hand should seek to restore what God had destroyed.

But in the degenerate days in which our history is laid such threats were not likely to be heeded. Accordingly, we read that, but a short time previously, Jericho had been rebuilt by one Hiel of Bethel, probably the head of an influential clan. He paid the penalty of his daring, for "he laid the foundation thereof in Abiram his first-born, and set up the gates thereof in his youngest son Segub" (1 Kings xvi. 34). So Scripture records in its own brief and graphic manner, naming names and recalling circumstances well known at the time, and describing the whole, as if Hiel had actually laid the foundation of Jericho in the tomb of his eldest, and hung up its gates within the framework of the coffin of his youngest child. We are not told whether the people understood this fearful visitation; but Jericho and its neighbourhood, although enjoying every advantage of situation and climate, continued as before—a sterile, unhealthy, and inhospitable region. The inhabitants felt keenly the contrast between what Jericho was and what it might be. Well might they point out to Elisha that "the situation of the city" was "pleasant." None more so in the land of Israel. With a rich alluvial soil and under an almost tropical sun, there was scarce a product of eastern climes of which the district might not have boasted. In later days, it was described by Josephus and others as almost fairy-land, a very garden and paradise of eastern beauty. Here the palm grew in wild luxuriance, while the balsam, a source of untold wealth, shed its rich perfume. But all this fertility depended upon a spring of living water, and without it the rich district of Jericho was barren and poor.

In the time of Elisha the spring which bursts from the desolate calcareous mountains in the background of the city, where tradition has placed the scene of our Lord's Temptation, was not sweet, but "naught" or brackish, and hence carried only sterility and desolation instead of freshness and life. The inhabitants well knew the cause of their poverty, and they pointed to these waters as the source of the evil. In the truest sense, the fruitfulness of a land depends upon good, living waters. The prosperity of a district, and the happiness of a family or of an individual, alike depend on the spring of spiritual life. Industry, learning, and our much boasted civilisation, without true religion, leave us, like Jericho before its spring was healed. There is abundant capacity for all that is fair and good, the "situation" is most "pleasant," "but the waters are naught, and the ground is barren." So it was in ancient Egypt, Greece, and Rome; so is it in the home of the most ancient of all civilisations—China; and so will it be in every country and district where true religion is not known. We may go even further, and say that the intellectual character of a district also depends in great measure on its religion. Under the influence of Scriptural truth the mind unfolds and is developed, the whole character, sometimes even the aspect of a man is changed. He who has come into right relationship to God will also learn to hold a proper position towards his fellow-men. But for this purpose what is vaguely termed religion is not sufficient, nor even religious earnestness. . Jericho had its spring, and yet the land was barren—not because there were no waters, but because they were "naught." In their superficialness men have come to be satisfied with *any* spring, no matter what the character of its waters may be. Even with those who are seriously disposed, religious earnestness, rather than religious truth, seems to be the main object. To use an illustration : It would almost appear as if it were of no importance whither the road led which a man pursues, provided he travels on it fast and far enough. But, surely, this is only to deceive ourselves and to mislead others.

The danger is all the greater, that this practice of calling evil good has almost become one of the conventionalities of society. There is scarcely a pleasure party, however worldly, nor design or undertaking, however far from God, for which the presence of some religious person is not sought, when straightway all seems to become sanctified thereby. The saddest point about it is the readiness with which religious people take their part in such matters. In return, there is not a banquet nor an assembly in which the sentiment to the piety, the devotedness, and the usefulness of those who do, or should represent religion in a district is not loudly cheered, whether or not those who are present believe in their hearts what they echo with their lips. But is this not virtually to declare that these are matters of secondary importance, of conventionality, of social respectability? and can it be right to share in this? What part supposed propriety, or else worldly regard for the worldly position of others, may have in this "deceiving and being deceived," will appear in the day that shall reveal all deceptions and all reality, and when our guilt in misleading others by calling darkness light shall be made manifest to us and to all.

Let us then be true in the truest of all things. The salvation of the soul is precious. Assuredly, it is not the spring, but its character, which is of vital importance. We must have not merely water, but good water. It is of comparatively secondary importance in whose company we get it, provided the waters be living. To attend a ministry of error, because we can attend it in fashionable company, or because the mode of service is in accordance with our predilections, is most dangerous trifling. There can be no obligation to sell the truth for the sake of any conventionality. Let us not say with Pilate, "What is truth?" The Scriptures will enable us readily to answer the question. Even a child of God cannot thrive where the water of life is partially or wholly "naught." It necessarily has a detrimental influence upon his spirituality, as a poisoned atmosphere would have upon the physical health. Not that we should indulge in a carping, critical spirit, so different from "the meekness of wisdom," which distinguishes "the love of the truth." Priscilla and Aquila acted very differently to many modern assertors of orthodoxy. They took Apollos to their home, and in quiet retirement of the family, and with the affectionate outpouring of Christian hearts they "expounded unto him the way of God more perfectly." Blessed be God, he learned it, and that far better than he could have done in noisy disputation. Yet, without giving way to captious criticism, the broad question still remains as to the character of the stream of which we drink, the waters of which are to be tested by no other standard than that of the Word of God.

It is most instructive to notice what pains Elisha took to show, that the position he occupied in the miracle about to be enacted was entirely secondary and subordinate. He was to act as minister, and only as such. For, first, he showed by his demand of a new cruse and salt, that the effect was not produced by his word, but that other means were to be employed. These means were, however, in themselves wholly inadequate to the purpose, that so the excellency of the power might be of God. Even these two considerations may tend to remind us of the ministry and its relation to the gospel. The spiritual effect which we seek to produce is not due to the word of man, far less is it magical. Means are to be used for healing the waters. Yet these means are in themselves wholly inadequate to the end, which is the production of spiritual life. What are these means? A new cruse and salt! The Word which we preach is indeed like salt presented in a new cruse, coming as it does, not in the oldness of the letter and the law, but in the newness of the Spirit. But how insufficient does the foolishness of preaching seem to save those who by wisdom had not known God!

Another instructive circumstance was, that Elisha "went unto the *spring* of the waters, and cast the salt in there." He went to the fountain whence the waters issued. A mere amendment of life, by which we become more serious or more religious than we had been, will not suffice. The waters are poisoned at their very spring. Out of the heart proceed sweet waters and bitter. It is not improvement, but an entire change of motives and affections which is requisite—a new heart and a right spirit. No amount of pruning or tending will change the nature of a plant; a fresh beginning must be made. We are not wrong nor deficient merely on one or another point. The whole head is sick and the whole heart is faint; and the first thing needed is that the salt of the Gospel of free grace in Christ Jesus be cast into the heart, as being the spring of the waters of life. We must believe, each one for himself, that Christ died for us, poor, guilty and sinful as we are; we must receive this "salt" into the spring of our life, and turn unto God as our Father in Christ Jesus. We must personally accept the offer of mercy; we must take Christ as the Father's unspeakable gift to us.

This *is* the salt in the new cruse, and will heal the waters. "Whosoever believeth in Him shall not perish, but have everlasting life." Why? Because Christ has died to reconcile us to the Father, because He has finished the work of our salvation, and because God is in Christ, reconciling the world unto Himself, not imputing their trespasses unto them. Whether we receive it or not, there is salvation provided for us; and ours it is simply, but most gratefully, to make it our own in joyous trustfulness.

Accordingly, when the prophet cast in the salt, it was with these words: "Thus saith the Lord, I have healed these waters." Three things here deserve special notice. First, that the prophet disclaimed all power. Jehovah, not he, had healed the waters. Secondly, that the Word and the Divine power seem conjoined in the healing of the waters, just as in the conversion of a soul the means and the blessing, the Word and grace, the offer of free mercy and the gracious willingness to receive it, are combined. Thirdly, the expression seems to point to the healing as a past act, wrought at the moment of casting in the salt. The work of spiritual healing is indeed a past act. "It is finished," said the Blessed Saviour on the cross. God *is* reconciled—the waters *are* healed. "Ho, every one that thirsteth, come ye to the waters, and he that hath no money, come ye, buy, and eat; yea, come, buy wine and milk without money and without price." The Gospel is simply the announcement of a fact. This fact so proclaimed as a fact is, that "God so loved the world, that He gave His only-begotten Son, that whosoever believeth in Him should not perish, but have everlasting life." Faith is merely our acceptance and crediting of this fact, our acquiescence in it, and consequently our reception of Christ as our Saviour, and our joy in the love of God, declared to us in His Son.

It only remains to observe, that the healing of the waters

of Jericho was immediate, permanent, and resulting in fruitfulness to a land which had formerly been desolate. "There shall not be from thence any more death or barren land. So the waters were healed unto this day." Most grievously do they err who fear that the Gospel of God's free grace may lead to carelessness of life and conversation. As no other consideration awakens such desire for the Gospel as a sense of sin, so nothing else causes such fear of and shrinking from sin as to realise our free forgiveness through the Gospel of His grace. When the spring is healed, "there shall not be from thence any more death or barren land."

Let us mark this twofold result: neither "death" in trespasses and sins, nor "barren land," but life and much fruit that may abound to the glory of our Heavenly Father. A new heart leads to a new life. Christ in the heart means Christ our life; and Christ as our life means that our living shall be Christ-like. "For the love of Christ constraineth us; because we thus judge, that if one died for all, then all died; and that He died for all, that they which live should not henceforth live unto themselves, but unto Him that died for them and rose again." And this change is permanent. It depends upon His Presence, which shall never be withdrawn. For who shall separate us from the love of God which is in Christ Jesus our Lord, or pluck His own out of His Hand? Those for whom Christ died shall live with Him for ever. Oh, blessed and most precious truth, the comfort of anxious souls! But in dealing with others, let us never forget that the one great need consists in this, that the *spring* of the waters be healed. For this let us pray and labour that in His mercy God may be pleased, by His Gospel, to heal the springs of our literature, of education, of society, and of every-day life, till "judgment run down as waters, and righteousness as a mighty stream!"

CHAPTER VI.

BETH-EL, OR BETH-AVEN.

"And he went up from thence unto Beth-el: and as he was going up by the way, there came forth little children out of the city, and mocked him, and said unto him, Go up, thou bald head; go up, thou bald head. And he turned back, and looked on them, and cursed them in the name of the Lord. And there came forth two she bears out of the wood, and tare forty and two children of them. And he went from thence to Mount Carmel, and from thence he returned to Samaria."—2 KINGS ii. 23–25.

THE ministry of Elisha was one of unusual length. It commenced under the reign of Ahab, and extended through those of Ahaziah, of Jehoram, of Jehu, of Jehoahaz, and partly even through that of Joash. Altogether it must have occupied more than half a century. Including his preliminary service of eight or nine years under Elijah, Elisha saw two generations in Israel coming and going. We have no means of judging how long he may have sojourned at Jericho, nor what his special activity there had been. His first recorded work was one of mercy, and bore some analogy to the miracle at Cana in Galilee, with which our Lord commenced His ministry. Nor does the analogy cease there. For, as our Saviour was immediately afterwards met and assailed by the unbelief of the men of Nazareth, who rejected His mission and derided His claims, so was Elisha at the outset of his public activity, on the way to Samaria, arrested and confronted by the blasphemous opposition of the men of Beth-el. Here, however, the points of resemblance end. Our Lord was the Son of God, and passed unharmed and unharming through the infuriated crowd which had pressed

Him to the edge of the cliff on which Nazareth was built. Elisha was only a prophet; his authority was delegated, not his own, and he had to vindicate it by an act of fearful judgment. It was, indeed, sad and trying, but yet most needful for his future work, that from the outset his authority as the prophet of God should be vindicated against all opponents, at least as publicly as it was challenged. His whole usefulness would depend upon his prophetic office being acknowledged and felt to be real; and hence, however incongruous with the rest of his life, his second public appearance must be in judgment, and not in mercy.

A more terrible illustration could scarcely be found than at Beth-el of the desolating effects of "water" that is "naught." It was one of the most sacred spots in the land of Israel. The memory of that vision, embalmed in the new name of Beth-el (house of God) which the ancient Luz had received, ought to have saved it from profanation. But, when Jeroboam usurped the throne of Israel, this ancient city and Dan, at the extreme northern boundary of the land, were selected as sanctuaries for the worship of the golden calves, in order that the people might be withdrawn from the service of Jehovah at Jerusalem. The place and the object of worship were equally suited to the purpose in view. For the first time in the history of the chosen people, the national establishment of religion was not only perverted from its sacred object, but prostituted to become the instrument of selfish statecraft. State and Church, whose union should be one of affection and free choice, were now wedded for the most sordid ends, and an unholy compact ensued, in which the Church surrendered conviction and freedom of action, yielding an abject obedience in return for worldly support, or from fear of worldly consequences. Jeroboam did not suppress the religion of Israel; he only sought to divert it into another and more convenient channel, by appealing to the darkest chapter in their religious history. The world does not ask us to surrender religion; it only opposes earnest, genuine religion. It has no objection to an easy, respectable form of worship. So far from this, the world approves, commends, and shares in it. We require the clergyman at baptism, marriage, and burial; we require him on the Sunday; we require him for religious ceremonies which will make life easier and the conscience unruffled; we require him at the sick-bed; we also require him at our entertainments and festivities. To be irreligious, at least outwardly, is nearly as much reprobated by the world as to be spiritually minded, which is always in the way, out of place, and out of season— even at a death-bed, where men are said to require "consolation," not uneasiness and disturbance. Clergymen would be the most respected of persons if they only closely resembled those idyllic personages, described in novels, with a "dear old face," "white hair," and very little religion— but very much tolerance of the devil, the world, and the flesh. In short, it is not religion, but its peculiar form and mode as spiritual, to which a Jeroboam and his imitators object.

And so Beth-el had, as a prophet describes it (Hos. x. 5), become Beth-aven, and the house of God was turned into a house of vanity. There are testing times in the history of every individual, household, district, and nation professing to be Christian, when the question, if truthfully put, really amounts to this: Shall it be Beth-el or Beth-aven; religion, or spiritual religion; respectability or godliness; the broad, or the narrow way; the world, or the Lord? That religion is not worth anything which is not worth everything, and does not pervade everything. So far as Beth-el was concerned, the question had long been decided. Nor must we in studying this history forget that, in a certain sense, Beth-el was a representative city, as the place where the idol-worship of Israel was set up and established. Accordingly, the opposition of its inhabitants to the prophet acquired more than ordinary importance. It may, in fact, be described as substantially the contest between the darkness and the light at that period.

Probably the intended visit of Elisha had previously become known in Beth-el. At any rate, there could be no difficulty in recognising Elijah's successor. Whether these "young men"—as the expression in the original should be translated, rather than "little children," as in our Authorised Version—had been incited to their conduct by the priesthood of Beth-el, or had gone out to meet him of their own accord and bent on evil, or else the meeting was accidental, is comparatively unimportant. Certain it is, that when Elisha reached the dense forest by which, as we know, Beth-el was surrounded, he was immediately recognised by a band of young fellows, and received with the repeated taunt, "Go up, thou bald head!" They had not yet learned the object of his visit, nor even become personally acquainted with him. His appearance among them was sufficient to provoke what we must regard as an insult to Elisha, and a challenge to Elisha's God. Baldness was regarded in the East as a reproach, and "thou bald head" was intended as an expression of contempt and ridicule. The challenge to "go up" referred to Elijah's ascent to heaven in the fiery chariot, and was meant to express their denial and scoff of the miracle by which God had removed him. Thus the taunt was similar in spirit to that addressed to our Lord Himself: "If Thou be the Son of God, come down from the cross." Contempt and ridicule of God's servant, blasphemy and denial of God's work: such then were the weapons employed against Elisha by these young men. And is not the same mode of opposition still employed? The two most powerful instruments which the Enemy wields against the cause of God are ridicule and denial of God's truth.

In general, it may be laid down as a principle, that we ought to distrust those who turn into ridicule that which is sacred to others. If an earnest man be tempted to doubt any of the truths of religion, he will do so with the deepest heart-sorrow. But a habitual scoffer must be destitute of feeling as well as of principle. The chief danger of ridicule lies in this, that few are proof against its shafts. Not unfrequently a man who could not for a moment sustain a serious argument on religious subjects, nor indeed on any subject, comes out triumphantly by dint, not of wisdom, but of small wit. And here much mischief is also often done thoughtlessly and unintentionally. All men have their foibles; and religious people and clergymen have not only their share of them, but sometimes a more than ordinarily large one. At any rate, their every weakness will certainly be searched out and dragged to public view, and often be grievously exaggerated. Nor do we seek to deny that in our days also not many wise, not many mighty, are found among those who are truly religious. The way is narrow, the company is small, and—be it so, for argument's sake—not always the most agreeable. This is part of the prediction—it may be, part of the cross. Besides, the angularities and oddities of natural character sometimes appear in magnified proportions under the strong light of the Gospel. Accordingly, it is not difficult to make merry at religious people and their supposed ways, as inferred from our partial knowledge of their eccentricities. But the thing ultimately aimed at is religion itself. But is there anything to laugh at in the Sermon on the Mount, in the teaching of our Lord, in that of His Apostles, or in their lives and martyrdom? It is the New Testament which represents our Christianity, not the eccentricities nor the supposed narrow-mindedness of its pretending or even real professors. Hypocrisy is a motive easily ascribed to others, partly because it meets our general suspiciousness, and, partly, because it is a charge which cannot easily be confuted. It seems to come readiest to the world as a motive for what they cannot understand, perhaps from their own abundant experience of the hollowness and selfishness of men. Any writer or teller of stories can readily draw with coarse chalk the caricature of an ill-shaped, ill-educated, canting personage, and represent this as an embodiment of religion. But the harm which may be wrought by this modern imitation of the cry, "Thou bald head, thou bald head," can scarcely be over-estimated. True, it is our weakness to be influenced by such things; yet more or less, consciously or unconsciously, we are all affected by them.

Perhaps, however, it may be even more important to point out, that persons not otherwise ill-disposed may unconsciously do injury in the same direction. We do not ask immunity, or even tolerance, for the sins and faults of religious people. But can it be necessary, is it wise, right, or kind to drag their every foible into the light, and to make them the butt of ridicule? Granting, or at least not controverting, that the critics are the strong, and the criticised the weak, is this the way to mend matters, is it Christ-like? If we are insensible to the wrong of such conduct, let us at least remember the claims of charity. One may be within hearing who has for the first time begun to think seriously, and your words may fall like a withering blight upon his soul. It will not be easy henceforth to listen with humble earnestness to those whom you have done your best to present in the most ridiculous light. In general, would it not be better to speak about these foibles to God in the way of prayer, rather than to man in the way of gossip? Another remark may be added on a kindred topic. Religious people are not unfrequently in the habit of indulging in puns and witticisms, which would possess nothing humorous if it were not that the point lay in a quotation, or rather misquotation, from Holy Scripture. With some this is a rooted custom, and what otherwise would be very trite becomes witty by the introduction of a verse or incident of Scripture, which, it need scarcely be said, was intended for a far different purpose. The practice is exceedingly objectionable, not only as being, in plain language, profane, but as familiarising the mind with an improper use of the Word of God. Never clench an outburst of supposed humour with Scripture, however tempting the occasion. Use the inspired Word reverently and for what it is intended—for conversion and edification.

By the young men of Beth-el, as in so many other instances, derision of God's servant was accompanied by denial of God's word and work. The shout "Go up, go up," which clearly referred to the ascension of Elijah, was intended to imply their discredit of the whole history. In this they would no doubt have been joined by many in our days. Fools rush in where angels tremble, and there is a kind of rough and ready infidelity which has its arguments and proofs current in the mouth of ill-educated conceit. As if the mysteries of our souls and of the eternal world could be solved by such shallow, hap-hazard talk!

Remembering the character of Beth-el as a representative city, the nature of the offence, the absolute necessity of vindicating the authority of the prophet, and the character of the times, we have little difficulty in understanding the punishment which befell these young blasphemers. Yet, as we read it: the prophet first "turned back and looked on them," as if to recall them to a sense of their conduct, which, irrespective of its religious bearing was cowardly and inhospitable. We need scarcely add, that it was in vain; for those who are not influenced by the fear of God are not likely to pay much regard to man. Then, and only then, was the dreadful judgment pronounced, which the beasts of the forest were so soon to execute. Let no one imagine that this was merely what in the cant phrase of modern infidelity is called "Old Testament vengeance." It is quite true that Divine Revelation gradually unfolded alike in the teaching of its truths and in its demands, till it reached the perfection of the Spirit's Dispensation. But the vindication of God's authority has remained the same in all ages. There is a maudlin sentimentalism which repudiates the punitive assertion of right and of truth, as if a world where truth and falsehood, right and wrong, were equally tolerated by the Supreme Ruler, could be God's world. The New Testament only repeats the Old in its assertion: "Vengeance is Mine, I will repay, saith the Lord." And not revelation only, but reason also, and the promptings of our inner sense, assert the supremacy of law and justice.

Perhaps the most instructive instance of the distinction which we ought to make between personal wrongs and attacks on the Word of God—a distinction which we are too apt to overlook—is afforded by a reference to St. Paul. We read in 2 Tim. iv. 14, "Alexander the coppersmith did me much evil. The Lord reward him according to his works." And yet there is not vindictiveness in this. For, happily, the reason of what otherwise might have seemed a strange denunciation, is immediately added. "The much evil" which Alexander did to Paul was not personal. "He greatly withstood our words," or, as it is more correctly expressed in the margin, "our preachings." Perhaps he was the same unscrupulous Jew (Acts xix. 33) who would have incited the assembly in Ephesus against the Christians, though on that occasion it only resulted in his own discomfiture (ver. 34). But St. Paul would have the youthful and ardent Timothy "beware" of the old and cunning impostor. As if to place in the clearest light the distinction between personal wrongs, however cruel, and public opposition to the word and work of God, St. Paul follows up his warning by giving us a glimpse into his own private history. "At my first answer no man stood with me, but all men forsook me." How cruelly unkind, that of all his converts none should have dared to own him in the hour of danger. When the grasp of an outstretched hand, or even a word of sympathy, would have been so precious, all turned aside and left the aged Apostle cruelly alone! What shall be done to them? Surely theirs must be punishment at least equal to that of Alexander? Not so; but "I pray God that it may not be laid to their charge." They had sinned against Paul, but Alexander had withstood the Word of the living God and hindered His work. "The Lord reward him according to his works." Let us then beware how we resist and oppose that Word! Though proclaimed by feeble men, the truth of God, not man's mode of presenting it, is resisted at our extreme peril. Not that we are absolutely to receive everything a minister may choose to say, or to be frightened by his denunciations in case of our non-submission. That which in itself is foolish or untrue becomes none the more wise or worthy of acceptation, because it is declared from pulpit or platform with denunciations in case of resistance. We have the infallible Word of God as our test, and to it, not to any real or self-asserting human authority, we are bound to submit. But whether the authority claimed be human or divine, we must examine for ourselves by a prayerful study of the Scriptures.

And so judgment was executed in Beth-el that day. With sickening hearts we turn to follow Elisha. He cannot stay in Beth-el; he cannot even go to Samaria. He must retire to the solitude of Carmel to collect and strengthen himself, no doubt, in secret fellowship with God, after " the strange work" which he has been called to execute. Little can they realise the import of what they say, who whole-heartedly and angrily hold forth judgment and hell to a world of sinners. Surely, on the evening of that day of judgment, there was not a sadder heart even in Beth-el than that of the lonely pilgrim to Carmel.

CHAPTER VII.

ELISHA AND THE THREE KINGS.

"Now Jehoram the son of Ahab began to reign over Israel in Samaria the eighteenth year of Jehoshaphat king of Judah, and reigned twelve years. And he wrought evil in the sight of the Lord ; but not like his father, and like his mother : for he put away the image of Baal that his father had made. Nevertheless he cleaved unto the sins of Jeroboam the son of Nebat, which made Israel to sin ; he departed not therefrom. And Mesha king of Moab was a sheepmaster, and rendered unto the king of Israel an hundred thousand lambs, and an hundred thousand rams, with the wool. But it came to pass, when Ahab was dead, that the king of Moab rebelled against the king of Israel. And King Jehoram went out of Samaria the same time, and numbered all Israel. And he went and sent to Jehoshaphat the king of Judah, saying, The king of Moab hath rebelled against me : wilt thou go with me against Moab to battle? And he said, I will go up : I am as thou art, my people as thy people, and my horses as thy horses. And he said, Which way shall we go up? And he answered, The way through the wilderness of Edom. So the king of Israel went, and the king of Judah, and the king of Edom : and they fetched a compass of seven days' journey : and there was no water for the host, and for the cattle that followed them. And the king of Israel said, Alas ! that the Lord hath called these three kings together, to deliver them into the hand of Moab ! But Jehoshaphat said, Is there not here a prophet of the Lord, that we may inquire of the Lord by him? And one of the king of Israel's servants answered and said, Here is Elisha the son of Shaphat, which poured water on the hands of Elijah. And Jehoshaphat said, The word of the Lord is with him. So the king of Israel and Jehoshaphat and the king of Edom went down to him."—2 KINGS iii. 1-12.

FROM Mount Carmel the prophet had next to proceed to the royal city of Samaria. He was now in readiness for whatever work the Lord had prepared for him. The call to it came sooner and in another form than could have been expected. Jehoram now reigned over Israel. King Ahab had died and been succeeded by Ahaziah, a wicked youth, to whom it had happened, as to many other weak and wicked persons, that nothing prospered to which he put his hand. At last he fell through a lattice, to his serious hurt. Instead of taking timely warning and turning to the Lord, he sent messengers to inquire of Baal-zebub, the "Fly-god" of the Philistines. But his messengers were not even allowed to reach their destination. They were met by Elijah, and sent back to Samaria with tidings of death.

Ahaziah was succeeded by his brother Jehoram. The concise summary which Scripture gives of his religious character, as working evil in the sight of the Lord, though not to the shameless extent of Ahab and Jezebel, and as putting away the image of Baal, but cleaving to the sins of Jeroboam, is abundantly confirmed by his history. He had the vices of his parents without the firmness of his mother. A more contemptible sovereign never ruled over Israel. Braggart and rash before danger arose, but cowardly and desponding at the first appearance of serious difficulty, he was always oscillating between boastfulness and utter despondency. Both Judah and Israel—but especially the latter—had terribly declined from the state of prosperity in which David and Solomon had left the country. Tributary neighbours gradually regained their independence, and would ere long impose their own rule upon a nation which, with its God, had lost its strength. But so long as the determined hand of Jezebel tightened the reins in the trembling hold of Ahab, such efforts could not be made unchallenged.

Ahab himself had died from a wound received in the battle of Ramoth-Gilead, fought for the purpose of rescuing that place "from the hand of the king of Syria." In that battle Ahab had the assistance of one similar to him in natural character, though, happily, different as regarded religious principles. Jehoshaphat, king of Judah, was a pious monarch. But that fatal weakness which tolerated "the high places" in his land proved the curse of his reign. To the invitation of Ahab to join him against the king of

Syria, he had replied in terms which mercifully were only in part verified: "I am as thou art, my people as thy people, and my horses as thy horses" (1 Kings xxii. 4). It was only after Jehoshaphat had entered upon that ill-fated expedition, that it occurred to him to consult the Lord about its rightness. And in this inversion of things he is, alas, not solitary. It is strange, how prone religious persons are to make alliance with the world. It sometimes seems, as if we almost witnessed a race who should most readily abandon his principles. Not only is an alliance accepted, but it is in these terms: "I am as thou art, my people as thy people." God forbid that this should prove true!

But all such compromises arise from this mistake, the more dangerous because practical and not theoretical, that religion and every-day life can be separated. We have our own principles, so it is argued, and others have their views. There need be no collision. On these points we may agree to differ, a saying which may be ranked among those specious platitudes, by which the great Enemy has deceived and injured so many. What! agree to differ! On what subject? Whether Jehovah or Baal is God? Yes, we shall differ, but never *agree* to differ on this point, till our faithfulness and strength have disappeared under the insidious influence of slow but certain spiritual poison. May we not go further, and, with sadness at heart, say that the meannesses and even the sins of which Christian men and women are sometimes guilty in entering upon such alliances, or to put it in modern language, in agreeing to differ, but really in lowering themselves and abandoning their principles, in order to be taken notice of by the world and worldly society, are mainly the reasons of the diminished spiritual life which we mourn in the Church? In some instances, the mischief may not spring from a deeper source than the weakness of a

Jehoshaphat. We are afraid to appear singular; we wish to occupy our proper place; we must be like our neighbours; our children, our connections, our business requires conformity to the world. But if, indeed, spiritual things have been a reality to us; if we have fled for refuge to the hope set before us in the Gospel; if we have been purchased with the precious Blood of Jesus; if we have laid up our treasure in heaven— let us consider and see what we are doing when thus identifying ourselves with the world, as we go to the ball-room or the theatre. Are we not, in very deed, surrendering our most cherished principles by such associations? Let us learn by the example of Jehoshaphat. Merciful indeed will be the dispensation, if ours, like his, be only outward and temporal harm, damage, and shame, and not, as too often, the impoverishment of our own souls, and deep loss to those of others.

Nor did Jehoshaphat on that occasion intend to go without the Lord. Before he marched to the battle-field he would "inquire at the word of Jehovah." But instead of seeking such direction before he went to Samaria, he asked it after he had gone, and when, consequently, it was too late. We also too often consult the Lord only after we have determined on our own course. We resolve to do a thing, though perhaps we may not confess so much to ourselves, and then we kneel down to pray—surely not for direction, but for success in what we have already chosen. This is to "ask amiss, that we may consume it upon our lusts."

To desire an Ahab "to inquire at the word of the Lord" (1 Kings xxii. 5) was but another, though a consistent, token of weakness on the part of Jehoshaphat. It was the way to be religious in Samaria. Of course Ahab consulted the prophets of Baal, and of course all the four hundred of them said with one accord, "Go up." Four hundred, or, for that matter, four thousand priests of Baal will be readily found to say at any time, and to any expedition or alliance, "Go up." And even when, at the request of Jehoshaphat, whose conscience was by this time increasingly ill at ease, a prophet of Jehovah is sent for, the messenger who brings Micaiah—like the hopes and wishes which accompany the prayers of those who, before praying for direction, have already settled what direction they want—entreats the prophet to let his word be like that "of one of them, and speak that which is good." But all was now too late; even the warning of Micaiah came too late. It is not easy to extricate ourselves from a false position; and Jehoshaphat had to suffer the consequences of his rashness. But he had at least so far profited by the lesson, that when Ahab's successor requested an allied expedition to Ophir, Jehoshaphat refused (ver. 49).

The ill-fated battle of Ramoth-Gilead had led to most serious consequences for the kingdom of Israel. No sooner had tidings of the defeat and death of Ahab reached Moab, than its king, hitherto tributary to Israel, resolved to cast off his allegiance. During the weak reign of Ahaziah no attempt was made again to reduce Moab to subjection. But when Jehoram came to the throne immediate measures were taken, in a manner characteristic of the new king. "He went out of Samaria," "and numbered all Israel." It was to be a grand national expedition. Having done thus much—and for the present begun, as he so often did, without calculating how he was to end—it occurred to him to solicit the alliance of Jehoshaphat, king of Judah. Perhaps he had postponed this step because Jehoshaphat's refusal, when Ahaziah had formerly applied to him, rendered his present consent doubtful. But any such fear soon appeared groundless. Possibly, the circumstance that Jehoram had put away the image of Baal, may have seemed to Jehoshaphat sufficient warrant for an alliance, especially as on political grounds it was evidently the interest of Judah to suppress rebellion on the part of vassal-kings. The success of Moab might prove a dangerous example to Edom. We always readily persuade ourselves to see a religious duty where it is in our interest or pleasure to find it. How often, for example, when an unequal marriage, or any similar alliance is about to be made, do we speak of "hopeful signs," such as "respect for religion," or "religious training," when after all there is no more evidence of real religion than in the case of Jehoram. Again, men flatter the great or those to whom advantage binds them, and discover marks of piety, where the most large-hearted charity would have failed to discover any, had not self-interest or inclination put it there. God forbid that we should judge others, or undertake to determine their state of heart! But there is great difference between pronouncing on a man's supposed irreligion and assuming his piety, when the latter alone would warrant our entering into close relationship with him. Let us hail every sign of good in others, but let us not call darkness light, nor evil good. Jehoram may put away the image which his father had made, and yet cleave to the sins of Jeroboam!

It is painful to find that Jehoshaphat on this occasion reiterated the very terms in which his former sinful compact with Ahab had been expressed. But perhaps it is better distinctly to understand, that, at least so far as consequences on earth are concerned, alliance cannot be made with the world on other terms than these: "I am as thou art." We cannot go so far, and then withdraw. When we are making such a compromise, let us not deceive ourselves by arguing, that otherwise we might repel a hopeful beginning, and so drive men farther from the gospel. But in order to be consistent it is not necessary to be disagreeable or unkind. There is, indeed, a species of sectarianism whose every principle—and its followers have a principle for everything—seems like a sharp point, wounding whatever comes in contact with it. We plead not for this, nor even for the obtrusion of what we may deem right. We plead not for repelling, but for attracting; yet while doing so, it must not be at the cost of lowering the truth.

In one respect, Jehoshaphat was more consistent on this than on the former occasion. After having resolved on his own course, he did not go through the ceremony of inquiring "at the word of the Lord." When at last the two armies joined, Jehoram, who by this time was retreating into his proper place, asked Jehoshaphat to propose a plan of campaign. The course suggested by the king of Judah was certainly the most prudent in the circumstances. As Edom stood to Jehoshaphat in the same relation as Moab to Israel, it would have been dangerous to have left a doubtful ally on the flank and rear. To march through Edom, and then with its deputy-king, against Moab, would not only swell the material forces of the allies, but show the people of Edom that rebellion would certainly not remain unpunished. This prudent scheme, however, well-nigh proved the destruction of the expedition. At first all seemed prosperous. They advanced through the wilderness of Idumæa, where Israel had of old suffered so much. Their wary enemy had retired before them. In the expressive language of Scripture, "they fetched a seven days' compass." For seven weary days the allies traversed the fiery desert. A fierce sun above, burning sand underneath, the withering sirocco across this fearful pathway, and not a drop of water for man or beast, not a cloud indicating the blessed approach of rain! The allies were shut up in the wilderness; they could neither go forward nor retreat. To all appearance they were a sure prey to the enemy lying in wait for them.

Jehoram was again the first to break the silence. "Alas! that Jehovah hath called these three kings together, to deliver them into the hand of Moab." And is this all? At last Jehovah is recognised, but only as an enemy, seeking vengeance, and laying snares! There is an almost incredible amount of folly and profanity about this coward monarch. The first to project the expedition, he is the first to despond; the first to ignore Jehovah, he is the first to tremble and to anticipate a long-merited doom. And is it not so with the sinner, when the lips, that had once poured forth blasphemy and defiance, blanched with fear seek to repeat long-neglected prayer, in the hope of thereby conciliating an angry God? Oh, how little they know God, alike in the pride of their hearts and in the abject despondency to which at last they give way! They know God only by His judgments; and His revelation to them is what an affrighted conscience suggests. Yet judgment is His strange work; He delighteth in mercy.

Assuredly, the time cometh when each of us will think of God. It is the time of trouble, it is the hour of death. To the unconverted He will then appear only the God of judgment and of wrath; to His own people He is always the God of love. Yet most awful though it seems, that the God of mercy should in such an hour be only realised as a God of terror, what right have unconverted men to take any other than this view? There is not a single promise to the unconverted within the compass of Revelation. There are invitations, declarations, offers, addressed to *all* without exception or limitation; but the promises are only to those who have believed on Him in Whom all the promises are Yea and Amen.

But now also appeared the difference between weak but pious Jehoshaphat and weak but ungodly Jehoram. How his conscience must have reproved him; how he must have recalled to mind the rash words with which he had entered into this alliance! But what under similar circumstances shall we do? Surely not despair. Judas will go out to hang himself; but Peter goes out to weep bitterly. "To whom shall we go? Thou hast the words of eternal life." "Is there not here a prophet of Jehovah, that we may inquire of Jehovah by him?" Why had this not been done before this alliance was entered upon? But even now it was not too late. For, it is never too late to go to God. Granted, that we have erred, and strayed, and sinned; granted, that we are most undeserving and most ill-deserving—what then? Even thus we will return to the Lord like the prodigal, like Zaccheus, like Saul of Tarsus, or, be it so, as worse than any or all of them. "The blood of Jesus Christ His Son cleanseth us from all sin." "Though He slay me, yet will I trust in Him." If we perish, let it be at the foot of the Cross. But none ever perished or can perish there. "To him that knocketh it shall be opened," no matter at what hour his weary feet seek the long-neglected path, and his trembling fingers at the door make known the return of the abashed wanderer. No exception here, nor limitation, for as yet the cry is not heard, "The Bridegroom cometh!"

It added to the painful humiliation, that the heathen king of Edom should have witnessed a scene like this. The impotent despair of an unbelieving Jehoram, on the one hand, and the acknowledged inconsistency of a weak Jehoshaphat on the other, must have conveyed to him a very erroneous impression of the influence of Israel's religion in adversity. Might he not have said, What is the advantage of your religion? In what stead does it serve? One of you has not faith, and the other has not works. And may not the world often address the Church in similar terms? What is the benefit of a religion that does not stand the test of adversity, but seems like a staff that breaks whenever we attempt to lean upon it? The test of real religion is, how it endureth affliction, whether it draws us closer to, or away from God; whether it softens or hardens the heart; whether it leads to repentance or to despair.

To the question of Jehoshaphat, one of the servants of King Jehoram replied by directing the inquirer to Elisha. Most pleasant is it to find another believer like Obadiah at the court of Samaria. God has always His instruments in readiness. Often, and for His most important purposes, they are of the humblest character. He, Who maketh angels His ministers, condescendeth also to use the lowliest instrumentality. We know not who this servant may have been, nor what strange accident may have brought him into the camp, or into the presence of the king at that moment. Yet perhaps this was his only, his life-work. Perhaps all the tangled web of his life had been so cunningly and curiously woven only for this *one* object and design. Little do we know the purposes of God. A man's position may be the humblest. It may be that of a poor, ignorant servant. His lot may seem strangely cast, and not in very pleasant places. Yet God may have a very great work for him, much greater than for his earthly master, or for the greatest and most learned men around. This man may have been specially kept in order to give this one answer about Elisha. This is work sufficient for a lifetime. Patiently wait, believingly wait. The hymn which you may have taught this child, the prayer that you may have offered, the lesson that you may have given, may come back many years afterwards, perhaps long after you have fallen asleep, all unconscious of the work you had done, and possibly thinking that you had lived in vain. How do we know what seed will take root? But assuredly, every one of God's people has some work to do; and perhaps one of the most blessed surprises of that day will be that expressed in the wondering words, "Lord, when saw we Thee an hungered, and fed Thee, or thirsty, and gave Thee drink? When saw we Thee a stranger, and took Thee in? or naked, and clothed Thee? Or when saw we Thee sick, or in prison, and came unto Thee?"

What sunshine and joy must have burst upon the heart of Jehoram's servant when he heard the reply, "The word of Jehovah is with him!" A ray of hope also broke upon the soul of Jehoshaphat. Jehoram followed him moodily to the prophet; the king of Edom wonderingly. At any rate all three are now in earnest, and Elisha, no doubt directed of the Lord, is in waiting for his strange visitors.

CHAPTER VIII.

AN UNEXPECTED ALLY.

"And Elisha said unto the king of Israel, What have I to do with thee? get thee to the prophets of thy father, and to the prophets of thy mother. And the king of Israel said unto him, Nay: for the Lord hath called these three kings together, to deliver them into the hand of Moab. And Elisha said, As the Lord of hosts liveth, before whom I stand, surely, were it not that I regard the presence of Jehoshaphat the king of Judah, I would not look toward thee, nor see thee. But now bring me a minstrel. And it came to pass, when the minstrel played, that the hand of the Lord came upon him. And he said, Thus saith the Lord, Make this valley full of ditches. For thus saith the Lord, Ye shall not see wind, neither shall ye see rain; yet that valley shall be filled with water, that ye may drink, both ye, and your cattle, and your beasts. And this is but a light thing in the sight of the Lord: He will deliver the Moabites also into your hand. And ye shall smite every fenced city, and every choice city, and shall fell every good tree, and stop all wells of water, and mar every good piece of land with stones. And it came to pass in the morning, when the meat offering was offered, that, behold, there came water by the way of Edom, and the country was filled with water. And when all the Moabites heard that the kings were come up to fight against them, they gathered all that were able to put on armour, and upward, and stood in the border. And they rose up early in the morning, and the sun shone upon the water, and the Moabites saw the water on the other side as red as blood: and they said, This is blood: the kings are surely slain, and they have smitten one another: now therefore, Moab, to the spoil. And when they came to the camp of Israel, the Israelites rose up and smote the Moabites, so that they fled before them: but they went forward smiting the Moabites, even in their country. And they beat down the cities, and on every good piece of land cast every man his stone, and filled it; and they stopped all the wells of water, and felled all the good trees: only in Kir-haraseth left they the stones thereof; howbeit the slingers went about it, and smote it. And when the king of Moab saw that the battle was too sore for him, he took with him seven hundred men that drew swords, to break through even unto the king of Edom: but they could not. Then he took his eldest son that should have reigned in his stead, and offered him for a burnt-offering upon the wall. And there was great indignation against Israel: and they departed from him, and returned to their own land."—2 KINGS iii. 13-27.

IT was, indeed, an intense relief to find Elisha in the immediate neighbourhood of the camp. We could have scarcely expected him there—as little as we look for God's mercies to follow so closely, as they do, upon His judgments. Yet Elisha was there, and the word of Jehovah was with him. And when troubles are around, and we see no way of escape, when our consciences condemn us for backsliding from the Lord, what comfort to discover that the precious Word of God is still near us, with its message of pity and forgiveness, ever meeting our wants.

And Elisha, what has he to say for God and to these three monarchs? Before him stands the proud, idolatrous son of Ahab and Jezebel, the abashed, pious Jehoshaphat, and the wondering, perplexed deputy-ruler of Edom. Of this one thing we may feel certain, that there will be no compromise on the part of the prophet. He will preach to this select audience of three kings as he would to the humblest in the land. He will not study what may conciliate them. There are those who, even when they speak the truth, speak it almost as if it were a falsehood, or else with bated breath and humble demeanour, as if, so far as God's truth is concerned, we were not all equal. Surely there cannot be a different method of preaching to rich and to poor sinners. If we believe that our message is sent by God, then let us speak it fearlessly; if otherwise, let us forbear. Nor let the truth be put before others in such manner, as that what small amount of it is doled out can scarcely be disentangled from the misleading platitudes with which it is overlaid and enwrapped. "Seeing then that we have such hope, we use great plainness of speech"—before Felix, before Festus, before King Agrippa, as well as before every one, be he Jew or Gentile.

The king of Israel and the prophet of Israel are apparently here meeting for the first time. How will each bear himself? In accordance with his true character. Before anything could be done, it was indeed necessary that matters should be placed on their proper footing. Elisha was not a magician to do or to foretell miracles at pleasure, in order to suit a king's caprice or necessity. God delivers His own people. If the wicked share in the blessing, let them not imagine that there is no difference between good and evil. The king of Israel was not only the descendant, but the spiritual representative of that Ahab who daily caused Israel to sin. "What have I to do with thee? get thee to the prophets of thy father, and to the prophets of thy mother." A most truthful and appropriate address. If your religion has been real, let it help you to the end; if otherwise, why hold by it? It is noteworthy that in trouble and in the hour of death men often change their views on religion. What formerly they had denounced as fanaticism, they now seek as of truth and importance. So far from resorting to the Word of God, they had derided it, while now they demand its consolations. If religion is to be called in for our deathbed, why set it aside in the time of our health? Or, again, if men would shrink from the thought of being surrounded, in the hour of their supreme need, by all the pomp of their worldliness, why give their soul and strength to it, while the outgoings of the heart are prompted by choice, not by fear? Oh, that it may never be too late! God forbid, that we should narrow the exercise of those mercies which we all so much need. Yet there may be a time when it may be too late, when only gloom, thickening into outer darkness, will close around.

Such, then, was the bearing of Elisha, not defiant, but truthful; not despising dignities, but faithful to his trust, and conscious of a higher dignity than this world could confer. And what was the bearing of Israel's king? If at any time, it is under the pressure of adversity that the real character of a man appears. He is not confident nor boastful now; only abject fear and utter misapprehension of the real state of things characterise the reply of the king of Israel. "Nay: for the Lord hath called these three kings together, to deliver them into the hand of Moab." It is as if he said to the prophet: You *are* concerned in the matter, for Jehovah your God hath entangled us as in a net, in consequence of the old controversy between you and our house. In truth, the words of Jehoram were substantially the same as those with which Ahab had, under somewhat similar circumstances, met Elijah: "Hast thou found me, O mine enemy?" For, it is the custom of a certain class to represent what is really rebellion against the Lord as merely a difference of opinion for which men cannot be held responsible before God. It is a question of differences between individuals, not of sin against God. They are as religious and as good as others; only that on certain subjects they hold different views. We say that such things are acts of worldliness, and incompatible with true religion, which requires a new heart and a right spirit. They differ from us— that is all; and they trust they are as good and religious people as others, though they may not take such exaggerated and unpractical views as those who profess more. But, after all, how are we to decide such questions? Comparing ourselves with ourselves, we are indeed foolish. The all-important test in this, as in other matters, is, What saith the word of the Lord?

At first sight, it may seem strange that Jehoram should have acknowledged Jehovah at all, or owned His power. But then the Jewish idolaters of those days did not deny the being of Jehovah. Only, instead of serving Him as the Living and True God, they recognised Him as only a national deity, by whose side other national deities, such as those of Zidon or Philistia, existed. Accordingly, it was rather a trial of power between them, and, perhaps, between their prophets, which of these deities would prove the strongest.

Heathenism identified the principle of nationality with religion; whereas the Old Testament, from the first, and with increasing clearness, declared, that in and by the truth of which Israel was the depositary, all the families of the earth should be blessed. But if Jehoram had made his choice in favour of Baal, why was he at that moment in the prophet's presence? The reason has already been explained. To Jehoram it seemed that somehow Jehovah had for the moment got the advantage; and, accordingly, his object was to make terms, if it may be so expressed, with the prophet of the Lord. In the same manner vows are still registered, promises made, and certain "good deeds" done when men are in distress or fear. Not that they are prepared to give up the service of Baal, but that for the time they are anxious to propitiate Jehovah. But, alas, there was not a trace of repentance in Jehoram. He had come to seek, not mercy, but water!

The prophet indignantly turned from him. It seems almost wrong to cast pearls before swine. There are times and circumstances when we need not, perhaps, ought not, to reason. True, at all times it is God alone Who can change the heart; but there are cases in which our speaking might only hasten the hardening process. Let it be ours to set forth the truth plainly, and then leave it to God and to each man's conscience, at least for a time. It was not for the sake of Jehoram, but for that of Jehoshaphat, that the prophet had been sent to the camp. And here we mark, how gracious is the watchful care of the Lord over His people. Even when they have strayed from Him, as the king of Judah had done, His eye pitieth and His hand saveth them. And not only so, but for their sakes He often dealeth mercifully also with the unrighteous. Thus the whole ship's company "was given" to St. Paul. The people of God are the salt of the earth. How often, and how many have not their prayers and their presence preserved from dangers, all unknown!

But before Elisha delivered his message, he called for a minstrel. His spirit had been ruffled and troubled, and in that state of mind he was not fitted either to receive the Divine light or to reflect it. What better to soothe his mind than soft, gentle music—perhaps some of those strains which Jehoshaphat's great ancestor, "the sweet singer of Israel," had learned from heaven and taught on earth. Here also there is a practical lesson. Religion can never thrive in an atmosphere of excitement. Neither an alternation of fear and feverish elevation, nor a succession of violent spiritual emotions, is favourable to the growth of true piety. Religion strikes its roots far and deep into the inmost recesses of the heart. True religion is calm, peaceful, earnest—far too holy to be exposed to every gaze, far too deep to be reached by mere excitement. The world confounds religion with fanaticism. Because we are thoroughly in earnest, and can never be too much so, they think we are fanatical or earnest without sufficient reason. It is not so; the very opposite is the case. Mere excitement forms no part of real religion. We choose Christ because we are fully, firmly, and calmly convinced that He is our Lord and Saviour. Not in haste, but deliberately, as having calculated the cost, we count all things but loss for the excellency of the knowledge of Christ Jesus. We do not give up the world because we are obliged to do so, but because we no longer love it, the love of the Father being now in us. Our chief motive is, not fear, but the love of Christ. And when that love of Christ can change a hard heart, and make it gentle, pitiful, full of holy shame and of holy resolve, of kindness, generosity, and love, let it not be said that fanaticism has made it such. No, it has been that the

Blessed Shepherd, Who gave His life for the sheep, hath found and brought back the wanderer to the fold.

It has been noted, that of old music was employed to soothe the spirit. Perhaps, on kindred grounds, it has always been used in worship. This raises wider questions, much agitated in our days—those of the connection between religion and art. Is there such a connection, intended by God—and, if so, wherein does it consist? The inquiry may be too complicated for such brief answer as alone can here be attempted. At any rate, we may dismiss at once, as unworthy serious consideration, the reasoning which would plead for a sensuous worship on the ground of a supposed connection between art and religion. The first and decisive question here would be, whether such a mode of worship is congruous to the Divine Being, Who is a Spirit, and will be worshipped in spirit and in truth. But putting this aside, there surely must be a link binding art to religion. For, art is God-given, and what is God-given must be capable of being in turn devoted to God. But how can this be done? The consecration of art, which is the highest expression of mind, is itself an act of homage. Our deepest feelings are poured forth in music as their most appropriate language; our highest thoughts in poetry; our most glowing imagination in painting. Not to produce religious feeling, but to express it, is the province of true art. Again, art calms and elevates the mind, and, if it takes us to its own high altitude, that there we may pray and worship, another of its objects is fulfilled. The mistake in sensuous worship lies in this, that it is wholly incongruous to God, and foreign to His service; that our service is supposed to lie in that which is artistic in opposition to that which is spiritual; and, finally, that art is expected to excite religious feeling, whereas it can never produce, although it may express, spiritual emotion. Thus, like so many of God's good gifts, when misapplied, art only leads from God, instead of serving as the handmaid of religion.

But to return. The minstrel had ended, and the prophet's spirit was restored to calm. The veil which hides the future from view was withdrawn, and he saw what would shortly come to pass. "Ye shall not see wind, neither shall ye see rain," yet full relief would come. And "this is but a little thing in the sight of the Lord," for the Moabites would be overthrown, and Israel's standard planted on their ruined cities. Meantime the Jewish host was immediately to fill the valley with ditches, and to await the result. This latter direction implied a trial of their faith. But what, we may ask, would have become of Israel if they had neglected what must have seemed such strange means of deliverance? And so it always is. God would have us employ means. Often He chooses for our deliverance such as to us seem wide of the mark. Yet success lies, not in the means, likely or unlikely, but in the blessing of the Lord. Faith can compass all; it has the promise of all. We may and ought to pray for all we need, temporal as well as spiritual, and we have the answer assured to us—God's answer, not what *we* imagine it should be. Thus, on the one hand, are faith and prayer always connected, while, on the other, prayer always implies moral and spiritual discipline. Nor is such praying the outcome of a *gift* of faith in distinction to the ordinary *grace* of faith. Whatsoever we ask in His Name, believing, shall be done unto us.

On the return of the three kings to camp, the occupation of the army was strangely changed. Instead of sword and spear, each man handled the pickaxe and the mattock. All day long they wrought under the burning sun; and when the shadows of evening fell, those strange ditches were dug, and the valley was full of them. As the weary labourers lay down, they must have wondered what would be on the morrow. Morning came, and with it the solemn time of the early sacrifice. And now, hark, the sound as of running water, coming nearer and still nearer! From the way of Edom, down the rocky sides of its steep and barren mountains, it rushed along the dry river-beds, and then rolled full and rapid into the valley, and filled the ditches. What wonder and relief! Now the sun had risen higher, and poured down his golden light, but no longer on a dispirited, stricken army. His glory was reflected on the water till its colour seemed changed, and in the distance it shone almost like blood. The scouts of Moab saw and reported it. The leaders of Moab imagined that they understood it all. In the distress of thirst and in face of death, so they argued, the incongruous alliance between Judah, Israel, and Edom had been broken up. "The kings are surely slain, and they have smitten one another: now therefore, Moab, to the spoil!" Oh, that we never gave our enemies better cause to infer that we are smiting one another! Our dissensions, alas, have too often led to the cry, "Moab, to the spoil!" But all unexpectedly to Moab, the host of Israel arose like a giant refreshed. They assailed their assailants; a panic ensued. In headlong flight the army of Moab passed from city to city. Smoking ruins covered the land; devastation of fields and orchards and universal waste marked the progress of the victorious host. At last Moab made a stand at Kir-haraseth, the capital. But the city was hardly pressed by the besiegers. Only one remedy seemed to remain. The king of Moab chose a picked band of seven hundred, with whom to cut through his way, selecting the direction in which Edom lay encamped, naturally supposing that this portion of his enemies might be the weakest, and perhaps the most ready to allow his escape. But the attempt proved unsuccessful; and diminished in numbers, dispirited and desperate, the king and his followers had again to seek safety within the walls of Kir-haraseth. There was evidently no help with man; let them try the gods. Alas! Moab has not an Elisha, nor "the word of the Lord" to "inquire at." Man, without the knowledge of God, ignorant of His love and compassion, and only realising the anger of an all-powerful Deity, seeks to appease it by the most fearful sacrifices. The Moloch-worship of old, the fasts, penances, and scourgings of our own days, all those penitential self-inflicted sufferings, what are they but a mute confession of ignorance of the one great and blessed truth, that God is in Christ reconciling the world unto Himself, not imputing their trespasses unto them? God *has* forgiven us all our sins in Christ. He *is* our reconciled God, stretching forth to us, even in our rebellion and disobedience, His hands of mercy.

Let us mark, by way of contrast, the horrible spectacle which heathen ignorance had in the present instance prepared. In view of all his people and of Israel, the king of Moab leads forth upon the wall his eldest son, the heir to the throne, and plunges the sacrificial knife into the bosom of his own child, to offer him as a propitiation to his offended deity. Moab's king had loved his people better than his son. It was a terrible sight, never to be forgotten, and must nave equally awed, almost paralysed, friend and foe. "There was great indignation against Israel." The campaign and the alliance were alike at an end. They left the half-ruined city, the bereaved king, and the desolate nation. Yet, horrible as this instance of heathen ignorance seems, is it quite without a parallel even among so-called Christians? Have we never heard of, or even seen, parents sacrificing their children on the walls of our city? And, if so, was the object for which such a sacrifice was offered perhaps even as noble as that of the heathen king of Moab?

CHAPTER IX.

THE WIDOW'S CRUSE.

"Now there cried a certain woman of the wives of the sons of the prophets unto
Elisha, saying, Thy servant my husband is dead; and thou knowest that thy servant
did fear the Lord: and the creditor is come to take unto him my two sons to be bondmen. And Elisha said unto her, What shall I do for thee? tell me, what hast thou
in the house? And she said, Thine handmaid hath not anything in the house, save
a pot of oil. Then he said, Go, borrow thee vessels abroad of all thy neighbours,
even empty vessels; borrow not a few. And when thou art come in, thou shalt shut
the door upon thee and upon thy sons, and shalt pour out into all those vessels, and
thou shalt set aside that which is full. So she went from him, and shut the door
upon her and upon her sons, who brought the vessels to her; and she poured out. And
it came to pass, when the vessels were full, that she said unto her son, Bring me yet
a vessel. And he said unto her, There is not a vessel more. And the oil stayed.
Then she came and told the man of God. And he said, Go, sell the oil, and pay thy
debt, and live thou and thy children of the rest."—2 KINGS iv. 1-7.

FROM the noise of the camp and the field of battle, the
sacred narrative transports us to a far different scene. The
preservation of three armies and the continuance of a kingdom are not now the object of the prophet's mission. It is
only the safety of a poor widow, and the liberty of her two
sons. Perhaps one of the sublimest lessons of all may be
learned from this sudden transition. When we look up to
those starry worlds above, which pursue their course in a
silence of which the solemnity is almost overpowering, and
whose glittering light comes through centuries and over
distances which the mind may calculate, but cannot realise;
when we consider what forces are perpetually at work, and
what a small place and part in this vast universe our earth
occupies, our hearts are well-nigh overwhelmed. Has the
great Maker of this machinery, to us incomprehensible in its
magnitude and complication, left it to the operation of those

laws which He has put within its every part to regulate and check its working? If so, what of the intellectual and moral aspirations within us, of that which constitutes equally the real being of man and his dignity? What of those thoughts and hopes which we instinctively feel to be heaven-born, since we know them to have not been earth-sprung? What of the high moral motives, the noble inward struggles and victories, the self-devotion and self-sacrifice, the patient bearing, the trustful waiting, and holy living? Truly, we cannot believe in man without believing in God. And, again, we cannot believe in God without believing in Jesus Christ. Jesus Christ is the Love of God and the Providence of God concentrated in One Individual, the Son of God; manifested in One Individual; and in Him extending to individuals as such. The first lesson He has taught us is contained in the first words of the prayer He has left us, even as it is expressed in the first utterance of the spirit of adoption in our hearts. These words are, "Our Father:" Father by His love which gave the Son; Father by His love in the Son; Father by His love through the Son—a love which called and keeps us, which in all things watches over, and will at last safely bring us to His heavenly kingdom. And *our* Father—ours, and the Father of all!

Does this God then condescend to men of low estate? In this small speck of His great universe does He regard individual men? Does He direct the smallest things concerning them, so that not even an event of slightest importance can happen without His active knowledge? May we believe this? Is it the presumption which deserves the ridicule of some, or the well-grounded trust which inspires others with such undaunted courage, firm hope, and continuous joy? Those of us who have attained Christian conviction have a real answer to this question, satisfying not only the mind but the heart. We believe in God, but we also believe in Christ; and we cannot believe in Christ without believing His words: "Lo, I am with you alway, even unto the end of the world." Thus far for the main point—and now for the inferences. Time is made up of moments, and life of fleeting breaths. The highest moral and spiritual life, like the mightiest river, may issue from small springs. Such a life may be made up of things in themselves small, if only heart and temper are subdued, self is sacrificed, and God served. It is this daily and hourly service which is real service. There are more martyrs in cottages, humble homes, and in everyday life—more witnesses for the Christ by suffering—than those whose names are recorded on the pages of history. The "noble army of martyrs" is every hour increasing, till, at last, in "the morning" of renewed earth, "the great cloud of witnesses" shall descend upon it "like dew." A spiritual life thus made up and perfected requires, but also receives special and constant grace; and, viewed in its moral aspect, it is an object not unworthy the special and constant Providence or providing of our Father which is in heaven.

But we have more than this to assure us of God's condescension and care: we have the special promises of God, and of Christ. And, to take a still wider view, the whole dealings of God with man, which were the object of Revelation, commencing with the first promise after the Fall, and embracing Old as well as New Testament times, may be characterised as the dispensation of condescension. Its lesson may be summed up in that one word, which is the last and highest outcome of St. Paul's teaching: *grace*—which ultimately means, that God condescendeth to men of low estate, and to things of low estate. This was the lesson taught throughout the course of sacred history: in the call of Abraham, in the birth of Isaac, in the selection of Jacob, in God's dealings with the children of Israel, in the history of that nation, as well as in the birth of Jesus Christ, in the manner of His appearance, in His death, in His gospel which is to babes, and in the history of His Church. And this also is the lesson which each of us must learn, till, at last, when fully taught it, we shall be where faith gives place to sight. Nor does the greatness of God appear anywhere so great as in this very condescension. To the Christian there is not a moment of day but bears with it some ray of heavenly light, not an event which is not full of Divine purpose in grace. Thus everyday life, even the humblest, may be holy and heavenly, full of God and of heaven.

Let us now mark the illustration of all this in the narrative before us. In one of the towns or villages of Israel lived a widow with her two sons. She was poor, very poor, and now about to lose what had hitherto made that poverty endurable, and even cast a gleam of hope upon her difficult path. For she was not only very poor, but in debt, and her creditor was hard and cruel. According to the law of Moses (Exod. xxi. 2), he might take her sons for bondmen in payment of his claim; and what he could, that he would do. Whether this was prompted by ill-will towards the family, by revenge, or by avarice, matters not in our present inquiry. If we have had experience of the world—not merely driven along its smooth highway, but climbed the rugged sides, and descended by the steep precipices of what is called Life—we shall have had occasion to learn, how apt was that prayer of David: "Let us fall into the hands of God; let me not fall into the hand of man." Nor can we except from this even professedly Christian men, so long as in the prayer taught us by Him Who best knew the heart, we are made to link our entreaty of forgiveness with that for grace to forgive others. It may be a sore trial to feel that we stand alone. But far sorer is it often to feel dependent on man, who, even in his charity, so mingles reproach with help, that we are sometimes uncertain whether to press or to cast away his outstretched hand.

We are not told how the prophet's widow had come into these circumstances of difficulty. To be in debt was certainly wrong on her part; yet, with her two children, she may have lapsed into it gradually and insensibly; for they only who have loved objects to care for, know how easily under such circumstances obligations of the kind may be contracted. Or she may have become involved by sudden reverses, or by misadventure without any blame attaching to her. Or, she may have been to blame. Perhaps, not accustomed to straitened circumstances, she may not have been prudent. It is difficult to be very prudent when one is very poor. God forbid, that we should make light of the sin of neglecting the direction: "Owe no man anything." But, on the other hand, we wish to check the harsh judgment of those who have never known such temptations or difficulties. Many who are free of outward debt are also in their own minds free from that other obligation which the same law lays upon us, when it excepts from all others this one debt: "save to love one another." It may happen, that some who pride themselves on the regularity with which they discharge their obligations are those who have least difficulty in so doing, and hence, whose merit in so doing is the smallest conceivable. But, in the present instance, the saddest point in the history of this poor woman was, that her husband had feared the Lord, and even sustained the official position of "one of the sons of the prophets." And her creditor was very hard; he had "come to take unto him" her "two sons as bondmen."

The law of Moses which authorised such proceeding was

not so cruel as might be supposed from the present narrative. That law was given not to a commercial, but to an agricultural people, whose transactions were few and simple; it was given at a time and among nations where such a code would be far exceeding in mildness every other legislation and custom; it was surrounded by strong safeguards to protect the bondman; and, best of all, there was the provision that servitude could not last longer than the seventh or Sabbatical year, when the debtor would return a freeman to his home. But little consolation to the widowed mother would for the present lie even in this provision. Josephus supposes that she had been the wife of that pious Obadiah, who, under the rule of Ahab, had hid and fed a hundred of the Lord's prophets, at a time when charity much less than this might have cost a man's life and estate. But whether the suggestion of Josephus be correct or not, there is sufficient in this history to raise serious questions of present interest. The Word of God gives to His people distinct promise of all that is needed for themselves and their children. This, we think, will be admitted by all. But had this Word now failed? Or, to take a wider view, Why were such calamities sent to one towards whom we should scarcely have expected such dealings? Such or similar questions often recur, in one or another form, as we watchfully observe the course of God's Providence. To mere onlookers it seems sometimes strangely devious. Why this calamity, or those repeated bereavements to the godly, and why such unbroken prosperity to the wicked? The inquiry is not new; it had so pressed upon the Psalmist that his "steps had well nigh slipped" (Psa. lxxiii. 2). Unacquainted as we are with the history of individuals, from its beginning to its close, we may be unable to trace either the lessons of His Providence, or the final deliverance of His people. But the Word of God can never fail, and He dealeth with His people only in love, not in judgment. Happily, in the history of this poor widow we are enabled to understand and follow all, and we therefore regard it as a sort of type of similar cases. The poor widow of the prophet stood *not* alone; never less than when most she seemed so. The promise of God did *not* fail either to her or to her children. The calamities which befell her proved real blessings; they brought help directly from God; they tried and trained her faith; and they issued in much fuller deliverance than could have been experienced, had her creditor been indulgent and patient, or her former friends mindful of her and charitable.

It may seem strange that we are brought into straits not only for our good, but for our happiness. And yet it is true. Surely the happiest moment to the Christian is when, utterly unable to find any help around, he finds grace in simple faith to cast his burden upon the Lord, quite content to leave it there, and quite certain that He is faithful in Whom he has believed. The *what* and the *how* of the deliverance form no longer subject of care; he has the Lord Himself as surety for good. Such exercise of faith fills the heart with intense peace and perfect calm. It is not victory, it is *rest*. The soul returns to its quiet rest; it rests upon the Lord. And this lesson we require to learn for our everyday life—for thus alone we come to live upon the Lord, and to live by faith. To open our whole heart to God; to tell Him all we need, not only in things spiritual but in things temporal; to spread before the Lord all that concerns us and others, is indeed not only our highest privilege, but our greatest happiness. And when, by reason of the forgetfulness of our hearts, we have become more rare and restrained in that fellowship, our wants and our trials drive us ever anew, with repentance, but also with restored joy, to the Throne of Grace.

In olden times when "God spake unto the fathers by the prophets," and not, as to us, directly by His Son, Whom He has appointed heir of all things, the suppliant, as this poor widow, would "cry" unto an Elisha. Indeed, it seems as if Elisha had been specially sent to that city for the purpose, just as in the evangelic narrative our Lord seems specially to pass through a place for the relief or the conversion of one person. The widow was evidently an earnest believer, for in her "cry" she referred to the promise made to those who fear the Lord. This is a claim never ignored in the court of heaven. But the help which the prophet would bring, he connected with the scanty provision still left in the widow's house. Though it be only "a pot of oil," it must be used. The world is frequently mistaken as to the interpositions of God. Because it can trace, it thinks it may deny them. Because God blesses our exertions, it ascribes success to them, not to the blessing upon them. But have not others equally exerted themselves and failed? Have not others been arrested in their exertions by sickness, or by circumstances which could not have been foreseen nor prevented? Two men partake of the same food; the one is nourished, the other is not; the one is healthy, the other is sick. The world, which ever denies the possibility of a miracle, ever clamours for miracles in their coarsest form. It will not believe that God directly helps the poor, unless it see the clouds part and the help come down visibly. It cannot imagine any interposition except the coarsest; it denies miracles, but believes in magic, which is the exercise of power without moral motive or spiritual object. The interpositions of God are generally by means, although by such as in themselves are inadequate to secure the object. And this because in such manner faith is called forth, which, in that case, is the use of the means without belief in the means, but with belief in the Living God—a constant spiritual negation of things that are seen and temporal, and a constant affirmation of things that are unseen and eternal. This is the moral aspect of faith. And thus the faith of this woman was tried: first, in being directed to the one pot of oil left to her; next, in borrowing from her neighbours "vessels not a few;" and, lastly, in pouring out of her one pot of oil with the expectation of filling all those borrowed vessels. All this was to be done simply on the ground of the prophet's word, just as we pray and trust simply upon the promise of our God.

Before entering on her strange employment, the widow was told "to shut the door" upon herself and her sons. To shut out the world, and, as it were, to shut herself in with God, was a befitting attitude. And now she filled the first, the second, the third vessel! As we use the gifts entrusted to us God will employ and increase them. Not to wait for more gifts or fresh opportunities, but to use what we have according to His direction, is the condition of increase. More oil, and yet more oil, till every vessel in the room was filled! Then only was the tide of blessing stayed. For, if we are straitened, it is not in Him, but in ourselves that we are straitened. The oil is stayed only when there are no more vessels to be filled. Whether it be the oil of personal religion, of usefulness, or even of temporal supply, it is equally true that we have not, because we ask not. If in simple faith we gathered our vessels, not for selfish purposes, but for the glory of God and according to His command; if we "shut the door," and in earnest prayer besought His blessing, the oil would continue to flow, and the measure of the supply would be, not that He stayed the oil, but that our empty vessels were full. Oh, what power is there in the Church and in Christians, lying in great measure unused, because we look to earthly resources, and human calculations! All things are possible to him that believeth. Given a work for God and living faith, and nothing is impossible or improbable; all things are certain. Do we believe this, and are we prepared to act upon it? Or shall we continue to live beneath our privileges, trusting in *uncertain* riches instead of the *Living* God?

The reasons which determined Elisha not to give the widow any directions about the disposal of the oil, leaving her to come back to him, are easily understood. To have foretold the full result might have interfered with the exercise of her simple faith. On the other hand, to make her tell the story of her deliverance would draw out her love and gratitude to the Giver of all. Nor does God ever give us directions for the morrow. He guides His people from day to day—surely, but not beyond the day. For duty and for trial, for faith and for hope, the day is ours; the morrow is His. The first direction of the prophet, "pay thy debt," is one which may not inappropriately be pressed on those who set light by everyday duties, as if beneath the scope of their religion. Yet, in these common engagements we are bound to take the Word of God for a lamp unto our feet, and a light unto our path. Having done this first needful duty, she and her children were to live of the rest. Here, then, was *sudden* relief, *complete* relief, *lasting* relief. Man might fail, but in any hour of future need, the same God Who had fulfilled His promise would be still near, and mighty to deliver her. This God is ours also, our Father in Christ Jesus. To Him we will go with our empty vessels, and in our every need. According to our faith it shall be unto us. The measure of our faith is alone the measure of His blessing; nay, He will do "exceeding abundantly above all that we ask or think."

CHAPTER X.

THE GUEST-CHAMBER AT SHUNEM.

"And it fell on a day, that Elisha passed to Shunem, where was a great woman; and she constrained him to eat bread. And so it was, that as oft as he passed by, he turned in thither to eat bread. And she said unto her husband, Behold now, I perceive that this is an holy man of God, which passeth by us continually. Let us make a little chamber, I pray thee, on the wall; and let us set for him there a bed, and a table, and a stool, and a candlestick: and it shall be, when he cometh to us, that he shall turn in thither. And it fell on a day, that he came thither, and he turned into the chamber, and lay there. And he said to Gehazi his servant, Call this Shunammite. And when he had called her, she stood before him. And he said unto him, Say now unto her, Behold, thou hast been careful for us with all this care: what is to be done for thee? wouldest thou be spoken for to the king, or to the captain of the host? And she answered, I dwell among mine own people. And he said, What then is to be done for her? And Gehazi answered, Verily she hath no child, and her husband is old. And he said, Call her. And when he had called her, she stood in the door. And he said, About this season, according to the time of life, thou shalt embrace a son. And she said, Nay, my lord, thou man of God, do not lie unto thine handmaid. And the woman conceived, and bare a son at that season that Elisha had said unto her, according to the time of life. And when the child was grown, it fell on a day, that he went out to his father to the reapers. And he said unto his father, My head, my head! And he said to a lad, Carry him to his mother. And when he had taken him, and brought him to his mother, he sat on her knees till noon, and then died. And she went up, and laid him on the bed of the man of God, and shut the door upon him, and went out. And she called unto her husband, and said, Send me, I pray thee, one of the young men, and one of the asses, that I may run to the man of God, and come again. And he said, Wherefore wilt thou go to him to-day? it is neither new moon nor sabbath. And she said, It shall be well. Then she saddled an ass, and said to her servant, Drive, and go forward; slack not thy riding for me, except I bid thee. So she went and came unto the man of God to Mount Carmel."—2 KINGS iv. 8-25.

THE character of a nation is best learned, not from abstruse study, but by mingling with the people in their everyday life. How events have in the course of history moulded the national mind; how the constitution and laws under which they live have affected their relations and habits; and how the religion which they profess has influenced them, can only be seen in the homes and by the hearths of the people. If we endeavour in this manner to make ourselves acquainted with Jewish life in those days, and, besides, to learn how the mission of the prophets affected, not only the nation at large, but families and individuals, we shall be able to form a better estimate of the polity which God had instituted, and of the religion which He had given.

The plain of Jezreel presented to the eye perhaps the richest tract in the land of Israel. The soil was particularly fertile and well cultivated. Although too often the battle-field of the nation, and drenched in blood, at the time of which we write it was smiling in peaceful beauty and laden with the treasures of husbandry. Far as the eye could reach spread rich fields, till the distant horizon was bounded on either side by the heights of Tabor and Carmel. About midway between these two points lay the quiet village of Shunem. If the people of that district could not boast of the wealth of commerce, their simple wants were easily supplied in their own homes; if they engaged not in extensive enterprise, they possessed in their fields and flocks all that they could wish. They were an exclusively agricultural population, whose primitive habits recalled the ancient days of Israel. Territorial aristocracy, of course, there was none, nor could there be, where, after a certain term, the land reverted to its original owners. But there were "great people" nevertheless; those whose sturdy industry had, with the blessing of God, brought them such wealth as there was, and whose position and character gave them influence in the district. Shunem also had its "great family," and to this home and household the footsteps of the prophet were now to be directed.

So far as we can infer, Elisha had at the time no fixed dwelling-place. Most frequently, indeed generally, he was to be found by Mount Carmel. In this grand solitude he could retire from arduous work within himself, or hold communion with his God. Those employed for God, indeed all busily employed, need seasons and places of retirement. It is a saying of Cecil's, that a business which does not allow of leisure for retirement and meditation, cannot be proper for a Christian. It certainly seems incompatible with the Lord's direction: "Seek ye first the Kingdom of God." The busier the life the greater the need for such retirement, and that not only on the Lord's Day, nor at certain times, but at a certain time every day, since daily grace and strength must be sought for daily work. It so happened that Elisha's way to Carmel lay through Shunem. On his frequent journeys to and fro the prophet had not remained unobserved. There was that in his appearance and bearing, which commanded attention and respect, even if his office were unknown, as at first it seems to have been to the Shunammites. The "great woman" of Shunem, as Scripture designates her, resolved to bid such a pilgrim welcome to her home. We know not why *she* is so singled out—whether because she was an heiress and proprietress in her own right, or because she, rather than her husband, represented the household. The latter may sometimes be necessary, and may be the case without implying either want of deference and respect to a husband, or obtrusiveness and self-assertion on the part of a wife. In truth, this Shunammite was one of the representative women of Israel. If her outward appearance corresponded to her character and conduct, it would not be difficult to imagine the picture. Gentle and respectful towards her husband, as when she afterwards sought his permission to use one of the beasts of burden for her lonely ride to the prophet; loving her own with all the ardour of a genuine and generous nature; frank, free, independent in mind —we had almost said lofty, if that term were not so often confounded with pride—yet so kind, tender-hearted, with such true womanly instinct, and, withal, so thoroughly and simply pious, this strong-hearted, soft-hearted woman would have deserved the title of "great" had she been the veriest beggar in the streets of Shunem.

General as the practice of hospitality was in Israel, whereby "some entertained angels unawares," hers was no ordinary invitation to the prophet. It is said, "she constrained him to eat bread." It was not the pressing and oppressing bustle which wearies rather than refreshes; nor was it, on the other hand, the stinted condescension which makes one feel, and perhaps rejoice in feeling, that one is only a guest. Elisha had not known her at the time, as he afterwards did, and he was unwilling to turn aside into her house. The "great house" and the "great woman" had no attraction for him. But, as at a later period Lydia, so the Shunammite constrained him. And the feast was simple and homely. It was an ordinary meal, but one at which a prince in Israel sat down at the board of an Israelite indeed, in whom was no guile. Let us here also learn a lesson. True hospitality bestows its favours, not as giving, but rather as receiving favour. It is the hospitality of the heart, not of conventionalism, of pride, of selfishness, nor of what is called "society," which ever seeks back its own with tenfold interest.

That word "Society" has a dangerous sound to many among us. Too often it is the idol to which is sacrificed that which is most precious. Let us be truthful with ourselves. Why do we desire this kind of society? Is it from pride, or because we think it due to our station, or, perhaps, because we would like it to be due to our station? Mostly we cannot but feel, that it is neither in the service of the Lord, nor yet for the benefit of our souls. Often it is not even to our worldly comfort. Yet how often have Christians denied their Master, or at least wounded their consciences, for the sake of "society"! But would we seek and cultivate the acquaintance of these same persons, if they were poor instead of rich, uninfluential instead of holding a certain position, obscure instead of being well known? How often has our choice been determined by the world, and only by the world! What endeavours are made, what ingenuity is wasted, what sacrifices and vexations are borne to "get into society;" and while an Elisha had to be constrained by the great woman to eat bread in her house, many would fain constrain her to allow them to pick up the crumbs which fall from her table. With what alacrity men go to the houses of the rich and the great, and with what reluctance to those of the poor! All this and much more holds true, alas, not merely of the world, but of the professing Church. Nay, this is perhaps the besetting sin of our days. It were hypocrisy to plead, that this is done in the interest of the gospel. It is not so; it is done in the interest of worldliness. And how can we hope to do spiritual good to others while we mix with them, as the worldliest among the worldly? In so saying we do not wish to ignore the legitimate place assigned by God to rank, influence, or even wealth. "Honour to whom honour is due." The hoary head is, indeed, a crown of glory—but only if wisdom and righteousness, not if folly and sin, are associated with it. The Lord has said in warning, "How can ye believe, which receive honour one of another, and seek not the honour that cometh from God only?" If we really believe that our God can fill the ditches with water without sound of wind or rain, and out of one pot supply with oil all the empty vessels, then why attach ourselves so much to man, and depend, or seem to depend, upon an arm of flesh?

Though Elisha had at first been an unwilling guest in the "great house" at Shunem, his intercourse with the family soon removed any latent misgivings. Accordingly, without further invitation or entreaty, "so it was that as oft as he passed by, he turned in thither to eat bread." Elisha was now the friend of the household, and the character of their intercourse, as well as the bearing of the prophet, appears from the proposal which the Shunammite made to her husband. We conclude, that at first she had been ignorant who her guest was. Her invitation was not, as so often in our days. Sometimes what is called a "popular preacher," is bidden —truth to say, on much the same ground as famous scoffers, or any one else who is famous, from idle curiosity, or because others seek such company, or from other selfish motives. It was far otherwise in this case. The Shunammite perceived, "that this is an holy man of God, which passeth by us continually." She would have "a little chamber" constructed for him "on the wall." She proposed not to assign to him one of the rooms in the house, but, as is common in the East, to build a little addition on the top of the house, to which there was direct access from the outside by a stair, so that he might come in and go out, without more contact with the family than he himself chose. In short, she studied his comfort and convenience, not her own gratification. Truly, this was womanly delicacy, mindfulness, and kindness towards one like Elisha. She would not have him pay dearly for his entertainment—for it is often bought much more dearly than with money's worth. But having first recognised him as "a man of God," she honoured and served God in honouring and helping His servant—and this also was "honour to whom honour is due." The little

THE GUEST-CHAMBER AT SHUNEM.

chamber was furnished with the utmost simplicity, consistent with the wants of the prophet—" a bed, and a table, and a stool, and a candlestick." And so it was ready against the time that Elisha should next "pass by."

Elisha was a man of like passions with us. Perhaps from the sternness of his calling and the consequent necessity of repressing his feelings, he was only the more keenly alive to all that makes social intercourse pleasant or desirable. As he spent his first night in his new and unexpected home, and noticed the delicacy and kindness with which the Shunammite had executed what her piety had planned, he felt that this was one of the instances in which in this life also must be fulfilled the promise, as old as God's mastership and man's discipleship, to those who give even a cup of cold water for the Lord's sake. But what that "reward" should be, must be left undetermined till God would show it in the course of His Providence.

Meantime, however, another figure had appeared on the scene. The prophet was no longer unaccompanied; he was attended by a "servant" named Gehazi; not one who sustained to him the same relation as he himself had done to Elijah, but simply a waiting man, who should take much needed care of the prophet. In some respects Gehazi was peculiarly suited to his post. He presented almost the exact opposite of his master. He was not good, nor was he even wise; but he was pre-eminently shrewd, a man of secularities, steeped in them, viewing everything through their medium, and with just enough of religion to pass off his worldly shrewdness under that favourite term which has almost come to be regarded as a religious virtue: "the wisdom of the serpent." Alas that this quality, so abundant in our days, should be so rarely combined with "the simplicity," or indeed with anything, that could remind us "of the dove"! There are few religious movements or religious persons that have not their Gehazi attached to them. They are not wise men, but shrewd men; men who are not to be taken in; in whose faces and on whose lips, when you ply them with spiritual motives, or take a different stand-point from that of secularity, you can almost read the answer: "Oh, we know that." They are not to be driven out by "this kind," nor by the views of unpractical men. They are eminently practical. *You* mean well, but *they* know better; and they hear you with a smile half of benevolence and half of pity which freezes the very heart-blood. And in one respect they are right. They know and can calculate far better than you the secular forces, probabilities and difficulties; only they have not, and know not the one element that constitutes all and in all to you—the spiritual and the eternal. They do not deny it—God forbid; they only ignore it. Yet even these men have their use, if you only know how to use them, or rather how *not* to use them. It is their misuse, which, alas, has led to such terrible secularity in the Church, in our enterprises, and in our religious societies.

Gehazi was a man keenly and quickly observant of all that passed around him. He could by a sort of instinct take in the whole situation without having gone through a process of elaborate reasoning. And his conclusions were, secularly viewed, generally correct. Where spirituality was not required, where secularity, "the wisdom of the serpent," was requisite, Gehazi was invaluable. With this, however, he combined vices, full of danger, as most vices in professedly religious men, not so much to others as to himself. He was weak and vain, boastful, and intensely covetous and selfish. Possibly all these things were unknown to himself; probably had he known them, he would have called them by other names, and thought that they could not interfere with his religion of secularities. But it would have been well for Gehazi, had he given heed to the first indications of the spiritual impossibility of such a religion, as this was gradually brought before him by his master.

Him Elisha sent to "call this Shunammite," on the morrow of his first stay in the guest-chamber. When she modestly and reverently stood before him, the prophet, with warm acknowledgment of her kindness, asked her what return he could make. Elisha was not "a practical man" in the sense of Gehazi. He had never taken in the outward circumstances of the household. He had no conception of the one and only want and sorrow of the family; they had never spoken of it before him; perhaps they had never confessed it to each other or even to themselves. "Wouldest thou," continued the prophet, perhaps rather thinking aloud than addressing the Shunammite, "be spoken for to the king, or to the captain of the host?" Elisha knew that these were the ordinary wants of the people, and his authority at court was just at that moment paramount. The answer of the Shunammite quickly recalled the prophet to himself, and convinced him that any return offered to her must come from a mightier Sovereign than him who ruled at Samaria. "She answered, I dwell among mine own people." Well and nobly spoken, daughter of Israel! Such were the laws of Israel, that even under the government of the weakest and most wicked monarchs one could say, "I dwell among mine own people:" I need not the protection, I ask not the favour of any man. Hers was that noble independence, which, without dealing haughtily with the most lowly, would scorn to abase itself before the most mighty. For, true independence of mind is something very different from independence of circumstances, though superficial onlookers may confound them. We may preserve our independence in the midst of the greatest outward dependence, and we may never attain independence, even while placed in the most independent circumstances. Indeed, true independence comes out quite as much in the mode of giving, as in that of receiving favours. From the way in which a person offers favours, we may judge how he would receive them, and whether under circumstances of outward dependence he would still preserve his inward independence. There is, in truth, only one way of reaching this. To be truly dependent upon our God in Christ makes us independent of men; serving one Master, we "have not many masters." What is it all? Our God reigneth. Such was the independence of the Shunammite. Blessed be God, that we also live in a land and under laws where we need not fear, nor seek the face of man. Yet much deeper praise and thanksgiving, if, through grace, we belong to the people of God, and looking up with perfect confidence to our Blessed Risen Lord, can say: "I dwell among mine own people."

Gehazi was much more "practical" than Elisha. With one glance he had taken in all, and discovered the one great want in "the great house" at Shunem.. Here were broad acres, and large herds, and full granaries, and plenty in barn and winepress; but here also was a mother's heart vainly yearning to feel that of a child beating against her own; and here was an Israelitish home of which the light was about to be extinguished, and which could never hope to see the great light of the Messiah kindled from its flame. All around were strangers, and all around was for strangers; and they themselves felt doubly strangers, soon to be remembered only as shadows of the past. Yet, and though childlessness was in Old Testament times far different from what it is in ours, there was neither murmuring nor repining on the part of the Shunammite. But Gehazi with his shrewd eyes had seen it all, and now, when the prophet said to himself, "What then is to be done for her?" he did not propose relief for her great sorrow—he was too shrewd to make *any* proposal—but he told how she had no child, and her husband was old, and he left the prophet to infer the rest. And so, after the prophet had, we cannot doubt it, first laid the matter before the Lord—the Shunammite was recalled, and in simplest words her coming happiness was announced to her. It was almost too great joy to be believed; but he was the "man of God" who had announced it. Another year, and she carried the babe in her arms. The prophet still came in and went out; but the home was no longer childless; and the infant grew up, an object of special interest to Elisha, and, no doubt, a child of many prayers.

Years had passed, and the period of helpless infancy was over. The father had now a little companion in the son of his old age. It must have been gladsome to watch how grey evening and rosy morning seemed here joined. And now the happy time of harvest had again come. A rich summer's sun was pouring his rays over hill and vale; the fields were waving with golden corn, and men's hearts were filled with thankfulness, for there was abundance in the land. The merry song of the reapers was heard as they went forth to gather the treasures of the field, and behind them followed, with modest step but lightened heart, the widow or her children, to glean among the sheaves, where some of God's rich provision had fallen unnoticed, or been purposely left on the ground. The sun had not yet risen high when the happy owner of all this plenty went forth to view the busy scene, his little son by his side. Incautiously the child removed his head-covering. The slanting rays of an Eastern sun struck him. All was such health and happiness around, that even the child's cry, "My head, my head!" failed to alarm his father. By his direction the boy, perhaps supposed to be only tired, was carried home to his mother. There, in the still and darkened chamber of the great house, upon the mother's knees and against her heaving breast lay the fevered child, his lips parched, his eyes glazed, his frame quivering. Slowly the hours crept on, and with the growing heat of the sun, grew the pain of the moaning child. With agonised heart she kept watch over him. She could only pray, but it seemed as if God did not hear her. The child moaned heavier, and tossed convulsively. The sun had now reached his mid-day height. Through the lattice he flung all his glare of brightness and of glory on the brain of this poor child, perhaps filling it with visions far more bright and glorious. For a moment the child seemed to stagger under it—the next the golden bowl was broken, and the spirit of the child had fled. The sunbeam of the Shunammite had crept up again to the Light whence at first it had issued. Look not down upon this heavy form! Where now is thine own, thine only child, O mother? Not here, O mother, no, not here. It is with the God Who gave it.

But *why* such a trial, and blasting of long-cherished, short-lived hope? Was it that prosperity was difficult to bear, and had the Giver been forgotten in the gift? Or, was the boy nurtured too much for the parents, and too little for God? Did they need this, or did the child need it? Perhaps, in the tumult of thoughts and feelings, the Shunammite had not yet asked herself any of these questions. For, it is only "afterwards" that affliction bringeth forth the peaceable fruits of righteousness. As yet the tree that beareth these fruits was only being planted deep down in the Shunammite's heart, and sore was the digging up of the soil in which it was to strike its roots. But amid all that passed in that mother's breast one thought stood out. In deepest sorrow we have only room for one thought. Whatever that thought may be, it wholly engrosses us. And now also only one object was before her, standing out high as a bluff of land in sight of the shipwrecked mariner. She must make for it, if she would be safe; she must concentrate all her woman's energies, all the strength of her strong heart, and neither look to the right hand nor to the left. She must reach that land, and then she may sink down weary and worn, but not till then, for then she is safe. Through all that blinding drift of sorrow, she sees it still; through all that storm she hears it: To Elisha! Come what may, through all that storm and tempest of feeling she must go to the Prophet. Yes, to *our* Prophet, to Jesus! Through all and every tempest, over the watery waste to Jesus, Whose word can hush the storm and bid the waves be quiet. Before we look intently at our sorrow, before we gaze on the dead face in the light of our shaded room, before we speak of it to any one, however near and dear, straight to Jesus! There, and there alone is safety—and what matters it though, when we reach His feet, we should sink down weary and worn? *He* will give us rest.

And so this strong-hearted woman, with this one purpose in view, has again become strong. Repressing the tide of her feelings, she has carried the child to the guest-chamber, and laid her dead boy upon the prophet's bed; for he belongs as much to the prophet, or rather to the Lord, as to her. The very action was like pleading the promises. Then, mastering her face and manner so that not even her husband could discover aught in her that was strange, she asked him for a fleet beast of burden that she might "run to the man of God and come again." The proposal was unexpected, for, as he reminded her, it was "neither new moon nor Sabbath," at which times Elisha was probably wont to gather around him those who loved to hear of the deeds of Jehovah. Not evasively, but from the very bottom of her heart, the Shunammite replied, "It shall be well." Having resolved to go to Elisha, even in that hour of bitterest agony she had no longer any doubt; she believed, and was not disappointed. In the hour of our keenest grief, when all seems empty and hopeless, and the one only child of our hopes lies dead in the upper room, yet looking to Jesus to be enabled to say, "It *shall* be well"—this is faith indeed, and victory over the world. To put Jesus over against everything, to take Him as our all in all! And why not? *He is* all and in all.

The sun was declining towards the west on the plain of Jezreel. Forward, still forward—"drive, and go forward, slack not thy riding for me." She knew not weakness, she felt not weariness, she rested not, but still urged on her way. For sixteen long miles she rode, in all that inward conflict supported by one thought, and seeing only that one object for which she made straight. "So she went and came unto the man of God to Mount Carmel."

CHAPTER XI.

EFFECTUAL FERVENT PRAYER.

"And it came to pass, when the man of God saw her afar off, that he said to Gehazi his servant, Behold, yonder is that Shunammite: run now, I pray thee, to meet her, and say unto her, Is it well with thee? is it well with thy husband? is it well with the child? And she answered, It is well. And when she came to the man of God to the hill, she caught him by the feet: but Gehazi came near to thrust her away. And the man of God said, Let her alone; for her soul is vexed within her: and the Lord hath hid it from me, and hath not told me. Then she said, Did I desire a son of my lord? did I not say, Do not deceive me? Then he said to Gehazi, Gird up thy loins, and take my staff in thine hand, and go thy way: if thou meet any man, salute him not; and if any salute thee, answer him not again: and lay my staff upon the face of the child. And the mother of the child said, As the Lord liveth, and as thy soul liveth, I will not leave thee. And he arose, and followed her. And Gehazi passed on before them, and laid the staff upon the face of the child; but there was neither voice, nor hearing. Wherefore he went again to meet him, and told him, saying, The child is not awaked. And when Elisha was come into the house, behold, the child was dead, and laid upon his bed. He went in therefore, and shut the door upon them twain, and prayed unto the Lord. And he went up, and lay upon the child, and put his mouth upon his mouth, and his eyes upon his eyes, and his hands upon his hands: and he stretched himself upon the child; and the flesh of the child waxed warm. Then he returned, and walked in the house to and fro; and went up, and stretched himself upon him: and the child sneezed seven times, and the child opened his eyes. And he called Gehazi, and said, Call this Shunammite. So he called her. And when she was come in unto him, he said, Take up thy son. Then she went in, and fell at his feet, and bowed herself to the ground, and took up her son, and went out."—2 KINGS iv. 25-37.

FROM one of the slopes of Mount Carmel an unusual sight met the eye of Elisha. Two travellers were urging their mules over the plain of Jezreel at the utmost of their speed. One of the two Elisha could discern, even at that distance, to be a woman. No ordinary travellers would have crossed the plain of Jezreel ere the heat of the day was past, nor hastened onward at such speed. As the two approached nearer, the prophet recognised the well-known form of her who, on Sabbaths and new moons, had so often come to wait on his ministry. Some very extraordinary event must have brought her at this time. In his anxiety to ascertain her errand, and with an undefined apprehension of some great sorrow, he hastily sent Gehazi to meet her, and to "say unto her, Is it well with thee? is it well with thy husband? is it well with the child?" Gehazi was not loth to execute the commission. He put the questions, doubtless, with not a little of personal curiosity, though without much personal sympathy. It is strange what trouble people will take to "know all about others," especially when they are in sorrow. Under such circumstances they seem prompted, not merely by ordinary curiosity, but by a morbid craving after coarse excitement. They would watch our every sigh, and measure our every tear; they seem to delight in every feature of the terrible. Or, is this another phase of selfishness—a wish to see their own faces reflected in our tears? Certainly it is not sympathy, for that is of delicate step, of tender hand, and of silent lips.

What other answer, than that she made, could have been expected of the Shunammite? She could not open up the story of her grief to any one without sinking under its weight, as she tried to lift it into view. Least of all could she have spoken of it to a Gehazi. She had locked it up in her bosom for Elisha, or rather for Elisha's God, and was she now to give up the key to Gehazi? Silence was her only strength, and that silence she would preserve till she had reached the spot, toward which she had toiled these sixteen weary miles across the plain of Jezreel. It seems incomprehensible—yet there are who can open their feelings and experiences, even to a Gehazi. But can these be the real wants of our inmost hearts, which are so readily spread to the eye of every onlooker? Can these have been real burdens of the soul which so lightly roll from the lips of religious talkers? Is this whole-hearted talk about being "powerfully awakened" and "peace" consistent with the anguish of a soul, striving to enter in at the strait gate, or with the holy calm when, after a night of wrestling, at morn the sun has risen upon halting Israel?

Still the Shunammite pressed on, till at last she stood before the well-known form of the prophet. The sight of him brought back the stemmed-up tide of remembrance. As crowded into one picture she saw it: Elisha's first morning in the guest-chamber of her house; she felt again, how, when the unexpected ray of hope had broken upon her, she could, in the confusion of her happiness, only say, "Nay, my lord, thou man of God, do not lie unto thine handmaid;" then the infant; then the boy; then her dead child lying in that same upper chamber! Like a mighty river, which having burst the feeble barriers that man opposed to its rush, sweeps them away in its torrent strength, so her feelings, long restrained, now unloosed, burst into a very agony of unspoken sorrow. She fell at Elisha's feet, and convulsively clasped them to her bosom. It was now that the contrast, as presented by the character of Gehazi, fully appeared. To the man of conventionalities and secularities, to the shrewd Gehazi, such an outburst of feeling seemed improper, unbecoming. He judged the outburst; he knew not what real feeling was. Perhaps he regarded it as unsubmissive, irreligious. He would have thrust her away; he would have rushed into what was most sacred, and applied his rules of common sense, or his religious platitudes, to the agony of an over-burdened heart.

Is it not still so? In the view of many, sorrow may wrap itself in orthodox trappings, and religion flow in well-worn channels. All beyond that must be sternly repressed. Similarly, we may speak to men from the pulpit, and tell them in their collective capacity that all are sinners, a charge to which, unless further applied, the most careless will not take exception. We may even at set seasons—as in times of trial, or at a sick bed—repeat this privately, though in a milder form. But to speak plainly on these subjects; to ask a person directly whether he is on the road to heaven or not, or to press upon him individually his duty towards God as regards means, time, or influence, that is beyond the conventional, and a Gehazi would thrust away the unwelcome speaker. There is indeed a twofold extreme here to be avoided. Personal religion is a matter between the soul and God, and we have no right to intrude. On the other hand, it is our solemn duty, not, indeed, to interfere, but to bring the truth to bear on the conscience. It is a terrible thought that some may fail finally and fatally for lack of our speaking plainly.

Or, to take a lower view, the duty of each one whether as regards giving, or working, or suffering, is as between him and his Master, and we have no right to prescribe. But to admonish the rich not to trust in uncertain riches, not to give of their means as if they were their own, but to offer as unto the Lord, meekly and in deepest humility, praying that He may be pleased to accept it; to do this, not seeking any personal advantage, is not interference, but Christian duty, and mostly a hard and trying duty to perform.

Such harm does a Gehazi-spirit work in the Church, that it would even thrust away from the feet of Christ. And yet there are true Christians who, in their intercourse with a hard, shrewd world, have allowed their hearts to be overlaid as with a layer of ice, although, thank God, the living stream flows underneath it. Like Gehazi, they imagine that they understand our motives also, and have sounded our depth, when in reality they have only paid out their own sounding line. Yet they are good and loving men. Beneath the crust of ice there is the flowing river, though it often needs, alas, the sharp pickaxe of affliction to break up that, which will not yield to such rays as pierce the wintry clouds overhead. Why should it be so, and why introduce the world if you have really forsaken it? Why not rather yield to spiritual motives, and live as true and consistent disciples of Christ?

But to return to our narrative. With brief words of explanation the prophet arrested the officiousness of his servant. A twofold sorrow now cast its shadow upon Elisha. The soul of the Shunammite "is vexed within her," "and the Lord hath hid it from me, and hath not told me." So constant and close had been the prophet's fellowship with God, that He almost spoke to him as a man to his friend. Yet even so, God had not told him. For, miracles are not magic, nor is revelation soothsaying. Extraordinary communications were only for extraordinary purposes. In ordinary circumstances Prophets and Apostles were subject to the same laws, and had only the same means of acquiring knowledge as ourselves. Nor does Scripture communicate knowledge, which might otherwise be obtained, any more than special Providence supersedes the wise use of the best means. St. Paul had his ship's company given him from the shipwreck, yet neither was the wreck itself prevented, nor were any of the means of safety to be neglected. It is vain to question disjointed words of Scripture for geological, or physical, or physiological information. There is nothing hid under obscure expressions, which require the ingenuity of after-information to elicit from them meanings which neither their writers nor their readers would otherwise have found in them.

It deserves special notice that Elisha did not seek to arrest the outburst of the mother's anguish. The most intense grief is not inconsistent with real piety. Only unbelief is to be watched against, lest, either in joy or in sorrow, we forget Him that sent it. Not so in the case of the Shunammite.

When she could find words, they showed that over and above the surging waves of sorrow this one grand fact stood out clearly before her—that the child had been God-given. She had not asked it; and when it had been promised, she had opposed human probabilities to the Divine promise, and only yielded because it was God-given. "Did I desire a son of my lord? Did I not say, Do not deceive me?" And thus she still saw God, and God only, in this dispensation. In this is real comfort and true help, if we can rise straight to God. Times of trial must also be times of searching, when we ask ourselves, "Did I desire a son of my lord?" We must not set our heart absolutely upon this, or any earthly object; nothing is certain but the Lord and His promises.

Even after this passionate outburst of the Shunammite, it seems as if the prophet had scarcely understood the full extent of her calamity. Accordingly he sent forward Gehazi to lay his "staff upon the face of the child." Perhaps this was intended to gain time for calming his mind; perhaps to try the faith of the Shunammite; perhaps to dispense with the company of Gehazi. Certainly it resulted in showing forth the mighty power of God. Gehazi gladly hastened to execute his commission. It flattered his self-importance; it corresponded with his carnal zeal; and it was to apply just such means as would commend themselves to him under such circumstances—to lay the prophet's staff upon the child, and so restore it to life and health. If a prophet's staff sent directly by the prophet could not accomplish it, what else could be expected to succeed? Alas, that in some respects, the same fatal mistake is still made. To go on the great errand of eternal life or death with no better qualification than that we bear the prophet's staff, is the fatal error of those who trust in mere outward means for spiritual results. But, alas, Gehazi is still and only Gehazi, even when he carries the prophet's staff on the prophet's errand. Even Elisha's injunction, neither to salute any man by the way, nor to return his salutation, did not awaken misgivings in Gehazi; perhaps it only increased his sense of self-importance. It was, no doubt, intended to express, that when on any errand for God all else must be forgotten—interest, friendship, ordinary acquaintanceship; in short, that all of self must be put aside if we are to be employed on this great errand of life and death. The ministerial work brings with it the obligation of entire self-forgetfulness, self-denial, and self-devotion. No other object, no other joy, no other engagement must occupy us, compared with that of serving the Lord in winning souls. Not to please men, but to awaken the dead, are we sent forth.

But the event which revealed the incapacity of Gehazi for imparting, also showed the preparedness of the Shunammite for receiving. With the strongest adjurations she declared that she would not leave Elisha. Not to Gehazi, nor that he might carry the prophet's staff, had she come! The mere use of means cannot satisfy the really anxious and burdened soul. No round of ceremonies, no religious ordinances, even though they be really of Divine institution, even as the staff was really Elisha's and not Gehazi's, will meet the wants of an awakened conscience. It must be Christ, and Christ Himself. None else can bring help, and to Him will we cling. "I will not let Thee go except Thou bless me." Have we ever wrestled in such manner with the Lord? The Shunammite had lost a beloved child; but we are in danger of losing our immortal souls. None else can save us but the Lord Jesus Christ—shall we rest satisfied with anything short of Himself and His word of life?

The prophet accompanied the Shunammite. Again two travellers hurried over the plain of Jezreel. The shadows of evening had lengthened, and from the deep blue canopy overhead shone out the stars, as if the clear light of each were telling of Him "Who doeth according to His will in the army of heaven and among the inhabitants of the earth"— just as these stars shone out, when Abraham looked up to them as pledges of the Divine promise; just as if each were a diamond knot by which heaven was fastened to earth. In view of these unnumbered worlds the two were travelling onwards, not arrested even by the perplexed Gehazi, who had come back to report that, notwithstanding the staff, the child had not awaked. As if any staff, however sent, if brought by a Gehazi, could wake the dead!

At last the house of mourning was reached, and Elisha passed into the chamber where the dead child lay. And now tremble, ye walls of Jericho, for the Ark of Jehovah compasseth you about; tremble, ye prison walls, for the voice of prayer, of effectual fervent prayer, is raised! He "shut the door upon them twain, and prayed unto the Lord." No staff now! It is the same as at the commencement of his ministry: "Where is now the Lord God of Elijah?" In that upper room there was wrestling and strong crying unto the Lord. It had been consecrated before by prayer and communion with God; but never before as now had Elisha wrestled. He pleaded the promise of God, the honour of His Name, the faith of His servant, the need of the mother, the grief of the household. One by one he took these burdens, and in earnest, believing prayer, rolled them over upon the great Burden-bearer. In faith he seemed to rise higher and higher, and to grow stronger and stronger, till, a spiritual Samson, he had almost burst the bonds of flesh, and seemed to hold visible communion with Jehovah. And now he turned to the child, and stretched himself upon it—the living upon the dead, and the body of the child waxed warm. Again he arose and renewed his earnest supplication, and again he brought himself into personal contact with the child—the living with the dead. And so must *we* also do in dealing with dead souls: earnest wrestling with God, and then personal contact, as it were, stretching ourselves, the living upon the dead.

And now once more the golden gates swung open, and once more the sun-ray from the eternal light streamed into the upper chamber. The child lived! The Lord had again given what He had taken away. We are not told how the last glimpse of the golden light, when he passed from heaven, had so dazzled the child, that, when he woke on earth, the scenes of glory now past from his view seemed all effaced. For soon fell on his ear well-known footsteps. The mother had been called, and with one quick glance had seen her living child. Ere yet she clasped him to her heart, she fell at the prophet's feet in speechless thanks; and then she took up her son and bore him away. What songs of praise and thanksgiving rose that night from "the great house" at Shunem! Our God is the Hearer and Answerer of prayer; our Saviour is the Resurrection and the Life. Were it necessary or desirable, how easily could He literally open the windows of heaven for the supply of His people's need. But, since Christ came and died and rose again, there is another restoration to life, when the dead soul is born again, not of corruptible seed, but of incorruptible. Thus to receive a child never to lose it again, or thus to receive again the wandering prodigal into a family whose union can never be broken up, and where now there can never be a vacant place, is joy indeed—joy in heaven, and thankfulness upon earth. And, not in one solitary instance only, but in the case of all His people, death is swallowed up in victory; and soon death shall be no more, for they who rest in Jesus shall come with Him, when His glorious Presence shall gladden ransomed earth. Meantime, we hold fast the firm assurance, grounded on His promise, and confirmed by our experience, that all prayer is answered; that if we have not, it is because we ask not; and, while with unlimiting confidence we ask, we ever learn it anew that believing, wrestling prayer has power with God and prevails. And though in this last dispensation of faith and patience, when the Bride on the eve of the Resurrection morning looks for the Bridegroom, God no longer literally restores to earth those who have once stood in the Presence of Jesus, He still answers, even in that respect, our prayers. Sometimes He gives sweet assurance concerning them, and their return with the Lord; always He wipes away every tear, and heals every painful wound. Not more marked is His love than His gentleness, nor His kindness than His tenderness. When man would bind up, he sometimes pains even where he would heal. But the Lord Jesus is the Balm of Gilead and the Physician there.

Living or dead? This the first question for each of us. And if living, have we learned to pray "with strong crying," with simple, child-like faith, not doubting—or do we still stand at the spot whence the Saviour beckoned His disciples onward, when He said, "Hitherto ye have asked nothing in My name. Ask, and ye shall receive, that your joy may be full." And then, when we look around upon those whom we know, still lying dead, or else upon the city, as at even the slanting sunlight, ere it parts, falls upon its reeking closes, and alleys, and dens, with all their mass of human misery, want, and sin, we will believingly remember the prophet's remedy. Let it be on our part earnest wrestling prayer, and then personal contact, the living stretched upon the dead, till life is poured forth into the dead, and praise rises to Him, Who is the Light of the world, and the Life of the world.

CHAPTER XII.

AN INTERRUPTED MEAL.

> "And Elisha came again to Gilgal: and there was a dearth in the land; and the sons of the prophets were sitting before him: and he said unto his servant, Set on the great pot, and seethe pottage for the sons of the prophets. And one went out into the field to gather herbs, and found a wild vine, and gathered thereof wild gourds his lap full, and came and shred them into the pot of pottage: for they knew them not. So they poured out for the men to eat. And it came to pass, as they were eating of the pottage, that they cried out, and said, O thou man of God, there is death in the pot. And they could not eat thereof. But he said, Then bring meal. And he cast it into the pot; and he said, Pour out for the people, that they may eat. And there was no harm in the pot."—2 KINGS iv. 38-41.

TIMES and scenes have sadly changed. Once more has a terrible drought withered the land, and famine and misery have swept over the people. Elisha is no longer at Mount Carmel, nor the Shunammite in her great, hospitable house. The famine has driven her from Shunem (compare chap. viii. 1, 2); and the famine has determined Elisha once more to seek out the sons of the prophets at Gilgal. In their company our narrative finds him, this time engaged in his favourite occupation of instructing them in the word and in the ways of the Lord. As the text expresseth it with pictorial brevity, "the sons of the prophets were sitting before him." But why the marvellous interposition recorded in the narrative above quoted; and why, when it had taken place, was it chronicled for all ages in the history of the kingdom of God?

Why? That it may be remembered in all time coming that God takes special charge of His servants, and that even imminent death can be turned aside at His bidding. This, indeed, is a truth which may be gathered from many other portions of Scripture. Not so some of the other lessons of this narrative. To begin—let us mark what the event would teach the sons of the prophets. As prophet of the Lord, Elisha had been instructing them in the Word of God, and now they had undeniable evidence that his mission, and therefore his message were of God. Death from poisonous food while "sitting before" Elisha would have been a practical contradiction of his teaching. Again, making wider application of it, this history means that death is *not* "in the pot." Nor yet is life "in the pot." It is as God sends the one or the other. There are who sneer at the prayer, "Give us this day our daily bread," when garner and storehouse are full. But what matters the outward provision? Bread is only really such if it feed and nourish the body. What though a home be furnished with all luxury, and provided with every delicacy, if disease and death have taken up their abode in it, or sorrow poison every spring of comfort! We know that the sun shines most brightly even on the darkest and most clouded day. What of that? We know it, and yet we all say, The sun shines not this day. It does not shine to us, for clouds intervene to hide its brightness. It is not as man has, but as God gives.

Yet another and a kindred lesson, and that of the highest application, may be learned from this history. Man liveth not by bread alone, but by every word which proceedeth from the mouth of the Lord. Thus the temporal and the spiritual—as we term them—are distinguished, and yet conjoined. And under the New Testament this, as every other eternal truth, was embodied and set forth in a visible form (which visible setting forth of the eternal constitutes the idea of a miracle), when the Son of God became Incarnate and appeared upon earth. Lastly, the event points forward

AN INTERRUPTED MEAL.

to the miraculous feeding of the multitude by the Lord Jesus, many centuries afterwards. It also points forward to that night on the Lake of Galilee, when the sleeping Master was wakened by the cry, "Master, carest Thou not that we perish?" and His command hushed the storm into a calm. And these many centuries afterwards, when the frail bark of the Church seems again tossed by the storm, we also say to ourselves, There cannot be shipwreck when the Master is in the vessel; and even if our meal is disturbed by the cry that poison has been mixed with our provision, there is not "death in the pot" while the Master presides at the board.

The presence of Elisha in the land preserved it not from the horrors of famine, nor did his company save the sons of the prophets from want. God's people are not preserved from the common evils of this world. They are sustained and helped in them. And famine was no light affliction in those days. We know something of its horrors in our own land, but what must they have been among a people which entirely depended upon agriculture, and at a time when the means of supply could not be obtained, as at present, from other and more favoured countries? But why did Elisha, under such circumstances, join the sons of the prophets at Gilgal? So far as appears from the sacred narrative, he had not been there since the removal of Elijah. Then *spiritual* dearth seemed threatening, now *outward* dearth prevailed. In both cases it was to appear that the "Lord God of Elijah" was still there, and in both cases was faith to prevail. Yes, to Gilgal he would go, to the poor and desolate sons of the prophets. In the time of famine he would not go to the rich; he would share the poverty of the poor. In days of prosperity he was the guest of "the great house;" in times of adversity we find him the companion of the sons of the prophets. For the shepherd must seek the weak of his flock, and tend them in the hours of danger. It is good for us to go to the house of mourning, not in order to make the heart sad, but to learn spiritual lessons. Some are afraid to witness sorrow, to hear of death, even to meet a funeral procession, as if by passing over to the other side they could for ever avert the lengthening shadow that is creeping over them. Why not rather think of all this as a reality, and prepare for it while there is time? But why should Christians be afraid of death? The grave may be lonely, dark, and cold; but it is not our dwelling-place. That is in the bright mansions above, and with Christ. As one has aptly said, "Christians may be afraid of dying," for nature shrinks from dissolution; "they cannot be afraid of death," for it is "swallowed up in victory." Assuredly, He Who has given grace for living, will also give it for dying. This also is one of the cares of "to-morrow," with which we ought not to burden ourselves.

There is another and a very precious comfort in such times of general danger and affliction, as that when Elisha arrived in Gilgal. Affliction brings God's people together and unites them. In the first ages of Christianity, when persecution prevailed, there was but one Church. As the visible Church grew in prosperity and worldly greatness; and, as worldly ideas made their appearance, the Church became disunited and divided, and so it has ever since remained. Not that we are really divided, for we all hold "one Lord, one faith, one baptism." But we have come *so* to hold our peculiar views on secondary points, which it is right for us to hold, that we hold them in a wrong manner—holding them, rather than anything else. Thus we hold out points of repulsion, and not of attraction, to our fellow-Christians. It is otherwise in days of trial and persecution. When the storm bursts over the mountains, and lightning leaps from crag to crag, the scattered flock gathers in the covering hollow, closely, head to head, and sheltering each the other. Then those which have strayed farthest, often come in soonest to their own fold! It is, indeed, most consoling, while watching the storm as it gathers in our days, and looking forward to the fast coming troubles of the last days, to be assured that we may then expect a larger union of all who really belong to the fold of Christ. In presence of common danger, and under common need, we shall no longer clamour, I am of Paul, I am of Apollos, or I am of Cephas, but all cleave closer to Christ, and rejoice in our new-found union. These will be both separating and uniting times—separating all true Christians from all incongruous and worldly elements, and uniting them among themselves; and no other separation or union is worth seeking. Meantime, we may, each in his own sphere, labour towards it. If any man preach Christ crucified, we own and welcome him as a brother; if otherwise, we neither recognise nor acknowledge him, under whatever name or by whatever outward authority he come.

But while Elisha was ministering to the souls of his hearers, he was not forgetful of their temporal wants. Not that he burdened himself with them; he knew that "the Lord would provide," and he acted in the spirit which alone befitted such conviction. He was content, however humble the provision might be. For, if while looking up for His supply, we were dainty of taste, and not ready to take with gratitude what His hand proffers, our faith would be presumption. But Elisha and his companions, knowing "both how to be abased and how to abound," were satisfied with the meanest fare. Some of us may have to lay our account with reverses and changes. The difficulty lies in the manner in which we submit to them—in other words: in *knowing how* to be abased and *how* to abound. To accept it all—

the former with cheerfulness, and the latter with meekness, and to feel that both come to us from the same Lord, is His gracious discipline to a chastened, believing heart. And if we really ask all of Him, and receive all from Him, why should we not prefer, if He so appoints, even the lowliest diet to the richest feast of the world? Can He not put gladness in our hearts, and with it vigour into our bodies, "more than in the time that their corn and their wine increased"?

A strange scene is next presented to our view. On the one side are the prophet and his hearers, and on the other is Gehazi at most congenial work, setting on the great pot and attending to its proper seething. We need those who will attend to the temporalities of the Church. At the same time there are peculiar and serious dangers threatening those who, if the expression may be used, attend to the seething of the great pot. The apostles committed "this business" only to men "full of the Holy Ghost" as well as of "wisdom"—not only for the sake of those to whom they were to minister, but also for their sakes who ministered. So far from choosing for such services "a novice," we ought to remember that not unfrequently men, who had given fair promise of commencing spiritual life, have thus become secularised and hardened. This, indeed, is at variance with the Gehazi theory, which proceeds on the assumption that a large pot sufficiently filled only requires to be set on and properly seethed, when a satisfactory meal will surely be the result. But the event proved otherwise. And, to continue our spiritual application of this history, it is still so. Take only one illustration. In regard to many of our religious institutions, do the results correspond to the means used? And why not? These are questions which deserve our most serious consideration.

As yet, however, none of the party gathered around "the great pot" at Gilgal was apprehensive of impending danger. Some had gone into the woods and fields, and, under the supervision of Gehazi, were adding to the common stock. One of them had gathered his lap full of "wild gourds," ignorant of their poisonous nature, and "shred them into the pot of pottage." The meal was ready; God had been owned and thanked for it, and they had sat down to enjoy their frugal feast. Of a sudden, whether from the acrid taste of the pottage, or from the commencing effects of the poison, they cried out: "There is death in the pot." The morsel lifted to the mouth was hastily thrown down, and helpless despair settled upon each heart.

We all know with what awful suddenness sometimes sorrow falls with crushing weight. Indeed, however long we may have looked for an event, we never fully realise it till it has come. But why these terrible surprises to God's people, and so often in the midst of calm and sunshine, or in the enjoyment of lawful happiness? Why should dreadful calamity befall the traveller from whom we parted a little while ago so well, so happy, so loved, so useful? Why should disease sweep over the circle in which all are so close to each other, as almost to seem holding each the other's hand? Why sudden, blameless poverty, why "death in the pot"? To this *why* we cannot return an answer, so far as the *Lord* is concerned. These are of the most secret of the secrets which belong to Him, and await the light of another than earthly day. In what order He gathers His sheaves, or what preparation for yet unknown service may be required, or what special purpose is to be evolved, we know not. But as regards the earthly aspect of this "*why*," it is perhaps remarkable that such questions are more frequently put by strangers than by the sufferers themselves. So far as their testimony is concerned, it bears that it had been good for them to have been afflicted, and that before they were afflicted they had gone astray, but now they have kept His word—all which the Holy Ghost seals to us by declaring that "all things work together for good to them that love God, to them who are the called according to His purpose."

It has already been stated that there could not be "death" in such a pot, and the course of the narrative vindicates the remark. Teaching symbolically by signs and wonders, God could not have disowned His servant, nor allowed such a feast to terminate in destruction. In the midst of his dismayed companions, Elisha alone remained calm. To their appeal he replied, "Then bring meal. And he cast it into the pot." "There was no harm in the pot," now. But what faith in the mission of Elisha and in the Presence of the living God must these sons of the prophets have had, when on his invitation they would resume their poisoned repast, the only antidote used having been so inoperative a substance as meal!

In the use of meal for removing the poisonous effect of the wild gourds, some have seen a symbolical reference to the meal of the Gospel, as removing the deadly effect of the world and of its elements. It suggests, however, another and an undoubted truth. In one sense, there is too often "death in the pot." Error, antichristian doctrine, and grossly superstitious practices are in our days but too frequently mingled with the provision set before the professing Church for spiritual nourishment. It is not difficult to understand how those who have not spiritual life nor health may, from certain outward motives, sit down to such provision. Painful though it be, in a land so long blessed with the light and liberty of the Gospel, to see so many encouraging by their presence and support what must result in the most fearful consequences, alike individually and nationally, we can, in the case of many, account for it on the ground of spiritual insensibility. But how those who have been taught by the Word of God can from Sunday to Sunday sit down to what is "death in the pot," well knowing it to be such—to be false, and even blasphemous—almost passes comprehension. If Elisha and his companions had known, *before* partaking of the pottage, that it was poisoned, would they have been warranted in sitting down to such a meal, or would God have wrought a miracle to deliver them from its consequences? Nor are we warranted in expecting to be preserved, if we neglect the many warnings in Scripture against false teaching. It does not imply any want of true charity to be jealous for the truth of God. We have no right to be charitable with that which does not belong to us; and the truth is His, not ours. Let us be as charitable as we may towards individuals, but let us not misname charity that which too often is only culpable weakness. Nor does it make the matter better, rather worse, if the error is promulgated in our own Church. It is right and solemn duty that each of us should search the Holy Scriptures, and, after most careful and prayerful consideration of all circumstances, attach himself to that part of the visible Church which, in his view, most nearly represents the New Testament ideal. It is also right that, having so chosen, he should closely adhere to it. But it cannot be right to surrender the truth as it is in Jesus, and, while professing zeal for the Church, to assist where its foundations are subverted and its Head is dishonoured. Be our Church ever so beautiful and dear to us, be it, in our opinion, ever so sound in its formularies—and all the more for that, we have no right to sacrifice truth nor to countenance error. We greatly prefer to hear the Gospel preached in connection with our own Church; but if we fail to find there wholesome and nourishing food for our souls, we may be even constrained to look for it elsewhere, and that, while all the time we continue to feel ourselves members of our own Church, and love its order and teaching. Only, do not let us take judgment to ourselves rashly or on insufficient grounds, nor yet be suspicious or censorious.

Before we leave the company of the prophets and the simple feast, which the mercy of God had now enabled them to enjoy without fear, some final thoughts suggest themselves. Surely, there is not any "pot" containing our provision for earth, however carefully selected its ingredients, which has not its wild gourds. There is not any pleasure wholly unalloyed, nor yet any cup of sweetness which has not its bitter dregs. Are there smiles which are never followed by tears? The happiest life, the brightest day, does not pass wholly without cloud. And what of the parting? In the case of the world, alas! all is poisoned. The good gifts of God nourish not, but rather destroy, through our abuse of them, our selfishness, and hardness of heart. Let us look back. How many years have we lived; how many mercies have we enjoyed; how much that was good and nourishing has He caused to be shred into the great pot from which so often provision has come, not only to satisfy our wants, but to exceed our utmost desires and hopes? And what have we put into this "great pot" for ourselves and for others? What of the wild gourds which spiritually have destroyed and poisoned all? "There *is* death in the pot!" Blessed be God, we are still in presence of our Elisha, and a handful of that meal—of the blessed Gospel of our Lord and Saviour Jesus Christ—cast by Him into this pot of life, and there will be "no harm in the pot."

CHAPTER XIII.

GRACE BEFORE MEAT.

"And there came a man from Baal-shalisha, and brought the man of God bread of the first-fruits, twenty loaves of barley, and full ears of corn in the husk thereof. And he said, Give unto the people, that they may eat. And his servitor said, What, should I set this before an hundred men? He said again, Give the people, that they may eat: for thus saith the Lord, They shall eat, and shall leave thereof. So he set it before them, and they did eat, and left thereof, according to the word of the Lord."
—2 KINGS iv. 42-44.

IT was no common privilege, when the saints of old were allowed to see the day of Christ afar off and rejoice. Ever and again did a ray of that heavenly brightness light up their horizon. From the glory which gathered around one of their own prophets might men infer what would be the power and goodness of Him Who was "before Abraham" and "greater than Moses." In such events, Gospel times and Gospel truths were anticipated, that so the mind of Israel might be prepared what to expect from Him Who was "the Desire of all nations." Rare as, comparatively speaking, such anticipations of Christ were, we are naturally led to look for a large proportion of them during the ministry of Elisha, not merely because his was specially typical of the ministry of Jesus, but also because he may be said to conclude the series of the *prophets of deed.* They were, in the onward progress of the kingdom of God, followed by the *prophets of word*, until, at last, both word and deed merged in Him Who was "the Word become flesh." Thus the marvellous feeding of the multitude upon the few barley loaves and fishes was foreshadowed in Gilgal, with such differences, however, as correspond to those between them who, in each case, spake the multiplying "grace."

It is this "grace before meat," this blessing of God invoked and bestowed upon the food, which makes it really nourishing. Why should it seem strange that, dispensed by the Hand of God Incarnate, the bread should have sufficed to nourish thousands? We too often fail to perceive the close connection between nature and God. Without God, nature were dead; its continual life depends on the continual Presence of God not only with it, but in it. As there is a false materialism which fails to recognise God in anything, because it identifies God with everything, so there is a spurious spiritualism which equally fails to recognise God, because it separates God from all, save that limited sphere which it designates as religious. The consequence of this is a morbid asceticism which is not gladdened by the beauties of nature, nor interested by the productions of art, nor elevated by the researches of mind, not even warmed by the joys of home and its circle, simply because it sees not God in any of them, and thus, looking away from God in all His gifts, at last settles into a half-desponding, austere gloom. But let us take a believing view of God's relation to His world and to His people. It is *not* strange that, by the touch of His Hand and the breath of His Mouth, the Lord Jesus could expand the scantiness of provision into sufficiency for all—for the creature only owned the power of its Creator, and we ourselves, in outward things, daily experience similar blessing. It was not even strange that, as recorded in the narrative before us, His forerunner could foreshadow this event by the fare increased to satisfy the one hundred sons of the prophets. But it was strange, that, in the infinitude of His love, Jesus should so have condescended to our human weakness as visibly, in the presence of all—believers and unbelievers—to breathe upon His creature of bread, that, for all time coming, it might serve as a lesson of Him and as a lesson also of multiplied food. And, to return to the present narrative, it was strange —at least to our human experience it seems so—that so unexpectedly there should have come from a wholly unknown quarter, what, under the blessing of God, proved not only seasonable, but sufficient relief to the prophets.

In reading the history of such a miracle, the thought involuntarily rises why an agency and means so manifestly inadequate were employed, and not the miracle wrought directly and immediately. We answer: They were not required, but God condescended to use them. And this, first, Because He is the God of nature, and employs His creature, nature. Secondly, Because He is the God of grace, and, in the use of such means, alike disposes the hearts of those whom He uses as His instruments, and prepares the hearts of those who are the recipients of His gifts. Who "the man from Baal-shalisha" was, we know not; we know not even his dwelling-place, nor anything connected with his history. Possibly he may have been equally unknown—at least, personally—to the prophet. At any rate, he appears as that exceptional character in the modern lists of religious societies: "An anonymous contributor." But whatever his name, rank, or condition, he was a just, a conscientious, and a liberal contributor. The Angel, whose recording pen enters the gifts offered to the Lord, has written it down for acknowledgment in heaven, and when the Spirit of God chronicled it for the instruction of the Church on earth, He allowed not the joy nor the reward of the giver to be minished by having his ministry known.

For, the seven long years of famine (2 Kings viii.) were at last drawing to a close. Once more the prospect of plenty gladdened the heart of the nation. Emigrants thought of setting their faces again homewards; and those who had wearily toiled, where toil was so long unrewarded, gathered fresh strength. In fact, the early harvest had actually commenced. Under ordinary circumstances the first-fruits belonged unto the Lord. It was the privilege of every family in Israel, as it were, to receive home and substance every year anew in fief from their God, and in the first-fruits to consecrate all unto Him. But times had sadly changed. To whom were the first-fruits now to be brought throughout the kingdom of Israel? Its established religion was Baal-worship, its established priesthood idolatrous. Doubtless there were who brought their gifts to Jerusalem, or offered them through the faithful among the Aaronic priesthood. But considering the difficulties in the way, these must, in the nature of the case, have formed a very small minority even among the small minority of Jehovah-worshippers left in Israel.

That we may learn present lessons, let us try to transport ourselves into the past, and realise the circumstances of the time. It would have been easy to argue, that one was released from obedience to a command of which the literal fulfilment had become well nigh impossible. But love is ingenious, and knows under the letter to discover the spirit of the law. The man from Baal-shalisha " brought the man of God bread of the first-fruits." There are, who are ingenious in their liberality, not in its eccentric application, which only argues folly or vanity, but in finding out the right mode of its exercise. There are others who always refuse—and somehow always refuse on principle. On principle they would on this occasion, of course, have refused to contribute to Samaria; and on principle they could not bring anything to Elisha, since he was neither a priest, nor in office in the Temple. And so "on principle" they would have held what they had, and this would have been their peculiar mode of "making the best of both worlds." Nor would their conduct have been singular. There are only too many, in all ages, who would fain combine the principles of the coming, with the practices of the present world.

Not so the anonymous donor in our narrative. Nor was his contribution inconsiderable. It was of "the first-fruits" after a seven years' famine. How many gaps had to be repaired in broken fortunes ! Ill could a man spare the best of the first for an object primarily religious, and therefore, in the view of many, unpractical. Even if contributions were to be made, the argument for postponing it to the end of the summer would be overwhelming—for, as the world would apply one of its sayings, not quite untrue in itself, but often thoroughly hypocritical on its lips : It is necessary to be just before being generous. As if man *could* be just while neglecting the claims of the Most High ! But, indeed, many mean by this saying rather to express that they must be generous to themselves before they can be just; and such is their generosity in this respect, that what between the claims of friends and of society, the exigencies of their station, and a future provision, there is little left for the exercise of charity. Let there be no misunderstanding here. Thank God, the Church has not lost the grace of liberality. It can point from among its members, high and low, rich and poor, to noble instances of devotion to the Lord, even although the organised system of advertising their bounty, as it were placing men with trumpets at every street-corner, has sadly broken in upon the music of their worship in offering gifts unto God. The system itself was, no doubt, well intended—but, on the whole, it seems a kind of

Gehazi-plan of encouraging those who have given, and at the same time of attracting by the noise others to the treasury so as to induce them also to give. But in this the Church has sadly declined from the liberality of Old and of New Testament times. The sin and spiritual loss are more serious than at first sight appears. Liberality is a grace—that is, one of the directions in which the Holy Ghost, if He dwell in a heart, inclines that heart. It is not a gift, but a grace, and cannot therefore be regarded as matter of small importance. A Christian may be wise or foolish, learned or unlearned, a babe or a man, in Christ. But a Christian can be neither without grace, nor yet without graces. In the latter case he will be incomplete and maimed, as is the human body which wants a limb. Nay, it is doubtful if there can be such defective Christianity, in view of the promise that we are all to be presented "perfect" before God. The discipline of God's chastening Providence will be directed towards the filling up of such a gap, if it exist in His own children.

For, there are some obvious, yet most solemn, considerations which ought to determine us on all such questions, if indeed these things be a reality to us. The first of these comes to us from the thought of how much we owe. Thus the Apostle pleads with his Corinthian converts: "the grace of our Lord Jesus Christ, that, though He was rich, yet for our sakes He became poor, that ye through His poverty might be rich." Other considerations come as inferences from our own profession as Christians. Thus, we profess to have renounced this world, and shall we continue to live for it? We profess to have been redeemed through the precious blood of Christ, and yet what have we done for Him, Who has bought us at such a price, and Whose we are? We believe that the world lieth in the evil one, and that its only remedy is the Gospel, and yet what are we doing for its spread? Again, if we believe in the promises, let us not live as if there were none. And, lastly, if we believe that time is fleeting and eternity at hand, then what of that to which we are devoting heart and money will remain, or receive us into those everlasting habitations?

In answering such questions, let us be honest with ourselves. And, in order to be so, let us be plain and straightforward. That scarcely deserves the name of Christian liberality which is not proportionate to our means. Rare as such contribution is, and large as it may seem, even to give a tenth may not be a fair standard. There are to whom a tenth may be more than a just contribution; for a man is to give of what he hath, not of that which he hath not. And there are considerations connected with the position which we may necessarily, and as appointed by God, have to occupy, which may involve what obliges to curtail our givings. This is indeed a principle capable of abuse; nor is it possible to lay down rules for its right application. Spiritually-minded Christians will rightly apply it; others will not, whatever be said or explained. On the other hand, there are in whose case a tenth would represent what is far below the right proportion of their giving, whether viewed by itself, or proportionately either to their other expenditure or to their savings. In this matter also no definitive rule can be laid down for others. Let the motive be love to Jesus, the act of giving one of worship, and let a definite and high aim be taken by each of us, as in view of the comparative value of things temporal and things spiritual.

There was another most pleasing feature about the anonymous contributor in this narrative. The "twenty loaves of barley" which he had given may be regarded as the necessaries of life. But the parched corn which he added ("full ears of corn in the husk thereof") was at all times, and must have been specially at that time, regarded as a delicacy. It was a mark of affectionate attention to the prophet, which expressed more clearly than words could have done, that the gift had come from the fulness of a loving heart. Let us beware of marring our gifts by the grudging manner, or the churlish mode, in which we bestow them. "God loveth a *cheerful* giver." Else, why give at all, if it be not regarded as a privilege; who hath demanded these things at our hands? It is well to learn, and to remember when we have learned it, that the cause of God does not depend upon us. It has for these thousands of years been carried on without us, and will prosper long after we and our gifts are for ever gone. But we may deprive ourselves of the honour of being used as His instruments, and of the reward promised to His faithful stewards. It were almost better not to give, than to give in a churlish spirit. Alas, how much more readily does a man bestow upon himself and his children, upon luxuries, or even follies, than upon the Lord. In this respect also: "When the Son of Man cometh, shall He find faith on the earth?"

Placing ourselves in the circumstances of those who formed the company at Gilgal, we may probably feel that we would have rejoiced as much, if not more, in the fact of the giving as in the gift itself. For, although even this small supply would prove seasonable and welcome, they must, long before, have learned to commit their daily wants unto the Lord. Similarly, must they have often experienced how easily their every requirement could be, and had been, supplied by their God. Seven years of famine must have been an excellent school in which to learn the practical lessons of faith. But in the present instance the hand of sympathy had been held out to them from a distance. A man apparently unknown had come to their relief. That there was such a man was in itself a relief. There might be many others whom God could employ for their help, were it needed. That he was unknown and unnamed was all the more precious. It is so to us; for his deed, like the gift of the poor widow, and not his name, is preserved. It was so to them, for it showed them that deliverance might come unexpectedly, and from unexpected quarters. "Let mine outcasts dwell with thee, Moab." Help comes sometimes through most unlikely channels; and it is in the experience of His saints that much more frequently it is given through means of which they had never thought, than through those which they might have deemed likely to be used. And herein lies our confidence, when this stay fails and that prop breaks, that God is not restricted to any instrumentality, and that He is the same yesterday, and to-day, and for ever. The less likely the helper, the more likely the help. How? By His own Hand, which has redeemed us; in His own way, which is of pleasantness; in His own time, which is the right time. Nay, and perhaps not only shall twenty barley loaves be sent, but with them "full ears of corn in the husk thereof."

The unexpected provision had been brought by the stranger *to* Elisha, but not *for* Elisha. He Who had sent His steward to the prophet had intended this, as all His other gifts, to be employed in His service, not to be consumed selfishly. In this sense also "none of us liveth to himself." All God's creature-gifts are good, if they are sanctified by the Word and prayer, and used aright. It is lawful to enjoy them, nor is it either wise or truthful to institute a comparison between God and them, as if, in order to love God, we had to renounce the good gifts bestowed upon us. Thus Scripture does not contrast love to a wife or child with love to God, nor represent them as inconsistent. If the love of God be really in us, our deepest earthly attachment can never come into comparison, far less into conflict with it, because it is of a totally different character. Our love to those around us is of a different nature from that towards God, nor would it in any way increase our love to Him if we had none on earth to love. It is, indeed, written, that we are to keep ourselves "from idols"—that is, from bestowing upon the creature what is due to the Creator. But this warning refers to a subversion of the right relationship, and no more proves the latter impossible than the direction, "Lie not one to another," would prove absolute truthfulness impossible, or make perpetual silence advisable, in order to avoid moral danger. We do not love anything in the world, nor any creature, in the sense in which we love God; and if we were to do so, the love of the Father would not be in us.

It is one of the peculiarities of receiving all directly from God that, like Elisha, we consider it not as our own, but seek to employ it in His service. Thus, whether we eat or drink, or whatsoever we do, we must learn to do all to the glory of God. Yet even in that happy company, gladdened by the gift of the unnamed friend, there was one whose brow was clouded, and whose speech betrayed dissatisfaction. It was Gehazi. "What, should I set this before an hundred men?" The arrangement proposed by Elisha did not approve itself either to his head or to his heart. Prudently used—and Gehazi would have taken care of that—the provision might have sufficed for some time for his master and himself. It had been brought to them, and the sons of the prophets had neither legally nor morally any claim upon it. It was just like one of Elisha's unpractical ways, which always ended in difficulty! Probably Gehazi expressed neither of these feelings. But he laid all the more stress on the obvious impossibility of extending such a meal to "an hundred men." It is the old argument of so-called "common sense" and probability against God and duty. Never has work of faith come to us, but common sense has called up a perfect phalanx of reasonable arguments against it. Could there be anything more unreasonable than to attempt passing through the Red Sea, or to encompass Jericho with the Ark and blasts of trumpets, or literally to spread a letter before Jehovah, or to build a wall which would break down if even a fox went upon it—or, to take even a higher view, to expect that the Son of God Incarnate would be laid in a manger, or that the Gospel, preached by a few illiterate Jewish fishers, would subdue the civilisation of Greece and the institutions of Rome, and in its onward progress conquer, renew, and civilise the world itself? Or else: Could anything seem more unlikely than that for sinners such as we are the Lord Jesus Christ should come into this world, and shed His precious blood? We have learned to call nothing strange nor unlikely which we have been taught to expect from the Word of God. And when, day by day, the ministers of Christ go forth to feed the company with provision, which it needs not a Gehazi to remind them is in many respects insufficient, their comfort lies in the assurance of the gracious power of God. In answer to prayer, He can, and He will multiply the scanty food. And we know that One greater than Elisha is with us. *We* may have only brought a few loaves and fishes; but He speaks "the grace before meat;" He takes and dispenses the food, and there is enough and to spare. Who is sufficient for these things? may often be the anxious enquiry of those engaged in this work. The answer is, "Our sufficiency is of God." It needs not power, might, imagination, eloquence, nor genius. After having used all the means at our disposal in preparing for the work, we may calmly, if believingly, go forward in His

Name, even if conscious of insufficiency. Just as in our outward want He can, if needful, send to our relief a stranger with twenty barley loaves and parched corn, so can He multiply the provision, temporal or spiritual, till it not only sufficeth, but there is "left thereof."

But Gehazi's prudential objection was silenced by the prophet's reply: "*for* thus saith the Lord." This is an argument which overrules all others. Gehazi obeyed, beheld, and wondered—yet, alas! he understood not, what was the grand lesson of this event, and that not only to them, but to us and to the Church in all ages, and with which the narrative emphatically closes—that all this was: "*according to the Word of Jehovah.*"

CHAPTER XIV.

THE CLOUD WITH THE SILVER LINING.

"Now Naaman, captain of the host of the king of Syria, was a great man with his master, and honourable, because by him the Lord had given deliverance unto Syria: he was also a mighty man in valour, but he was a leper. And the Syrians had gone out by companies, and had brought away captive out of the land of Israel a little maid; and she waited on Naaman's wife. And she said unto her mistress, Would God my lord were with the prophet that is in Samaria! for he would recover him of his leprosy. And one went in, and told his lord, saying, Thus and thus said the maid that is of the land of Israel. And the king of Syria said, Go to, go, and I will send a letter unto the king of Israel. And he departed, and took with him ten talents of silver, and six thousand pieces of gold, and ten changes of raiment. And he brought the letter to the king of Israel, saying, Now when this letter is come unto thee, behold, I have therewith sent Naaman my servant to thee, that thou mayest recover him of his leprosy. And it came to pass, when the king of Israel had read the letter, that he rent his clothes, and said, Am I God, to kill and to make alive, that this man doth send unto me to recover a man of his leprosy? wherefore consider, I pray you, and see how he seeketh a quarrel against me."—2 KINGS v. 1-7.

RANK, distinction, and wealth are undoubtedly good gifts of God, which only a morbid asceticism could affect to despise. They can procure much; yet, after all, they can effect very little. Indeed, it would be easier to enumerate what they cannot, than what they can, effect. As in many other things, so here, the Unknown exercises its charm. While beset by outward difficulties, we are prone to imagine how much could be effected by money, or to suppose that easy circumstances must mean circumstances of ease. They mean nothing of the kind. It is only after we have all that we want, and when there is no rational outward wish which cannot be gratified, that we see how very little money can really effect, and how small an element it forms in securing happiness. The springs of human life rise much higher than often seems even to ourselves, and our happiness or unhappiness depends on causes over which outward circumstances have little, if any, control. But over all reigns that Divine Providence which orders all, and which, out of seeming confusion, brings calm and beauty.

Few events could apparently bear less reference to each other than the disease of Naaman, and the capture of a little Jewish maiden. Few events also could, at the time, have seemed more untoward. Yet, in reality, few events could have been more deeply and closely connected, or were fraught with richer blessing, than these two. Far from Samaria, in fair Damascus, Naaman held state—the general-in-chief of Syria's armies, and the trusted adviser of Ben-hadad. Under the reign of that monarch, the relations between Israel and Syria had changed. Cunning, cruel, and determined, the Syrian king had known how to combine for his purpose all the elements hostile to Israel. It was a day of bitter humiliation and terrible disaster when, at the head of thirty-two kings, Ben-hadad laid Israel low, and long did the land feel the consequences of Ahab's sin and folly. In that battle Naaman must have done signal service. According to Jewish tradition, it was from his bow that the arrow sped which smote the king of Israel. The war ended with that battle, but not the defeat. The army of Israel was dispersed; Syria no longer encountered resistance, and a constant marauding border-warfare henceforth desolated the land, and distressed the people.

The services which Naaman had rendered to his king and country were not forgotten in Syria. He was elevated to the highest post in the state; nor was he undeserving the honour. As his figure is drawn in Scripture, it is that of a frank, generous, proud, and bold soldier. "He was a great man with his master," "and honourable," a favourite with the people, a dashing leader—as the narrative bears, open-handed, open-hearted, though quick-tempered, just the man to be idolised by the populace. Moreover, if we may be allowed to interpret his name as a designation, he was Naaman, or "handsome," his outward appearance corresponding with his natural character. Here, then, was everything that could procure happiness—rank, glory, wealth, influence, together with a natural disposition that would fit him for a keen relish of it all. And yet there was a worm, and a sting in it all; the drop that had fallen into his cup made all its contents most bitter. At the end of all, the Hand of God had written the word "*but*"—"but he was a leper." To be stricken with such a loathsome, hopeless distemper, marred all else—home and palace, honours and popularity. Wherever Naaman went, or whatever he did, he was still the leper. How his pride must have chafed under what he could neither conceal, nor subdue, nor remove! His was the least curable of all, the white leprosy (as we learn from the sequel), and neither man nor god in all Syria could deliver him from his misery. What could have turned into his life-stream that poisonous current which polluted it, and made the meanest soldier, who gaily hummed by the watch-fire his song about home, a man happier far than his chief, powerful and renowned though he was? Alas, this little word "but" seems to follow men through life, like the shadow of death. How soon may the unfinished sentence which begins with this "but" be filled up! He was rich, honoured, happy—"but" God laid His Hand upon him! What folly then to live in a sense of imaginary independence, and in forgetfulness of the Most High! Even if we not only retain what we have, but could add indefinitely thereto, yet, with this unwritten sentence to be inserted in the vacant space, does it not seem as if the lengthening shadow were falling across our path? But is it really so? Not if we recognise God as our Father—if we feel that all is lovingly and well ordered by Him, and if we can trust in, and cling to, Him.

And it was this God Who, in sovereign mercy, was now about to lead Naaman unto Himself, though by a strange and tangled way. Surely all the paths of the Lord are mercy and truth. Nay, long before this, the Eye of the Lord had been upon Naaman for good. "By him Jehovah had given deliverance unto Syria." This not as implying that Syria had been used as an instrument for chastising apostate Israel, but in a much wider sense. For, though God looks down upon His own people with special condescension, and causes all events to contribute towards the purposes of His covenant of grace, yet He is also Lord over all, "and doeth according to His will in the army of heaven, and among the inhabitants of the earth." He openeth His hand, and sustains and feeds *all* His creatures. The eyes of all wait upon Him. Accordingly, to feel oneself a creature of the great God is in itself an unspeakable privilege. It almost seems like an earnest of redemption. That we walk upon the earth, and breathe the air; that we eat of the bread, and drink of the water which our great Creator supplies; that we are surrounded by tokens of His goodness; carry within us His image, however defaced; cherish within our souls thoughts of immortality, however dim and clouded; that we are continually within the range of His Providence; that Jehovah gives deliverance to Syria,—all this sounds like a call and an encouragement to go and fall upon our knees before God our Maker, to tell Him all, to humble ourselves before Him, and to ask of Him all that we need for body and for soul. We know, indeed, that between Him and us stands an awful cloud of guilt, which separates and estranges us from Him, but ever and again, like sunlight through the cloud, come luminous thoughts concerning Him, such as those which chased from Manoah and his wife the fear of death. And so may Nature and Providence be to us as a schoolmaster unto Christ, leading us to hope that this God will not let us perish, that He has provided a refuge for sinners, and opened some way by which He can be just, and yet justify the ungodly.

Blessed be God, we are not left in doubt or to mere speculation on this subject. With a clearness that cannot be misunderstood, He invites one and all to partake of His promised mercy in Christ Jesus. Comparatively insufficient as the knowledge of this appears to have been under the Old Testament, God supplied means by which the same, or a similar, spiritual result as at present was obtained. They possessed in those days but a small portion even of the Old Testament; nor can the Scriptures have been diffused through the households of Israel. But here we see the value of the symbolical teaching, and of the special institutions of the Old Testament. As the child, which could not otherwise have learned it, full well remembers what he has been taught pictorially, so did Israel read, as it were, the whole Bible in the types which surrounded its life. And when, thrice a year, the great festivals summoned every household to the Temple, lessons of the past, the present, and the future, most precious and spiritual, were taught to the thousands of Israel. Then there was the mission of the prophets. Here, there, everywhere, like a meteor in clear sky, appeared the prophet, with burning message, direct from Jehovah. Not a household in the land but must have known it—not a child but must have heard of "the man of God," and in its excited imagination, with wonder and awe, tried to realise something about this living path between heaven and earth, or to picture to itself this witness to the God of its fathers. Each story of old gained new interest, since every day it might be re-enacted. Like lightning, it lit up, with sudden flash, the whole sky; like thunder, it leaped from rock to crag, till its distant echoes were heard in the remotest homes of the land: The Lord God of Israel liveth!

Notwithstanding the general corruption, there must still have been many pious households in Israel. While there were mothers like the Shunammite, children like the captive Jewish maid of our narrative could not be wanting. Often, no doubt, had the child heard the story of God's dealings with her fathers. Often also must she have listened with breathless, rapt attention, as they spake of "the prophet that was in Samaria." Her Old Testament training had ripened into Old Testament piety. At the foundation of it lay that quality so rare in our days—*reverence*. Familiarity has made many of us irreverent; not, indeed, that this familiarity is real, but imaginary. We imagine we know everything, though we see little beyond the reflection of our own narrow vision. In Old Testament times: "Honour thy father and thy mother" was a real commandment; and love and reverence towards God and man went hand in hand with happiness and humility. Moreover, the maiden's was a child's religion—very defective, perhaps, but genuine. Children have personal religion, and that real and spiritual; but it were a great mistake to expect it to manifest itself in the same manner as in older persons, or to test it by the same standard. It is, indeed, easy to excite the feelings of children. But the result is equally unsatisfactory to us, and detrimental to them. True, their tears are honest, the outcome of their feelings; but they exhaust their little wealth of feeling in those tears. Similarly, it were easy to teach children the formulas of orthodoxy. A child is naturally imitative; but in this case imitation is dangerous, for familiarity with solemnities takes away their solemnity, and hardens the heart. A child's religion ought to appear much more in its deeds than in its words. Not that they will cease to be the deeds of a *child*, but that all around the child and its deeds there will be the halo of having been with Jesus, and of having received His blessing.

What terrible desolation must have swept over that family, when, after the Syrian raid, referred to in our narrative, they crept from their hiding-places, and vainly searched for the maiden. They would call her by name, and look for her where she had been wont to play; they would seek her with neighbours, perhaps as desolate as themselves. Was she dead; or, worse than death, had she been carried away to heathenism, shame, and slavery? And why had God allowed this child to be taken—so meek, so modest, so loving, so good, so pious? Alas, how often do similar questions rise in the heart and to the lips. Ask them not. Only believe. Perhaps "the Lord has need" of this child. He had need of that Jewish child; perhaps He has of yours, though you know not on what service. Yet how difficult is it under such circumstances to believe—to shut our eyes against all present appearances, and to look up straight to our God in Christ Jesus.

It must have been so in the history under consideration. In the morning all had been peace and happiness in this Israelitish village and home. Suddenly one of those marauding bands which kept up a continual border-warfare made its appearance. Before the mid-day sun had reached his height, mangled bodies, smoking ruins, wasted fields, and desolate homes marked the track of the Syrians. But there was something which parents would dread for their loved ones, far more than even death. It was slavery, and this was the sorrow which had now fallen upon a quiet, pious household.

For the little maid had been carried captive to Damascus. It may seem a strange coincidence, that in the slave-market of Damascus, amidst that cowering band of captives, this little Jewish maiden should have attracted the notice of Naaman's steward, and that he should have purchased her for his master. Perhaps it was an enviable lot; perhaps it might prove a sad one, even for a slave. But whatever it might seem, we cannot doubt that it was so appointed both in answer to her parents' prayers, and in fulfilment of the expectations of her own simple faith. Thus it came that, while those who loved her best mourned her most as one for whom death would have been happy deliverance, the Lord placed her in the position where she was to serve Him efficiently, and where of all persons this little slave could best advance His Kingdom. Indeed, it may be doubted whether any other could have done this special work.

In such circumstances, surrounded by heathens, far from the ordinances of religion, with little knowlege, and no help from without, we could scarcely have wondered if the maiden had forgotten her early training and lapsed into idolatry or carelessness. Perhaps few of our so-called Christian children would have stood the ordeal. It was otherwise with her. What day by day she saw around her would only remind her of the contrast between heathenism and the faith of Jehovah. There was one thing especially, and which she could never forget, one outstanding personality which seemed to her to embody the religion of Israel. It was the prophet in Samaria. Something like this is requisite to give reality to a child's religion. For, to make present application of it—in the case of children it is always not so much doctrine as a Person, around which spiritual experience grows up, and to which it clings. That Person is Jesus. If a child has come to Jesus, really learned Who He is, how loving, how mighty to forgive, to help, and to save, then its affections and thoughts will henceforth cling to the Person of Jesus. In whatever circumstances, even though adverse, such a child may be placed, Jesus will always appear to its mind as the one grand outstanding Reality, as the ever ready refuge at all times and in all wants—and the child will be safe. Therefore, we teach Jesus to our children; nay, in this sense, we must all become children, since our religion also must be centred in that one outstanding Personality, Jesus.

With this firm faith in the truth of Jehovah and of His word, as to her childish mind it seemed all embodied in the prophet of Samaria, the maiden in Naaman's palace continued pious, calm, and, as we infer from the narrative, not unhappy. Her stedfast adherence to duty, and the quietness which a religious heart imparted to her outward bearing, soon brought her into notice, and the little Jewish maiden became the favourite personal attendant of Naaman's wife. This modest little girl was, however, very observant, for she was very interested in all that she observed. And she had a great secret of her own, which had probably spoken out of her eyes long ere she ventured to entrust it to words. It was connected with this one thought, which was always present to her, about her God and the prophet that was in Samaria. But how would she dare to utter it? Yet she was so firmly convinced that the prophet could do anything, that she felt she must no longer keep such a secret. And so it came out one day, bursting, as it were, straight from her heart: "Would God my lord were with the prophet that is in Samaria! for he would recover him of his leprosy." It is a child's speech, and a child's theology, but it is that of a pious child. We find it the same still. To the faith of children who know Jesus, all seems so simple; there is such conviction in their going straight to Him with every want, that we verily feel their angels always behold the face of our Father Which is in heaven.

But besides, her mistress would look on her with special affection and confidence. For she was the very pattern of a little maid-servant. Modern society has become so practical, that it has introduced the idea of machinery even into the family. Servants take no interest in their masters, and masters take no interest in their servants; the thought of the one is of self in the form of pay, that of the other of self in the form of service. Meantime, the idea of the *family* has been lost from view. Instead, there is mutual suspicion and utter want of mutual regard. We have lost the evil of slavery; but we have also lost the good in slavery. Our cold individualism has separated us into so many units, as if God's world were an aggregation of atoms. In too many instances, if servants profess religion, they seem to hold the truth rather in impertinence than in love, and to use it rather for forcing their masters into toleration of their misdeeds, than for animating themselves to Christian interest and dutifulness. On the other hand, there are only too many so-called religious masters and mistresses, whose words savour rather of selfishness and spiritual pride than of Christian sympathy. Still, domestic service often offers almost unsurpassed opportunities for the service of Christ. But, be this as it may, the fact remains, that a pious little Jewish maiden became the means of converting the Captain-General of Syria, and of first introducing into Damascus the service of Jehovah.

Taken all in all, that little Jewish maid offers one of the most remarkable evidences of what the teaching and training of the Old Testament must have been. Were it for no other than this reason, her story would deserve permanent record in the annals of Scripture. We learn how a child, far from home, friends, and religious influences, surrounded by idolaters, remained a consistent religious professor. Possessing herself very little knowledge of religion, never having handled nor probably even seen a Bible, or that portion of it then existing, she preached successfully the faith which her master despised. She had known little, but felt much; and at Damascus she remained a true Jewish child, with her heart on her God, and her trust in Him. Syria and its idolatry were nothing to her; the God of Israel was the only True and Living God, and He could do all. By her beautifully consistent walk and conduct she gave constant testimony to her religion; and her religion was first seen before it was heard. And so, when she had been faithful in little things, she proved such in great things also. When the occasion came, she spake out for God; nor did she hesitate to preach Jehovah in the palace of Naaman. Yet even so, she did not forget her station; but when she spake, it was evident that she was under the influence of two very strong motives. She was convinced of the reality of the help offered, and she was most deeply and lovingly interested in the family for which she would fain procure that help. Then she spoke so modestly, yet with such wisdom and discretion, as guided by the Living God; her words were so earnest, clear, and full of conviction, that she succeeded in convincing her own mistress, and at once engaged her on the side of truth. From the character of Naaman, we can have little doubt that his consent was not so easily obtained. His heathen notions would ill consort with thoughts of the God of Israel; his national pride could ill brook the humiliation of being dependent for anything upon vanquished Israel, or receiving any boon from its religion. To his mind, a conquered people meant also an inferior national religion. For, nothing is more characteristic of the very essence of heathenism than this identification of religion and the state, irrespective of truth or falsehood, right or wrong.

Therefore, a less promising mission could scarcely be conceived than that which soon afterwards prepared to leave Damascus for Samaria. It seemed to contain all the elements to ensure its failure. In what spirit Naaman had ultimately consented to try this remedy, so firmly believed in by "the maid of the land of Israel," appears from the subsequent narrative. Then, before leaving, Naaman had applied to his king, and Ben-hadad had encouraged him to go, either under the influence of some superstitious notions, or with the same well-meant untruthfulness with which, in our own days, friends and relatives so often try to deceive the hopelessly sick, saying what they know to be false, and planning what can never be carried into execution. And, as if to make matters still worse, Ben-hadad himself proposed to interfere. "I will send a letter unto the king of Israel;" as it were, he can rule his prophets, his religion, and his God; he is my servant, and I will give him to understand that in this case I will brook no disobedience on his part, and, if anything can be done, it shall be done.

Passing strange as this conceit on the part of the Syrian king may seem, it is not without its parallel among us. Indeed, we meet with only too many similar manifestations. There are some, much inferior in rank to the Syrian king, who seem to speak, act, and think as if the world were made specially for them, and as if its inhabitants were to move as satellites around their orbit. Strange to onlookers, terrible to unhappy dependants, they profess no other religion than that of the most approved character, and they bear themselves in it like people who in so doing are performing a lofty duty. They can order anything so far as they can see, anything for this world and for the next—except that corruption shall not feed on them, and their bodies crumble into unsightly mould. Their anger at finding any person or thing impossible is unbounded; their only remedy is to ignore it or him. As for religion and its ministers, it lies within easy reach of a "letter," like that of the king of Syria, or some similar mandate. How much have such men to learn and to unlearn, before they can be prepared for the wonder of healing at Jordan! How much had grace to do in repelling and in attracting, before even Naaman was prepared to receive the Divine benefit!

Proud and unbroken in heart, with such retinue and presents* as befitted a Syrian prince, he set out on his journey to Samaria. If this had been all, neither his gifts, nor his honours, nor the command of King Ben-hadad would have availed him. But in infinite mercy the eye of the Lord —of Him Who afterwards healed the leper by His "I will," and Who restored the servant of the heathen ruler by the word of His lips—was upon Naaman. And all along the journey there followed that proud, unhumbled man the humble prayers and the childlike faith of that little Jewish slave in his palace at Damascus.

* The sterling value of the silver and gold which Naaman took with him (10 talents of silver and 6,000 pieces of gold) amounted to about £12,000.

CHAPTER XV.

THE WASHING OF REGENERATION.

"And it came to pass, when the king of Israel had read the letter, that he rent his clothes, and said, Am I God, to kill and to make alive, that this man doth send unto me to recover a man of his leprosy? wherefore consider, I pray you, and see how he seeketh a quarrel against me. And it was so, when Elisha the man of God had heard that the king of Israel had rent his clothes, that he sent to the king, saying, Wherefore hast thou rent thy clothes? let him come now to me, and he shall know that there is a prophet in Israel. So Naaman came with his horses and with his chariot, and stood at the door of the house of Elisha. And Elisha sent a messenger unto him, saying, Go and wash in Jordan seven times, and thy flesh shall come again to thee, and thou shalt be clean. But Naaman was wroth, and went away, and said, Behold, I thought, He will surely come out to me, and stand, and call on the name of the Lord his God, and strike his hand over the place, and recover the leper. Are not Abana and Pharpar, rivers of Damascus, better than all the waters of Israel? may I not wash in them, and be clean? So he turned, and went away in a rage. And his servants came near, and spake unto him, and said, My father, if the prophet had bid thee do some great thing, wouldest thou not have done it? how much rather then, when he saith to thee, Wash, and be clean? Then went he down, and dipped himself seven times in Jordan, according to the saying of the man of God: and his flesh came again like unto the flesh of a little child, and he was clean."—2 KINGS v. 7-14.

THE road from Damascus to Samaria is among the most celebrated highways of the world. Natural beauty and historical interest combine to lend it a peculiar charm. The first glimpse of Damascus from the west, and, of course, the last look of it from the road to Palestine, have inspired every pilgrim with almost poetic enthusiasm. Such a perfect wilderness here of luxuriant vegetation, such wealth of verdure and trees, such bubbling of fountains and sparkling of waters, and under such a sky—it seems an enchanted region, an earthly paradise, in the midst of burnt-up desolateness all around. And then, when turning away from Damascus, the snowy peaks of

Lebanon rise into view; next, we reach winding Jordan; then the deep blue Lake of Galilee appears in sight, and, still travelling onwards, we pass "Jacob's well," and finally come to queenly Samaria! What thoughts would crowd on the mind along this road. This is the plain where the Hand of the Lord arrested Saul of Tarsus, and where he was blinded by the light which afterwards guided him all along his path, and unto glory. And by the way are places consecrated by the memory of patriarchs; there the Blessed Lord Himself walked, and taught and wrought; by this well were the words spoken which first opened the Kingdom of Heaven to all who sought it "in spirit and in truth;" and there lies buried in vast silence the ancient city of Israel's kings. So gently has the breath of time swept over all, that even the ruins of ancient cities are not destroyed, only covered with the dust of ages. Everything around is like what it must have been many, many centuries ago, when Naaman and his followers pursued the same road. But with far other thoughts than those of pious remembrance did they follow its course. Naaman was a Syrian, a warrior, proud and unbroken in heart. He had, indeed, his recollections, but they were not of spiritual scenes. They were of battles fought and victories won on this very soil; and of circumstances far different from those of a suppliant. Damascus had, at that period, reached the highest point of its power and glory, and to this result Naaman had contributed not a little. Each of the five or six days of his journey must have been one of bitter humiliation. Yet this offered the only prospect of recovery open to the Syrian. And how often do we still find a similar state of mind in those who seek help in Israel. Numberless difficulties will always beset the first application for spiritual cleansing—perhaps, more or less, every access to the throne of grace. The recollections of the past; the humiliation of lowly kneeling, of confessing ourselves sinners, and seeking pardon in the old way; the irresolution, the doubt, the fear, the ill-suppressed shame: all contribute to keep us from the healing stream. Only under the pressure of felt necessity do we yield.

At last Samaria was reached, and Naaman proceeded to deliver to King Joram the missive of Ben-hadad. Probably we have all experienced that commonly disappointment is the first sensation, after we have gained the goal for which we had long toiled and hoped. We had quite set our hearts on a particular interview with a person, on some particular place, on one particular book, on one particular object. Here it is—and we are thoroughly disappointed, to begin with. The reason lies not in the thing, but in us. We had expected too much. There is only one direction in which there never can be disappointment. The Lord and His grace always exceed our utmost thinking and hoping. But the scene which now ensued was one for which Naaman could scarcely have been prepared. It was, however, quite in character with what we know of Joram. The arrival of an embassy, with Naaman at its head, would be sufficient to throw the king and his court into a flutter of excitement. Joram was a man of many devices, but of little wisdom; arrogant and boastful, where he should have been modest; craven-hearted where he should have been bold; a man of little weight, who would always alternate between the extremes of despondency and exultation. Joram and his counsellors received the Syrian general, and he delivered the letter of his monarch. It was brief and plain, a letter such as a Ben-hadad would send to a Joram, and ran as follows: —"Now, when this letter is come unto thee, behold, I have therewith sent Naaman my servant to thee, that thou mayest recover him of his leprosy." No farther explanation of this strange demand was added, no salutation nor compliment wasted. The terms were certainly sufficiently imperious and contemptuous to have made any request unpalatable; but this demand, as addressed to poor, bewildered Joram, was so utterly and ludicrously inappropriate as to set all explanation at defiance.

The king glanced from the read letter to Naaman, and from Naaman to the letter, and then all around. Had Joram been other than a coward, he would have given way to a burst of passion. As it was, he yielded to the other extreme of petulant despondency, and losing all heart, and forgetting all dignity, he rent his clothes in token of despair and mourning. "Am I God, to kill and to make alive,"* he at last found words in his childish mood to exclaim, "that this man doth send unto me to recover a man of his leprosy?" There was sense and religion too in the speech. Would that the speaker had only acted upon his own words! It is strange how much sense and religion there may be in the words of some, who never apply to themselves the moral of their own reasoning. With some it is a new form of an old hypocrisy to attempt teaching honest-hearted, earnest men, and to set before them burdens which they themselves would not touch with their little finger. Over his wine or in a novel, a man will discourse eloquently on religion, and alternately scold, picture, and moralise, while his own heart is utterly wicked, and his own conduct intolerable. The most foolish of men will talk wisdom on other people's affairs, and the most godless glibly moralise, and blame those to whose moral height they never can attain. Let us denounce all such folly and hypocrisy, and tear the mask from its face; and, when a Joram talks to us religion, let us tell him that for very shame's sake he should, at least, do so with rent clothes. Yet if Joram

* In the symbolical teaching of the law leprosy was regarded as equivalent to death (Num. xii. 12).

really believed that there was a God, and that He had power to kill and to make alive, why did he rend his clothes? Why not rather appeal to that God Whose prerogative Ben-hadad had so blasphemously usurped by his imperious command? Had Israel and its king not had experience of the wonder-working of Jehovah of old? But it is always so, when the realities of religion are brought before godless men. They know and feel the impossibility of help, so far as they are concerned; but they know not, and see not any way out of the difficulty.

What a wretched spectacle this craven king, in the midst of his discomfited courtiers, must have presented to the Syrian general! Similarly, we say it deliberately, there is not a sadder sight, than a Christian who desponds and distrusts his Lord. If the world have no hope, we can understand it; but when a Christian, in the hour of need or sorrow, sits down in impotent despair, as if there were no God nor help, it is a spectacle to make devils rejoice, and angels and men weep for very shame. There is nothing so dishonouring to God as unbelief. He often exceeds our belief and expectation; but He will not do any other thing for unbelievers or half-believers than to confound their distrust and bring them to shame. Joram, not finding comfort in his religion, which only showed him the impossibility of complying with Ben-hadad's demand, quickly turned to another subject. Dismissing the idea that Ben-hadad could have been in earnest about the cure, his fertile imagination saw in the letter only a pretext for commencing a dispute. Verily, the wicked flee when no man pursueth. And so, alternating between fear and resentment, the king and his counsellors were as incapable of understanding God's ways as either Ben-hadad or Naaman; nor was there in that proud assembly even a Jewish maiden, to speak of that prophet who "would recover" a man "of his leprosy."

THE WASHING OF REGENERATION. 155

Here began a series of trials by which the Lord prepared Naaman, step by step, for receiving temporal and spiritual benefit. For the bewilderment at the court of Samaria was not the only trial to be encountered. Even when help came, it was from a quarter and in a manner utterly humiliating to his pride, disappointing his expectations, and breaking his hard heart so as at last to make him willing to believe and obey like a little child, that so he might enter the Kingdom of Heaven. And this also is the object of many of those trials by which the Lord converts us unto Himself. Meanwhile, tidings of what had passed in the palace of Samaria must have quickly spread through the land; for such a guest from Syria on such errand would arouse general attention. In his humble abode the man of God heard of it. With what holy indignation and shame must he have learned that the king of Israel had, in his unbelief and cowardice, prostituted to a scene of almost incredible self-degradation one of the noblest opportunities of glorifying the God of Israel. If anything could have brought the blush to Joram's cheek, it might have been the prophet's question, "Wherefore hast thou rent thy clothes?" But if the country was degraded, not so religion. "Let him now come to me." There are times when it is the duty of Christ's ambassadors to rise not only to the full height of their commission, but to declare it in plain terms. *You* cannot deal with the ills of the world; you cannot cure the distempers of society; you cannot by your interference restore to it health or happiness. *We* have and hold the sole remedy: it is the Gospel of our Lord and Saviour Jesus Christ. Let them come to us—or rather to Him Whom we preach—and they "shall know that there is a prophet"—ay, and more than a prophet, a Saviour —"in Israel."

Encouraging as this message was, it involved great humiliation to Naaman. Elisha did not come to Naaman; Naaman had to go to Elisha; and most incongruous must have seemed the retinue at the head of which the Syrian chieftain now repaired to the humble home of the prophet. "Naaman came with his horses and his chariot, and stood at the door of the house of Elisha." At this point the conduct of the prophet becomes almost unintelligible, were it not explained by the character and bearing of Naaman himself. At any cost he must learn, what otherwise he could never have understood, the vast difference between Jehovah and the idols of Syria; and that simple faith and implicit obedience were the conditions alike of man's worship and of God's help. Elisha did not even go forth to meet the splendid *cortège*. He sent a messenger to direct Naaman to wash seven times in Jordan, with the promise that this application would prove effectual to his cure.

The special reason for each part of the prophet's conduct appears clearly from Naaman's indignant reply. He was disappointed at the bearing of the prophet; he was brought into contact with a religion utterly at variance with all his old notions; his pride rebelled against the distinction bestowed upon the waters of Israel over those of Damascus, and he held the latter to be as good, if not better, than any that flowed through the Land of Promise. But why should the prophet not have met him, and explained the reason of these directions? That reason could not be explained. An explanation would have destroyed the meaning and purpose of the direction itself. We *cannot* understand the meaning of many trials; God does not explain them. To explain a trial would be to destroy its object, which is that of calling forth simple faith and implicit obedience. If we knew why the Lord sent this or that trial, it would thereby cease to be a trial either of faith or of patience. Nor was Elisha uncourteous in his studied neglect of Naaman. This was Elisha's answer to the heathen mode of approaching God with horses and chariots, with talents of silver, and pieces of gold, and changes of raiment. It was intended to teach in the only manner in which a heathen could understand it, that the God of Israel could neither be overawed nor influenced by worldly greatness—that He was "the Most High."

And these are lessons, which, if only we have faith in our Master and in our mission, we must hold before this generation also. There is no sacerdotalism in all this—only the dignity of the Gospel. The complaint so rife in our days about the decadence of the Church must be traceable, either or both, to the inefficiency of the pulpit and the worldliness of its occupants. Efficiency in the pulpit depends, we are convinced, not so much on talent, as on godliness, and with it on *directness* of utterance. Much of our preaching is inefficient, because it is not *direct*. The least gifted man will secure attention, and does secure it, when he is distinct and direct. We must have something definite, not roundabout, to say, and say it in plain and clear language. And it is a good test of a sermon, whether or not, after having preached it, we begin to feel how infinitely more there is in the text, than we had ever formerly seen in it. This shows that the Spirit of God has been opening to our minds His own Word. A still greater source of danger, however, lies in the worldliness, probably often more seeming than real, of ministers. A Naaman is left to think that, after all, horses and chariots, and gold and silver, are qualifications for inheriting the Kingdom of Heaven, instead of learning that all these things must be denied, and that each man must enter in as a little child. The deference which is paid to the rich and the great of this world, the eagerness with which they are welcomed, their every religious platitude is cheered, their worldliness condoned, their approbation courted, and their every contribution or patronage received, however churlishly or self-righteously bestowed — all this is fraught with terrible consequences. We deceive these men, and contribute to the ruin of their souls, encouraging them to walk proudly where they should kneel humbly, and we grievously misrepresent Christianity, as if its existence or support depended on such help. True and living faith in our Master should produce in us consciousness of the dignity of our office, preserving us from stooping to degrade, not ourselves, but the office which we hold, and with it Him Who has called us to His work.

And now the meaning of Elisha's directions will become apparent. Contrary to Naaman's expectation, the prophet did *not* " come out," nor yet did he, calling " on the name of Jehovah *his God*," "strike his hand over the place, and recover the leper." This would have been magic, Syrian miracle-mongering, such as Naaman had looked for. He must learn that not the prophet but Jehovah recovered the leper; not by the putting forth of the power possessed by a man, but by the quickening Spirit of the Living God. We cannot pardon, nor give absolution, nor make a man whole. For the pretence of that, men may apply to a spurious priesthood; for the reality we point to the Living God, keeping ourselves entirely in the background. Nor was there need for any extraordinary measures. " Wash in Jordan seven times," the covenant, or sacred number. Use the spiritual provision of Israel, and it sufficeth.* Whatever your sin or

---

* Both the washing and the sacred number "seven" bear reference to the typical ordinances in the Levitical law on the purification of the leper (Lev. xiv. 7, 8, 9, 16, 27).

need, go to Christ. His blood cleanseth from all sin; His grace is sufficient for you. We have no other remedy, and we need none other.

But why wash in Jordan—why not in any other river? Because it was Israel's provision, and because, though Israel was humiliated in consequence of its guilty monarch and apostate rulers, there was yet infinite power in its spiritual provision. To us also is this the lesson. There is none other way than that of God's provision for Israel, Jesus Christ; and though the Church seem weak and small by the side of earthly kingdoms and powers, yet the gracious provision of our Lord is all-powerful. And this is the last and most humbling lesson of all, which every Naaman must learn: to deny the "Abana and Pharpar" of the world's wisdom, power, and greatness, and to choose that humble, humiliating way of coming to God, and receiving benefit at His Hand. From Naaman's point of view, it is easily understood how he would fail to perceive the need of such humiliation, and indignantly refuse to submit to it. For, in the opinion of many, is not one religion as good as another? But the point of the direction lies not in the command to wash, but to wash in Jordan. It matters not what distinctions surround, nor what earnestness is exhibited in connection with false religion. The Gospel of our Lord Jesus Christ is that truth which alone can save us. Then, however humiliating to our natural pride to submit to come in this manner, let us go, or we shall never "recover this leper." Let us learn that religion which is not associated with brokenness of heart, is not of the Holy Spirit's working, and as destitute of result to our eternal good, as washing in the rivers of Damascus would have been for the recovery of the leper. The hard heart must be broken, and natural pride laid low. We must feel ourselves lost sinners, see that there is no other mode of recovery than by the Blood of Jesus, and be made willing to come in the Gospel way, no matter at what cost to pride and natural unwillingness. This may require and imply a very painful process to the natural heart. "Flesh and blood cannot inherit the Kingdom of God." The Gospel is a humiliating way, which we enter by the strait gate, when all must be left behind, all renounced, and all given up, that we "may win Christ and be found in Him." We must come as sinners, who so need Christ that they need nothing else, and count all as loss for the excellency of His knowledge. The soul is most precious; it can in no other way be recovered. Here flow the waters of Jordan, sufficient for the healing of all, and free to all. Here is Christ sufficient for all, and offered to all. The hindrances are within, not without our own hearts. It is most easy to believe—we have only to go and wash, and we *shall* be clean. Yet it is most difficult so to believe; its very ease constitutes its difficulty. We cannot believe without a broken heart, without such a sense of need as will bear anything if it can only get Christ. The work is indeed finished for us; but the pride of the natural heart rebels against this simple, humble way. Except we be converted and become as children, we shall not enter into the Kingdom of Heaven.

Do we then ask, What are we to do to be saved? If we feel our need of Christ, let us simply go to Him, and just as we are. Let us tell *Him* our case, and ask Him to give us the broken heart; let us come in faith, for He has never turned from any who so came to Him; let us wrestle and persevere till we are heard, answered, and saved. As guilty and unclean, as lepers, let us come in faith to that Blood which cleanseth from all guilt and uncleanness; let us submit to God and believe in His Christ, and so shall we with joyous hearts learn that verily there is a God in Israel.

CHAPTER XVI.

THE RENEWING OF THE HOLY GHOST.

' And his servants came near, and spake unto him, and said, My father, if the prophet had bid thee do some great thing, wouldest thou not have done it? how much rather then, when he saith to thee, Wash, and be clean? Then went he down, and dipped himself seven times in Jordan, according to the saying of the man of God: and his flesh came again like unto the flesh of a little child, and he was clean. And he returned to the man of God, he and all his company, and came, and stood before him: and he said, Behold, now I know that there is no God in all the earth, but in Israel: now therefore, I pray thee, take a blessing of thy servant. But he said, As the LORD liveth, before whom I stand, I will receive none. And he urged him to take it; but he refused."—2 KINGS v. 13-16.

THAT Syrian soldier must have been kind and considerate, as well as brave, since so many of his dependants had learned to love him. It seems so easy to gain the affections of the poor, unless they have been spoiled by our own folly; and it gives them such joy to find an outlet for their affections, that one almost wonders that the rich should be so sparing in bestowing this luxury upon themselves and their humbler neighbours. Indeed, in this matter the world too often shames the Church. Too often it even seems forgotten that courtesy is expressly enjoined by the Holy Spirit on Christians; and that the principle of courtesy lies in considerateness for the *feelings* of others: in quickness and delicacy in understanding, and in kindliness and readiness in meeting them. So far as we can judge, the household of Naaman was bound together by affection. The same spirit seemed to animate all its members. As we recall the words of that Jewish maiden, we think of Naaman's wife as loving and earnest. And again, the heartfelt wish of that little Jewish maiden was for the recovery of her master. And even in the moment when Naaman "turned and went away in a rage," his servants were not afraid to "come near," and oppose their advice to his passion, addressing him in language which shows the cordiality of their relations.

On how small a matter may our whole life turn—alike in its bearings on time and eternity! Upon an outburst of temper on the part of a kind, quick-tempered man; upon the presence of some prudent attached servant; upon a remonstrance, upon a word fitly, calmly, seasonably spoken! Upon all these—and yet in reality on none of them, but on the gracious arrangement of all things by the Lord in His purpose of mercy. On this occasion at least, a sullen temper, or a self-sufficient manner would have deterred unbidden but interested counsellors. But even this open, kindly temper of the Syrian was the good gift of the good Lord. Its value in the Church also is apparent. The sullen and the generous may be alike converted; vessels for the Master's use may be made of both; yet it seems difficult to understand how a golden vessel could ever be made out of hard wood. And though we know that all is of grace, and that He giveth more grace, we feel none the less grateful for His gifts. Nor will grace supply that which can otherwise be obtained. And kindliness, openness, and generosity can in great measure be got by our own efforts, grace making us watchful, influencing us to covet the best gifts, rendering us self-observant, and leading us to seek Divine help in overcoming our natural failings. Again, it deserves special notice, that God has His instruments always in readiness when He needs them, and that often they are of the humblest character. Once more were slaves to become the means of effecting their master's true freedom. Nor were they even religious servants; only, not having the same temptations as Naaman, they saw the more clearly how unchecked pride might deprive him of the hoped-for benefit. Quick and sharp temptation puts an end to reasoning, and leaves us open to the sway of impulses, from which may God in His mercy deliver us!

It is scarcely necessary to indicate, how terrible the consequences, if Naaman had been allowed to carry out his purpose, and had returned "in a rage" to Damascus. The last hope of relief would then have passed away for ever, and body and soul been doomed to perpetual leprosy. And how near he had been to complete recovery! Here was certain relief, and it had been freely offered. Only "wash in Jordan seven times, and thy flesh shall come again to thee." And yet he was about to turn away from it, when the Hand of the Lord arrested him. Whose would have been the blame and guilt, if he had gone back to Damascus unhealed? So is it in the case of each unconverted sinner among us. Cleansing, pardon, and salvation are freely offered to all. We have God's gracious provision; and His invitation to all is: Go, wash, and be clean. But if, in the pride or the unbelief of his heart, the sinner turns away, whose is the blame and guilt but his who has destroyed himself? On the part of God, there is neither exception nor limitation in the Gospel-call. It is made earnestly and most lovingly, even as a father entreats his child not to destroy himself. There is intense agony of disappointed love in the declaration, "As I live, saith the Lord God, I have no pleasure in the death of the wicked; but that the wicked turn from his way and live." Songs of joy are said to be raised in heaven over every repenting sinner. How terrible that, when such free and full salvation is within reach of every one, any should be lost. And let us fear, "lest, a promise being left us of entering into His rest, any of us should seem to come short of it."

There was so much, not only in the manner in which the servants of Naaman addressed their master, but in the calm and sensible words which they spoke, that even a more harsh hearer than he would have been soothed by them. "My father, if the prophet had bid thee do some great thing, wouldest thou not have done it? how much rather then, when he saith to thee, Wash, and be clean?" Calm words, kindly spoken, have been the means of recalling those, who otherwise might have rushed on to destruction. Faithfulness does not mean bitterness, nor yet sternness. It is surely most desirable to make the Gospel as attractive as possible, by showing its transforming influence, even upon our outward conduct. And how true it is, as these servants said, that a man is much more ready to do some great thing for the recovery of his leprosy, than simply "wash and be clean." So immense a result as salvation seems unattainable by such simple means. Then, we all seem to feel as if we must do something ourselves to rescue our souls. "Some great thing" on our part meets the expectation of the natural heart. Yet they know very little of what vital Christianity is, who deem Evangelical doctrine consistent with an unchanged heart and life. Unquestionably there are who profess these doctrines, whose hypocrisy casts, in the mind of the ill-informed, suspicion upon all religion. Nothing is more easily imitated than the semblance of religion; nothing more difficult of attainment than its reality.

But let us view the matter in its real bearing. When a sinner goes to Christ, it is under a deep sense of felt spiritual need. To accept Christ is to accept the heavenly, the spiritual gift of God's love; to become imbued with that love, to yield to it, to surrender to it, to be constrained by it. So-called acts of religion may be easy; a life of religion is unattainable, except by grace. The heathen devotee scourges, chastises, and immolates himself precisely on the same principles and in the same manner as the Popish bigot. But there can be no real service to God or man in this, nor yet can any other results ensue than those produced by the nervous excitement consequent on such "exercises," which is equally wrought by heathens, Mohammedans, and so-called Christians, and which, indeed, may any day be produced by other means wholly unconnected with religion. But a life of godliness, the quiet inward walk with God, the constant upward look, the heart full of faith and prayer, the joy even in tribulation; a life of self-denial and of aiming, all unknown to others, after what is good and holy, yet still rejoicing most of all in fellowship with God; and all this as on the part of children ransomed by the Blood of Jesus, as in gratitude and love, as indwelt by the Holy Ghost, as looking for the coming of the Lord—surely such inward life ill accords with the charge that Evangelical doctrine may be dissociated from holy living. We are now replying to those who are sincerely inquiring, not to a class of writers who preach to others what certainly they do not practise themselves. No thoughtful man would accept criticism on scientific subjects from those who are notoriously ignorant of them. What then shall we say of the declamations on what religion is, or should be, by male or female writers, whose lives are sometimes of scandalous character, and prove them to be destitute not only of religion, but even of ordinary morality? We honour the wise and the good, who instruct us in what they themselves have learned in the school of life. But of all the cant, hypocrisy, and sensationalism to be denounced and ridiculed, the worst is that of those moralisers, whose personal character and conduct would, if properly judged, debar them from the company of all but the hardened.

By the influence of God on Naaman's heart, the remark

of his servants proved sufficient to arrest him. A little reflection, and his obstinacy and prejudice gave way. Not, perhaps, that he believed; but that he felt disobedience utterly unreasonable. Naaman returned to Jordan. How much depended on every step he took; and how much depends on every step *we* take in our return to God! To draw back is to be lost; to hesitate is to risk all. Never let us hesitate to yield to a religious impulse. Let us kneel down when we feel the need of it, or retire within ourselves. Let us give thanks, or pray, or act; but let us never suppress the emotion, which in its nature is fugitive. It is like cutting the bud off a flower, or the blossom off a tree. Nay, worse far, it is to suppress the rising effort of spiritual life to unfold and develop. Not a few may date the commencement of their hardening and ruin to the first religious emotion suppressed. The Spirit of God will not always strive with man.

But Naaman yielded, and turned towards Jordan. And now he stood by the brink of the river. The longer he looked at its quiet, swift course, the less likely must it have seemed to him, that its waters could be fraught with such healing powers. But he must not so look; he must simply comply with the direction of God. The very essence of the matter lay in this; and to this was added the trial that he had to wash seven times before any result could be expected. We can almost imagine with what feelings Naaman must have descended into the river. Once he plunged, and no result; twice, thrice—and still no result. Each time his anxiety would naturally become greater. Four times, five times, six times, and still no result! Only one more hope remained. Is it too much to imagine that, in such circumstances, he would pour forth an untaught prayer, springing from his heart up to the God of

Israel, and appealing to His own Word, as he was now about to make trial whether or not Jehovah was the living and the true God? At least, his after-confession before Elisha (ver. 15), as indeed every true confession of faith, reads like the substance of a former prayer, although not cast in the form of a petition. And so he washed a seventh time. And, behold, with joyous heart he emerged from the waters, his flesh like that "of a little child." What tumult of feelings must have swept through his soul, what vigour and ardour through his being, it is not needful nor indeed possible to describe. He only who has known the sudden rebound in having passed from death to life, from despair to assured joy, from bondage to liberty can, on looking back, understand what caused that rush of feeling in which all seemed at the time confusion, except the one gladsome sense of safety and rest.

It can be scarcely requisite to say, how closely here the analogy holds to the Gospel mode of salvation. Wash in the precious blood of Christ, and immediately, wholly, permanently, you are clean. But, while this is obvious, it cannot on this occasion be pointed out without a feeling of sadness. It is one of the most painful things connected with religious error, that it so often attaches itself to the most precious portions of the Word of God. In this instance, it is well known that the washing of Naaman has in its effects been compared to Christian baptism, and that what is known as the doctrine of "baptismal regeneration," has again and again been sought and found in this passage of Scripture. The criticism and interpretation may safely be left unnoticed; not so, perhaps, the doctrine in question.

Let us not be misunderstood. The remarks which we are about to make refer not to those who speak of "baptismal regeneration" in the sense of a new relationship to God, with all of blessing that it may imply, but to those who regard it as a change of state, disposition, or nature. Further, in justice even to those who hold this view, it should be understood that some at least of its advocates, while asserting that baptism implies in every case this regeneration, do not maintain that baptismal regeneration ensures salvation. They distinguish between regeneration and conversion; the first, they say, is imparted in baptism, the other is our own spiritual act and choice, necessary because we have fallen from baptismal grace. In that case, conversion is, of course, only a kind of supplement to regeneration, necessary on account of sin after baptism. But if so, what becomes of those who have been converted without having been previously baptized? What of the Old Testament saints, for example? But, in general, how do *regeneration* and *conversion* stand related; are they connected, and does the one presuppose the other? Must a man be first regenerated before he is converted? If so, what becomes of adult converts to Christianity, who must be converted before they can be regenerated in baptism? Or, on the contrary, must a man be first converted, and then regenerated? If so, what becomes of infants? Or, is there no connection between regeneration and conversion; may the one take place without the other; and if so, on which of the two does salvation depend? Was the penitent thief converted, but not regenerated; and were Ananias and Sapphira regenerated, but not converted? We repeat, if we take the words in their subjective aspect, as marking, not a new relation to God, but an inward state and condition: Regeneration means being begotten again, conversion means turning unto God. In such case, the one marks the Divine, the other the human aspect of the work of grace. In that view a man cannot be regenerated or begotten again of God, born from on high, without conversion or turning unto God;

and, on the other hand, a man cannot be converted, or turn unto God, without having received the new nature, or being begotten of God and born again.

We return from a controversy which, in some aspects of it, is equally strange and painful, to the history before us. The interval of time between Naaman's washing in Jordan and his return to the prophet must have been very short. Yet what changes had taken place, alike in the outward condition, and in the feelings of the Syrian. All things had become new to him, all bore a different aspect. The world, and all that was therein; religion, and all that its thoughts involved, were seen in quite another light. So, when we rise from our knees pardoned, accepted, and adopted children, all appears to us changed, not only in the spiritual, but even in the outward world. At first it may be difficult distinctly to trace and set in order the feelings which agitate the mind, but amidst them all, in our case as in that of the recovered leper, two thoughts are always uppermost. In assured consciousness, Naaman realised that he was healed; and with the firm conviction of experience, he now believed in Jehovah, the God of Israel. And if we have passed from death to life, it seems difficult to understand that we can be unconscious of the great change that has passed over us. Doubts as to its reality can only spring from lurking unbelief in the adequacy of the remedy. True, internal healing is, indeed, not palpable to the eye, like an external cure; but the sense of pardon and acceptance is unmistakable. *If we would only learn to trust it!* But our reluctance springs from remaining unbelief. Nor can there ever be so strong conviction of the truth of Christianity wrought in us as that produced by personal experience of its benefits. The remark of Calvin, at the close of his elaborate discussion on the evidences of Christianity, to the effect that the Holy Ghost and spiritual experience were the best and most convincing evidences, is profoundly true. Hence, in dealing with the opponents of our religion, it is always desirable to address primarily the conscience, while at the same time ready to give a reason for the faith that is in us.

The first impulse of Naaman was to return to the house of the prophet, to make public avowal of his conversion to God, and in some manner to express his affection and gratitude. Coldness on the part of a genuine convert is, to say the least, most incongruous. Only selfishness, or a Gehazi-spirit, could counsel caution under such circumstances. If ever, surely this is the occasion for distinct avowal of feelings, the deepest and the holiest. In our days, when the difficulties of a full profession are not to be compared with those encountered by Naaman, an outright, warm, and joyous confession is still, alas, the exception. Some fear that they may be made the subject of remark; others, that they may be taken advantage of; yet others, that at some time they may fail in consistency—thus beginning their service of God by refusing to serve Him. The consequence is an uncertain sound, which does not arouse any one to prepare himself for battle.

It deserves special notice that Elisha now no longer refused to meet Naaman. The convert could no more misunderstand his conduct or motives. Rather did he welcome him as a brother, beloved in the Lord. And what gladness must have filled the prophet's heart, when Naaman burst into a child-like confession, which renounced all the past and opened such a new future. "Behold, now I know that there is no God in all the earth, but in Israel." It was not merely that he owned belief in one God, and in Him as the God of Israel, but that he owned Him the only True and Living God in all the earth. Here was Elisha's first-fruits from among the Gentiles—a man entirely changed in heart, thought, and behaviour, and that on the ground of his conviction, that there was no God but in Israel. Tongue cannot tell, nor the mind of a stranger conceive, the deep joy of gratitude and affection which fills the heart of a minister of Christ on beholding the fruit of his labours. It is worth a life's toil, care and sorrow, burden, misrepresentation and weariness to behold one genuine convert. If men only knew what gladness a good confession sheds in our hearts, what consolation it offers in our trials, what encouragement in labours, carried on as it were in the night, when we can at least *see* no progress, they would not be so slow nor so niggardly in avowing or showing their experience of God's goodness to them. Not that we wish any one to make parade of religion, far less to employ it for controversial purposes. But if ever, it is in our days, when religiousness passes for religion, and carelessness shuts itself up behind miserable platitudes, that men ought not to hesitate making full confession that there is no other God in all the earth, but in Israel. If otherwise, their hesitation can only arise from fear, or from love of the world. Can we wonder that a religion of indecision and weakness worketh no good to others, and that it yieldeth neither happiness nor peace to our own minds?

Probably the first and most natural manner, in which a real sense of benefits received shows itself, is in seeking some mode of utterance. Affection and gratitude are never dumb. They have a hundred ways of speaking. They always speak warmly; they always speak earnestly; and they always speak modestly. Gratitude to Christ speaks warmly, earnestly, and modestly. "Behold, Lord, the half of my goods I give to the poor; and if I have taken anything from any man by false accusation, I restore him fourfold." The precious ointment in the alabaster box, the price of lands and possessions laid at the Apostles' feet, the diligent, loving search for the captive Paul among the prisoners of Rome by the friendly Onesiphorus, the abounding liberality of some in the midst of their deep poverty, are all manifestations of the self-same spirit. And such gratitude is ingeniously inventive, and finds a thousand ways of asserting itself. It asks, moreover, as a favour, what it offers as a gift. "Now, therefore," pleads Naaman, " I pray thee, take a blessing of thy servant." The gift, which is not offered as bestowing in its acceptance far more on the giver than on the recipient, may be taken by man; it is not accepted by the Lord. To offer of our own unto God is an act of humble service, allowed us as a great privilege. To present it in any other spirit, grudgingly, boastfully, proudly, as bestowing, not as receiving favour, would be an act of daring presumption, to which the Scripture applies : "Who hath required this at your hand? Bring no more vain oblations."

Though earnestly urged by Naaman, Elisha resolutely refused to receive any token of gratitude. Not from pride, for he had received the bounty of the Shunammite, and only lately the gift from Baal-shalisha; but, undoubtedly, for reasons connected with the spiritual welfare of those assembled around, both Jews and Syrians, and for the interests of the Kingdom of God. For, strange as it may sound in these days, the reception of contributions is not the highest aim to be sought by Christians. There is something much higher than this—the good of souls and the glory of God.

And so, for the first, and perhaps for the last time they have met on earth, these two noble, loving, believing men, Elisha and Naaman. How like, and yet how unlike each other! We hope to meet them in heaven, and then, perhaps, we shall learn more of this history, and how passed that hour of brotherly fellowship between the Jewish prophet and the Syrian general.

CHAPTER XVII.

DANGERS BY THE WAY.

"And Naaman said, Shall there not then, I pray thee, be given to thy servant two mules' burden of earth? for thy servant will henceforth offer neither burnt offering nor sacrifice unto other gods, but unto the LORD. In this thing the LORD pardon thy servant, that when my master goeth into the house of Rimmon to worship there, and he leaneth on my hand, and I bow myself in the house of Rimmon: when I bow down myself in the house of Rimmon, the LORD pardon thy servant in this thing. And he said unto him, Go in peace. So he departed from him a little way. But Gehazi, the servant of Elisha the man of God, said, Behold, my master hath spared Naaman this Syrian, in not receiving at his hands that which he brought: but, as the LORD liveth, I will run after him, and take somewhat of him. So Gehazi followed after Naaman. And when Naaman saw him running after him, he lighted down from the chariot to meet him, and said, Is all well? And he said, All is well. My master hath sent me, saying, Behold, even now there be come to me from Mount Ephraim two young men of the sons of the prophets: give them, I pray thee, a talent of silver, and two changes of garments. And Naaman said, Be content, take two talents. And he urged him, and bound two talents of silver in two bags, with two changes of garments, and laid them upon two of his servants; and they bare them before him. And when he came to the tower, he took them from their hand, and bestowed them in the house: and he let the men go, and they departed. But he went in, and stood before his master. And Elisha said unto him, Whence comest thou, Gehazi? And he said, Thy servant went no whither. And he said unto him, Went not mine heart with thee, when the man turned again from his chariot to meet thee? Is it a time to receive money, and to receive garments, and oliveyards, and vineyards, and sheep, and oxen, and men-servants, and maid-servants? The leprosy therefore of Naaman shall cleave unto thee, and unto thy seed for ever. And he went out from his presence a leper as white as snow."—2 KINGS v. 17-27.

THERE is to observant minds a peculiar taint about many religious biographies. They may be exceedingly well meant, and very devoutly written. But, viewed as biographies, they are simply not true. The statement may seem startling; it is only too correct. Who has ever met such people in real life? And thankful we are that the answer will be in the negative; since otherwise no hope of being Christians would be left to us, nor to any persons living outside printed books. For, assuredly, there is not a warp without a woof, nor light without shadow, nor yet a life without failings, foibles, and the thousand and one little things which give to character its individuality, and to life its peculiarity, but which are carefully left out of so many biographies. The religious phase alone is presented, and even that from the peculiar point whence it falls within the visional range of the interested onlooker, the spiritual adviser, or the religious writer. The result is, the record of lives which none of us can recognise as human—which are neither true nor real, in that they present only one phase of life, and even that in a manner distorted and exaggerated. Not so Scripture, which even in this respect proves its claim to Divine authorship, that it is so unlike human books. It has no predilections, and no passions—no heroes, caricatures, nor exaggerations. It is simply true; it gives the *whole* character and history of a man in all their phases; and what it says about a man's religion is neither unreal nor unnatural. We feel that even the farthest advanced, and most favoured of God's saints, were men "subject to like passions as we are." The bewilderment which this altogether unusual truthfulness of Scripture produces in the minds of good men appears in the discordant opinions of interpreters, whenever the subject of comment is some act which, to the honest Christian onlooker, viewing it in the light of our own days, seems, to say the least, doubtful. That it should, perhaps, be viewed in the dimmer light of Old Testament days, does not occur to them, nor yet that the standard of perfection should not be applied to the commencement of a religious life. And so they condemn, or seek out reasons for excusing, as they are severally disposed.

The request and the inquiry, which formed part of the interview between Naaman and Elisha, were simply what we might have expected under the circumstances. They were neither absolutely right, nor were they absolutely wrong. They were simply natural on the part of a convert like Naaman. So was the reply of Elisha, and so is the narrative of Scripture; and these details make the whole much more real and life-like to us than it could otherwise have been. It was certainly not in accordance with our more advanced knowledge concerning the spirituality of religion, when Naaman asked for his proposed altar to Jehovah "two mules' burden of earth" from the Land of Israel. But although the proposal accords not with our ideas, and indeed to some may seem to savour of the superstitious, its tolerance, not its approval (for the former, not the latter, was accorded by Elisha), *does* agree with the practice of St. Paul, who would have the strong bear the infirmities of the weak, and himself would have yielded to the utmost verge of Christian endurance, in order to preserve a brother from offence or stumbling. But did Elisha, by his reply, encourage his convert in superstitious notions and practices? What did he reply, or what indeed could he reply, other than "Go in peace"? Probably, some of us might have judged differently, and been inclined to reason the point with Naaman, till, before we had reached our sixth or seventh argument, the young convert would have become bewildered and confused. Similarly, not a few might have refused to baptize the Ethiopian eunuch, unless he had consented to learn by heart a good many things before re-entering his chariot. What really was most important for Naaman was simply what the prophet said, that he should "Go *in peace*."

But supposing, for the moment, that the request of Naaman did savour of the superstitious, Elisha's reply raises the broader question, so often forced upon us, how far we are warranted in tolerating certain practices, not in themselves sinful, on the ground of bearing with the weak, or how far it is our duty to resist them, as opposed alike to the truth and spirituality of religion. Of the danger of such practices, it is scarcely necessary to speak in our days. In view of this, the question of Christian duty becomes all the more urgent. Our first distinction must here be as to circumstances. A dim grey light precedes the dawn of day; it also precedes the commencement of night. That which may be matter of forbearance in him who is only just beginning the Christian life, or finding the truth (as Luther, and the other early Reformers), would be sinful compliance if tolerated in those who profess to be advanced. Again, if any outward thing becomes part of a system, is put forward, insisted upon, defended and advocated as such, we must not take part in it, but, so far as we can, in consistence with charity, resist it to the uttermost. It is no longer harmless; it will strike deeper, and spread wider; it is the leprosy of superstition. Anything, however indifferent, ceases to be indifferent if absolute value is attached to it, and they who practise it regard it not as indifferent, but as necessary, or most important. Superstition is to place a thing above its proper value, and above its proper place; it is misplaced religion, the putting a value upon things which they do not possess in themselves. Weakness should be borne with; superstition must be resisted. Any practice, however indifferent in itself, becomes absolutely sinful, when, ceasing to be indifferent, it is made the object of superstition to our neighbour. The same law of love which demands our tolerance in the one, requires our utmost resistance in the other case, and, more than that law only, our duty also towards the truth, and towards Him Who is the Truth.

But in the case of Naaman, this question could scarcely arise. Naaman spoke under the Old Testament dispensation of types and shadows, when such a request could not have been designated as superstition, whoever had proffered it. Naaman spoke as a young convert, just emerging from heathenism, with a heart full of ardent attachment to the God of Israel. He had renounced the religion of Syria as a lie, and made public avowal of Jehovah as the only God. He purposed, in the midst of Damascus, to rear an altar unto the Lord, and there openly to serve Him. And so thorough was his repugnance to Syrian superstitions, and his attachment to the religion of Israel, that he would not construct even that altar from the earth polluted by idolatry, but would testify to his entire separation therefrom by building it from Israelitish earth. It was, so to speak, an Old Testament mode of showing that he hated even "the garment spotted by the flesh." And if Naaman did "take pleasure in her stones, and favour the dust thereof," do not our grateful memories also cling, with peculiar affection, to the place where we first heard the truth? There was certainly nothing of superstition in what was made matter of request, since it was not urged as necessary for his worship. And if there was aught of weakness in the desire, let us remember, before casting a stone, that while few attain the decision of the Syrian who proposed to rear an altar to Jehovah in the very midst of Damascus, many far surpass him in the weaknesses which attach to their religion. To whatever section of the Church we may belong, have we not our own predilections, one for this, another for that form to which we have been accustomed, or which we have, perhaps, lately adopted? Far be it from us to assert that deep Scriptural truths may not underlie some of these feelings and convictions. Yet, in regard to some of them, after all, may it not be, that they are love for the "two mules' burden of earth" needed for our altar, associated, perhaps, with our conversion unto God. Some may choose to call this a sentiment connected with religion; and sentimentalism is dangerous. Yet far rather a sentiment, than no religious experience to call forth sentiment. "Go in peace;" the Lord will teach thee, and the Lord will keep thee.

Far more serious was the inquiry of Naaman regarding his official attendance upon his master in the temple of Rimmon. If it involved moral wrong, untruthfulness, or conformity to idolatry from worldly motives, it could never, nor on any plea, have been tolerated. But, fairly viewed, it implied none of these things. The very avowal and statement of the case removed it from the category of those odious compromises, of which the essence lies in the attempt to deceive ourselves and others. A man, who had built an altar in the midst of Damascus, professed that there was no other God than Jehovah, and worshipped none other, could not be supposed by any one to share in the idolatrous services of Rimmon. His presence in that house was imposed upon him by his official position as the king's nearest attendant, "on whose hand he leaned," and even that passive attendance was dreaded by Naaman, and its lawfulness submitted to the Lord, ere he would resume it. Of course, had it involved idolatry, his duty would have been, at any sacrifice, to relinquish his official position. But with such an avowal and such a testimony for Jehovah, his conduct was not sinful, because it could not be misunderstood. On the other hand, the inquiry itself is perhaps one of the clearest proofs of the genuineness of Naaman's conversion. So tender was his conscience, that what might seem the appearance of evil he felt to be intolerable; so decided was his religion, that from the first he clearly saw its bearing upon every department of life, and that he set himself to carry it out not only in acts of devotion, but in every act of his private and public life. His deep earnestness on the subject shows itself even in the twice repeated plea, "The Lord pardon thy servant in this thing." Henceforth his whole life was to be a service of God, and he dreaded lest in any action of his the presence and power of that religious element, under whose absolute control he now felt himself, should seem to be wanting. Thus, from whatever point it is viewed, we say once more with the prophet, "Go in peace"—and in such peace may the gracious Lord help each of us to go onward!

If this sketch of Naaman enables us to realise the young and ardent convert, still retaining his natural characteristics, though under the influence of grace, his spiritual experience just commencing—the companion picture in the narrative is equally true to life. We can almost see and hear Gehazi; and if we did not see nor hear him on this occasion, our knowledge of him would enable us to tell what he would have said, and how he would have acted. That Gehazi did not approve the conduct of his master, scarcely surprises us. Probably, he rarely approved what men like him would designate as Elisha's well-meant, but ill-applied and far too high sentiments, which might be good in theory, but were unsuited to practical life. Why should any one refuse money, that had been offered from the purest motives, and which might be applied to the cause of God, as for the support of those many dependent sons of the prophets, who were daily resorting to Elisha? Was it better to take the money back to Syria, where it could not be so profitably employed?

Besides, the whole transaction may have presented itself to Gehazi in quite another light. It was a Syrian who had received benefit from Israel. What claim had he upon Israel, and why should he obtain healing, who was a stranger, an alien, an enemy? The smallest return he could make would be to give of his riches; he had gotten of ours, let him give of his. It was a fair exchange in which the advantage still lay with Naaman, whatever money he gave. We recognise in this the old principle of "so much for so much," which is, alas, characteristic of the Gehazi-spirit in the Church. So to speak, the two sides of the ledger—so much spiritual work and so much money—must be made to balance. So much annual income, so many converts—or else how much does each convert cost? To whom; to Christ or to us? So much preaching, so much return! But spiritual labour and work, be it proclaimed and known, has no equivalent in money. We cannot pay a minister; the object is to give him the means of support, that he may be able to give himself to the work of the Lord. God alone pays ministers, whether faithful or unfaithful. We may pay a Gehazi; we cannot pay an Elisha. We can pay for the occupation of a pulpit, for what is curiously enough termed "the performance of Divine service," and for the outward routine of clerical labour, but spiritual work cannot be paid for, since it has no equivalent in money. It is the privilege of the Church to enable the servants of the Lord to live by the Gospel, but there can be no arithmetical calculation of the balance on either side.

Surely nearness to grace is not grace. On the contrary, it sometimes seems, as if familiarity with religion and religious men brought into broader relief the natural evil dispositions of the unrenewed heart. Such religiousness is like a mirror which reflects indeed a face, but presents its features so distorted, false, and out of proportion, as to make the likeness a caricature. The similitude of religion reflected from such a glass is truly repulsive. Here the worst passions of man, and the most intense selfishness, are made to shelter themselves in the shadow of religion; while hypocrisy, falsehood and vice, look and talk religiously. It is this kind of religion which makes our most zealous sectarians, just as Gehazi here appears in the character of a zealous Israelite. "Behold, my master hath spared Naaman, this Syrian." All is lawful that can be done to, or got from " this Syrian "—and my master has had regard to his personal feelings! Presently Gehazi waxeth even more righteous, and appeals to conscience and to God. "But, as Jehovah liveth, I will run after him, and take somewhat of him." *I* have no such scruples as Elisha. It has been said that the devil quotes Scripture; if so, he does it most glibly, when he incites us to evil. Never has any one who made a profession of religion, and who was not a conscious deceiver, said or done wrong, but he could quote chapter and verse in vindication of his conduct. He will convince himself, "as Jehovah liveth," that "this Syrian" should not be spared. Christian union is beautiful and most desirable—but it can never be; which practically means, that, so far as we are concerned, it *shall* never be. A dream this of Elisha, which Gehazi sees to be unpractical, because *he* is an Israelite, and the other "this Syrian"! And yet we are told there is "a principle" in it all; for when was wrong ever said or done without some "principle" being involved in it?

It is not impossible that there may have been a semblance of truth about the story with which Gehazi, when he hastened after Naaman, to "take somewhat of him," met his surprised inquiry. There may have been in waiting distressed sons of the prophets from Mount Ephraim, sorely in want of outward help. But it is scarcely necessary to say that the whole body and substance of the story was a lie. Untruth consists not only in saying what in the wording of it is contrary to fact; but what, though perhaps literally true, leaves on the mind of another a different impression from that which we know to be the correct one. And yet it is so common a practice, even on the part of those from whom better might have been expected!

Most saddening also is it to mark, how this whole solemn transaction between Naaman and Elisha had apparently not made the least spiritual impression upon Gehazi, not even such as might have been expected on a generous character, uninfluenced by grace. The reason of it was, that one all-absorbing passion held rule in Gehazi's breast. The love of money is designated in Scripture as a root of all evil, perhaps chiefly on the ground that it is a sin from which the man who has surrendered to it cannot shake himself free in any transaction of his life. If we yield to it, it will follow us everywhere, cling to us at all times, and mingle with all our thinking and feeling. Every other sin comes and goes, so to speak; covetousness never goes nor comes again; it is always there, and always casts over us its broad shadow. And, even in the rear of an Elisha, there is always a Gehazi who can apprehend nothing about any spiritual movement except the bags of Naaman, and, all the time a miracle is enacting, only calculates how much it may be worth, when transformed into money or money's worth.

Yet it were a mistake to paint Gehazi wholly in dark colours. Scripture presents him not as a caricature, but as a real man. He was not consciously irreligious. On the contrary. Only his religion was simply sectarianism; he was an *Israelite*, and nothing else than an Israelite. Just as many of us are not religious, but party-men, so Gehazi was zealously affected in *this* cause, but in no other. That he must have succeeded in deceiving himself, appears from his adjuration, "as Jehovah liveth." Profession without experience hardens the heart, and deadens the conscience. Again we say: Let us beware of undue familiarity with holy things. There is a danger of turning what is holy into meaningless phrases; or using it as cant, which means words coming from the lips but not issuing from the heart. Thus, for example, even the use of such terms as "if the Lord willeth," has become a mere form, or degenerated, till sometimes the words are employed to cover the very opposite. And so from one offence to the other, till a Gehazi will lie and deceive, and not heed what terrible havoc and ruin his offence may cause, so far as the spiritual interests of a Naaman are concerned. But the Lord will take care of His own people. All the more deeply touching, in contrast to the hypocrisy of Gehazi, appears the unfeigned humility of Naaman, as he alighted from his chariot to meet the prophet's servant; and, with an affectionate earnestness which might have moved any but a covetous man, urged upon his apparent reluctance the double of the miserable demand which he had made.

God preserveth the simple; and Naaman, speedily rejoined by the servants, who had carried to the city-gate the ill-gotten treasure of Gehazi, pursued his homeward journey, no doubt, all the more joyously for the service which he had been allowed to render. The reward of what we may do for the Lord shall not be lost, because of the misapplication and deception of any Gehazi to whom we may entrust our offerings. If we have offered our gifts as unto the Lord, He will own and receive them. But the discovery of the hatefulness of sin shall not be long delayed. The boldness with which Gehazi tried to turn aside his master's searching look and question was foiled. No doubt Elisha had followed in prayer his departing convert, when, to his mind, divinely enlightened, the whole scene of Gehazi's sin and degradation presented itself. It needed no elaborate reasoning to put aside Gehazi's self-deception and sectarianism, and to show him that his real motives had been self and covetousness. But was all that is highest and holiest to be used as the means for gratifying the lowest, meanest, and most sordid kind of selfishness? The work of God, the soul of Naaman, the truth of religion: were all these to be made only the occasion for a Gehazi to acquire wealth? Oh, terrible discovery, which left him no excuse; oh, still more terrible discovery, which will burst upon men when the great Judge shall sweep away all self-deceiving pretexts, and show to men their real motives! And so, as he had sought what was Naaman's, he should have it; but with it also would Naaman's curse of leprosy cleave to him for ever. God be merciful to us—and in nothing more than in keeping within us a holy dread and awe of His work, that we may never touch His Ark with unhallowed hands, and ever beware of making godliness a gain, remembering that our God is a jealous God!

CHAPTER XVIII.

A VERY PRESENT HELP.

"And the sons of the prophets said unto Elisha, Behold now, the place where we dwell with thee is too strait for us. Let us go, we pray thee, unto Jordan, and take thence every man a beam, and let us make us a place there, where we may dwell. And he answered, Go ye. And one said, Be content, I pray thee, and go with thy servants. And he answered, I will go. So he went with them. And when they came to Jordan, they cut down wood. But as one was felling a beam, the axe head fell into the water: and he cried, and said, Alas, master! for it was borrowed. And the man of God said, Where fell it? And he showed him the place. And he cut down a stick, and cast it in thither; and the iron did swim. Therefore said he, Take it up to thee. And he put out his hand, and took it."—2 KINGS vi. 1-7.

NEXT to the assurance of our salvation, the conviction most necessary to our comfort is that of God's continual Presence with us. Without it we would feel as orphans in this world, exposed to numberless unknown dangers, yet unable to meet them. But the object of the Incarnation of our Saviour, and the fact that our Great Advocate was "in all things made like unto His brethren," convey to us the assurance that He is "a merciful and faithful High Priest." Having "suffered, being tempted, He is able to succour them that are tempted." The Son of God in heaven still wears our human nature. He is with us even unto the end of the world. Afflicted in all our affliction, saving us by His Presence, having redeemed us in His love and in His pity, He bears us and carries us all the days of our lives. Still, in our weakness we too often doubt and distrust, and feel as if it needed ocular demonstration to convince us of these facts. How much more must this have been the case under the Old Testament dispensation, which was pre-eminently one of faith and hope. We can scarcely realise how precious to them would be those records of God's dealings, which proved so clearly that Jehovah was " a very present help in trouble."

And certainly, if in any circumstances, there could not be failure, loss, impossibility, nor defeat where the prophet of the Lord was. He appeared as the representative of the Lord. His failure would have been failure on the part of God. If the prophet could not be absolutely relied upon, neither could the message which he brought be implicitly trusted. A messenger direct from heaven requires to bring credentials direct from heaven. If our Saviour could not have procured the tax-money for which Peter had rashly engaged, the confidence of His disciples might have been rudely shaken. If Elisha had failed in any emergency, the whole character of his mission would have been changed. It was intended to show that Jehovah is the Living and the True God; that if He claimed homage and service, His thoughts were all of mercy and of love; and that never, nor for anything, could any one apply to Him in vain. In short, it was designed to prefigure the blessed truths which now in Christ are exhibited in all their fulness. And thus we also say and believe, that no application to our Prophet can be made in vain, and that to believing prayer there can be neither failure, loss, impossibility, nor defeat.

The labours of Elisha had not been in vain. Indeed, labour in the service of the Lord, however humble, can never be in vain. Wherever the Gospel is faithfully preached some will gather around to bear testimony to its power, and though the patience of His people may be long-tried, in due season we shall reap, if we faint not. We must learn to work, as well as to live, in faith. Sometimes God enlarges our opportunities.. Such increase should be received, not in a spirit of self-congratulation, but with gratitude, with meekness, and with fear. In the present instance, God had evidently blessed the work. The number of disciples around Elisha had grown till the place was too strait for them. The proposal made for meeting this emergency was sensible and modest. Contented with humble accommodation so long as they had Elisha in their midst, the "sons of the prophets" suggested that each man should do his own part in the work, and that, availing themselves of the material so abundant in the neighbourhood, they should "take every man a beam," and "make a place there," where they might dwell. The presence of the true and faithful word with them would richly compensate for any discomforts connected with their new mode of living. Let us have the Gospel in its purity, no matter what outward drawback may be connected with it. Rather the Gospel among the most illiterate people and in the least attractive form, than well-bred, faultless indifference, or worse than that, Antichristian error. It is strange self-delusion to imagine that we can escape damage or guilt, if we take part in other men's sins.

It is wonderful how much can be accomplished by hearty, cheerful labourers, where each is ready to undertake his own share, and all are content with humble appearances, provided the great object be attained. There is much undeveloped power in the Church and in each of us, if we were not so starched up in conventionalities, and would rather attend to present necessities than to worn-out precedents. It was a healthy sign of healthy religion, when, as the place became too strait for them, each set himself not to beg, but to labour as best he could. Is there work to be done in our neighbourhood? Then, do not let us wait for eventualities, which may never occur, but set to it with right good will, as we can, each man taking a beam. There is abundant opportunity and abundant material everywhere, if there be only willing hearts and busy hands.

Yet work, without having Elisha by their side while working, would have been hard and unpromising. "And one said, Be content, I pray thee, and go with thy servants. And he answered, I will go." Moses prayed, "If Thy presence go not with me, carry us not up hence." An enterprise in which God does not take part can never truly succeed. We wish not only to work for the Lord Jesus Christ, but to have Him with us in our work. The sense of His presence makes labour sweet and easy. It ceases to be labour, when carried on in the service of love and under His Eye. If the missionary and the visitor on their daily rounds can speak as in the hearing of Jesus, and with His approbation, and invite others to come to a present Saviour; if, realising His pity and love, they will, in gladness and earnestness, seek to draw souls unto Him, then, while blessing others, they will be richly blessed themselves. By all means, let us seek enlargement, enlarged opportunities, and enlarged success. But not for carnal purposes, not that we may become secularised. The Master must go with His servants; let it be not merely work, but work with Christ, till we enter into His rest.

For some time the labour had been steadily progressing. The banks of Jordan resounded with the noise of axe and hammer, all the more energetically wielded, perhaps, because, in great measure, probably by unpractised hands. There are lessons here for young and still unskilled workmen. It does not appear what speed they had made when their work was suddenly interrupted. With the best will, but with little knowledge, one of these labourers had been dealing heavy, but probably, for the most part, aimless blows, as some of us are apt to do in our most elaborate efforts. At last, by the violence of his strokes, the axe had become separated from the wooden handle to which it had been attached, and, heavily whirling over his head, fell into the river, not to rise again to the surface.

One of the most difficult lessons in life and in work is, how to aim our blows. Not violence in the blow, but skill in the use of the weapon, is effectual. It is quite possible, even for a good man, and in a good cause, to let zeal outrun discretion. If we constantly strike, no matter where, only taking care to strike with all our strength, we may end by doing harm instead of good, by losing the axe-head instead of felling the timber. In going to others, especially to the poor, the outcast, and the sunken, let us remember that it is by the message of love, and not by the violence of religious assaults, that we are to subdue the heart. If we strike blows, and only blows; if we have nothing else to wield than the law, destruction, and reproaches about their sins and their general wickedness, the axe has, to all intents and purposes, whirled over our head and disappeared in Jordan. It needs wisdom, kindness, gentleness, not noisy laboriousness, to be a successful workman.

Another truth, equally plain, but almost equally overlooked, is, that the iron head, not the wooden handle of the axe, does the work. The Word of the Living God is sharp and two-edged; it alone can bring down the proud and lofty, and lay him low before the Lord. Our official position, learning, eloquence, and influence, are the handle by which the axe is wielded. Let the axe-head be of the genuine metal, tried, and in keen edge; almost any stick on the banks of the Jordan may be cut down for a handle. Many are zealous in plying the handle, who have long lost the axe, if indeed they had ever possessed it. In ignorance of the real cause of failure, the wooden handle is perhaps all the more earnestly applied, that the blows fall harmless. Be it ours, whether we labour in public or in private, to remember that conversion is the work of God, and that the great instrument of it is His Word. Let us prize and apply it, and ever act as realising that, however necessary the handle may be, it is only for the purpose of wielding the axe itself. In that respect the sequel of the story almost reads as if Elisha had foreseen the dangers which would threaten the Church many centuries afterwards, and had intended by his conduct to forewarn and to teach us. For, when afterwards he restored to "the son of the prophets" the lost axe, he entirely discarded the old handle, which had become loosened from the iron, and cast into the water another stick which he had cut down, and to which the iron rose. Nor let it be thought that there is no lesson here even for those who are true witnesses for Christ. Merciful, indeed, will be the dispensation which brings us to a knowledge of our need, and leads us to cry for help. For, we also are in danger of overlooking the axe while we grasp the handle. In our Christian living, as in our working, much that is unreal—hay, wood, and stubble—may be built up even on the true foundation, only to be destroyed in the day of His coming.

The cry of distress soon brought Elisha to the spot. It came from the most laborious of the workmen, who had been suddenly brought to a stand-still. "Alas, master!" And yet it may be good for us to be so arrested, that we may receive back from the master the old axe with a new handle, and learn how to use it aright. It will be the old axe, the old truth; but we may formerly have handled it wrongly, and so ultimately lost it. Our involved periods, our drowsy discussions of worn-out controversies, and our aimless preaching; or else our stiff officialism and fussy zealousness, may have been the wrong handle to which the old axe would no longer hold in these days of felling tall, strong, heavy trees of the forest. We live in times when nothing is taken for granted, and earnest work demands suitable instrumentality. Men will not listen to us, because we are clerical officials. The earnest Christian should humbly accept this state of things, though he may tremble for those who, ignorant and unprepared, have broken away from the past, and are entering upon a new and untried path. Yet the cause of Christ will ultimately prosper only the more, if what too often was a hollow, unthinking assent be succeeded by genuine and earnest inquiry after truth and conviction. Believing as we do in the Divine origin of Christianity, we cannot shrink from such inquiry; having experienced its power, we are not afraid to have its vitality and suitableness to the wants of men tested. And blessed indeed will be the result, however painful the process by which it is attained, if it ultimately lead the labourers, as in this case, to cry out, " Alas, *master!* "

May we not carry the analogy still farther, and say that many an axe-head is not our own, but "borrowed,"* that too often that with which we work is not our real possession, got by ourselves and belonging to us, but borrowed from others, and that work with borrowed tools generally miscarries? But to return. In this, as in every similar instance, the cry of distress was a healthy and hopeful sign. For, when the gust of sudden trial laid bare the inmost feelings of this man, it disclosed an honest, upright heart. This we say,

* The rendering "borrowed" gives the correct sense, though not the literal meaning of the original, which is "requested," "entreated" from another.

taking the lowest ground, that of common honesty, although on reflection we may find it not quite so low as it may appear to some. To mourn most of all, because that which has been lost is not their own, but another's, is not so common among the men who have to borrow other people's tools. Downright honesty, concern not for the consequences, but for the fact of injury to another, a kind of reverential respect for the property of others, is the quality of a noble and generous heart. And surely true religion ought to inspire us with this feeling. The first outcome of love to our neighbour—one might almost say its lowest application—is regard for that which belongs to him. No amount of religious profession will make up for any infringement of this, whether in trade, in business, in government, or in any other department where the mine and the thine bound each other. And in this application also the saying of Holy Writ holds true, "He that loveth not his brother whom he hath seen, how can he love God Whom he hath not seen?" One other consideration, in connection with this matter, we may profitably set before ourselves. When the sudden gust of distress lifted the curtain from that man's heart, it was seen to be an honest, true, and noble heart. Sudden affliction makes us truthful, because it finds us unprepared, and shows us as we are. What would be the result in our case? Would we appear loving or selfish, truthful or unreliable, religious or destitute of genuine trust?

As on other occasions, so on this, Elisha provided help. It could not have been otherwise, nor, so far as we can see, could it have been done otherwise. The same simplicity and absence of assumption which had characterised the prophet before, were still marked in his conduct. Again, as at the spring of Jordan and in the widow's house, means, though in themselves totally inadequate, were used. He cut down a stick, and cast it in where the axe had sunk, "and the iron did swim." *

In the perfect conviction of the truthfulness of his narrative, the writer makes no attempt to disguise, or to explain, the miraculous nature of the event. There is in these few words, "the iron did swim," a world of argument, in this respect, that the writer did not deceive himself as to the fact that the laws of nature seemed here infringed, and that yet he believed the event to have actually taken place, as here related. How "the iron did swim" is not told, nor do we understand it; nor perhaps would we have understood it, even if it had been told. For, perhaps in this seeming disordering of the order of nature, there may have been a higher order, as yet unknown to us; beneath this apparent disturbance of laws, the operation of a higher law. We simply do not know the circumstances under which this sudden up-flowing of water took place, in consequence of which the iron came to the surface. But the question as to our belief of the fact itself cannot be discussed separately from that of our belief of the Scriptures as a whole. If, on rational and sufficient grounds, we believe the truth of the Scriptures, we shall, of course, believe the reality of this event. This, however, may be safely said, that in answering the question *whether* this event took place, we have nothing to do with that other question, *how* it took place. We

---

* Here again our Authorised Version is *substantially*, though not literally, correct. The word rendered "to swim" occurs only in two other passages of the original: in Lam. iii. 54, "Waters *flowed over* mine head," and in Deut. xi. 4, "He *made* the water of the Red Sea *to overflow*" their horses and chariots. The parallel, both in the miracle and in the wording, seems to lie in this latter passage. The *quality* of the iron was not permanently changed, but He miraculously caused it to "flow up," or by sudden agency in the water beneath to come to the surface.

believe many things, of which we neither know nor can explain the "how." The "how" of many of the commonest events and processes is as much beyond our ken, as how "the iron did swim." *How* our bodies grow, *how* food is turned into nourishment, and nourishment portioned off into the various constituent elements of the body—*how* these, and a thousand other processes, which daily and hourly pass under our sight, are carried on, is quite as much a mystery as *how* "the iron did swim." That we observe them so constantly does not help us to understand their *how*, any more than hearing every day an unknown tongue would make us understand it. Yet we believe these events, and on good grounds. And there is the most abundant evidence for the truth of the Scriptures; so that we believe what they record, even while, confessedly, we may not always understand *how* these events took place.

Yet, in a certain sense, we possess a test of their truthfulness. We may almost bring them to the test of experience. We believe that, in answer to simple, trustful prayer in the Name of Jesus, all difficulties can be overcome, and will disappear; we believe that all things will be overruled for good, contrary to what might seem the ordinary course of nature, as contrary to it, and as unlikely of occurrence, as that "the iron did swim." And so firmly do we believe this, and so truly is this belief grounded on the words of our Saviour, that we are willing to stake our belief in the Scriptures and in Christianity itself on the result of applying this test of experience, that men make trial of it, and go to God through Christ in the Scriptural manner—but without prescribing *how* "the iron is to swim." Would that we could persuade men to make the experiment, and they would see such things, and greater things than these, because Jesus is gone to His Father!

A VERY PRESENT HELP.

The poor we have always with us, and to them there may be some special lessons of hope and trust in the story of the restored axe. That the Hand of God supplies daily wants, that He succours in the humblest labour, and gives relief in pressing difficulties, is indeed most precious, alike for rich and poor. For before Him, and in deepest reality, we are all poor; we all need Him; we all live upon Him. It is simplest truth, though clad in most gorgeous imagery, "The eyes of all wait upon Thee, and Thou givest them their meat in due season. Thou openest Thine hand, and satisfiest the desire of every living thing." But to receive directly from the Hand of the Lord the axe with which to cut down the trees of the field—to recognise God, and to have Him with us in our daily work, to receive from Him the instruments even of humblest labour, is to have that labour sanctified and glorified, and in anticipation already to experience how the curse of labour's sweat is wiped away from the brow of His ransomed children.

CHAPTER XIX.

AN UNSEEN HOST.

"Then the king of Syria warred against Israel, and took counsel with his servants, saying, In such and such a place shall be my camp. And the man of God sent unto the king of Israel, saying, Beware that thou pass not such a place; for thither the Syrians are come down. And the king of Israel sent to the place which the man of God told him and warned him of, and saved himself there, not once nor twice. Therefore the heart of the king of Syria was sore troubled for this thing; and he called his servants, and said unto them, Will ye not show me which of us is for the king of Israel? And one of his servants said, None, my lord, O king: but Elisha, the prophet that is in Israel, telleth the king of Israel the words that thou speakest in thy bedchamber. And he said, Go and spy where he is, that I may send and fetch him. And it was told him, saying, Behold, he is in Dothan. Therefore sent he thither horses, and chariots, and a great host: and they came by night, and compassed the city about. And when the servant of the man of God was risen early, and gone forth, behold, an host compassed the city both with horses and chariots. And his servant said unto him, Alas, my master! how shall we do? And he answered, Fear not: for they that be with us are more than they that be with them."—2 KINGS vi. 8-16.

POLITICS and religion—what have they in common? This fundamental principle: "The Lord reigneth." With this conviction we look at passing events, not as uninterested, far less as dismayed, spectators. The saying of a German divine, that next to the Bible, a Christian cannot find more edification than in the newspapers, may seem paradoxical. Yet a deep truth underlies it. If the progress of human affairs were merely a struggle of forces, evenly or unevenly balanced; if it depended on the cunning or craft of men who shall prevail, or what shall obtain, we might give way to anxious thoughts. But it is not so. Through the tangled web of human affairs runs one great design. The government is upon His shoulder, Who sitteth at the Right Hand of the Father. It is indeed true, that trial awaits every child of God, and a conflict sharper than any yet waged, the Church as a whole. As soldiers of the Lord Jesus, we are prepared, and look for the day of battle, not boastfully, but confidently and calmly. We know that the result will not only be victory, but a far brighter and happier morrow, without divisions and heartburnings, and without watchful enemies around; not a lonely morrow, but one in the sunlight of His Presence.

We take an interest in everything: in politics, in science, in art, in society, in life. We would not, even if we could, put an arrest upon anything. These are all streams, tributary to the great River of Life. These must all contribute to the Redeemer's Kingdom. Every progress is really progression towards that perfection, though at the time it may seem otherwise. Every truth is another treasure gained, every achievement another voice raised, every progress another advance made; and each treasure must be laid at His feet, each voice proclaim Him Lord, every advance bring us nearer to the end. We are not jealous of the discoveries of science; we hail them, though we may mourn the aberrations of some of those who make them, and who, while enriching their kind, themselves remain poor in the toil. We are not distrustful of art, though we may deplore its misapplication. We are not afraid of progress, of the spread of thought, of knowledge, or of free inquiry, though we would fain save those who are trampled down by the crowd in the onward movement. We are not afraid; "our craft" is not in danger, our Church is not in danger, our truth is not in danger, our heaven is not in danger, our God is not in danger, and therefore our faith is not in danger. From every seeming evil, as from a root deep buried in the ground, springs high and lasting good;

and if "the whole creation groaneth and travaileth in pain together," it is in the birth-throes of a holier and better life than earth has yet witnessed. God is not merely in heaven: He reigneth; and there is not a secret design whispered in the council-chamber of a Ben-hadad which is not known to Him, or which can come at unawares upon His cause or people.

Such precious consolation have the children of God, that their assurance is derived not from the promises alone. To them the lessons, and even the facts, of the past are really not of the past, but of the present, for they are of Him Who is "the same yesterday, and to-day, and for ever." All Scripture history contains present fact for reproof, for instruction, and for comfort, and all is to us "yea and amen" in Christ Jesus. Scripture genealogy runs up into that of the Christ; Scripture miracles into His Incarnation; Scripture types into His work; Scripture prophecy into His Kingdom. Therefore, when we read the Scriptures, we live not in the past. The history of Israel is as full of instruction to us, as it was to the fathers thousands of years gone by; the Psalms of David are as rich in consolation, as to the exiles in Babylon; the prophecies as full of glorious hope. To this hour the lowly sufferer, far off in some mountain-glen or distant island, or the Church in her present contendings, pores over that sacred volume, forgetting the past in the present, and reading it all as applying to present times and to present circumstances. And rightly so. There is no other book, no other history, no other truth like this: it is God-given, not of the past, but always and to all of the present. And so to us Ben-hadad and his counsellors still sit and plot in Damascus; Elisha is still watchful over Israel; and Israel is still safe.

The healing and conversion of Naaman had not in any way removed or softened the hatred of Ben-hadad against

Israel. Even if he did not view it as merely a case of individual benefit and individual acknowledgment, he would have failed to derive from it any lessons concerning Israel and Israel's God. At any rate, it had no influence on his plans and pursuits. And so it always is. Even the most striking case of conversion unto God, as undoubted in its effects as the cure of Naaman, will not turn worldly men from their ways. They see it, and hear it, but they do not see or hear in it the God of Israel. Accordingly, expeditions against Israel, rather of a predatory than of a regular warlike character, continued to be planned in Syria. In these there is no reason for supposing that Naaman took part. The contrary seems implied in the fact that the king of Syria himself devised and executed them. Perhaps, indeed, the withdrawal of the favourite general may have increased the animosity of Ben-hadad. The principal object of these expeditions seems to have been the capture of the king of Israel. The terms in which the narrative explains how Joram "saved himself"—or rather, as in the original, "was ware,"—and this "not once nor twice," by sending "to the place which the man of God told him," or by not passing "such a place" to which the Syrians were "come down," convey to us the idea of personal rather than of public danger. And the Jewish historian, Josephus, relates how Joram had at last to give up his hunting expeditions, on account of the frequent ambuscades laid for him by the king of Syria. It was not the purpose of God that these devices should succeed, for Israel's day of grace had not yet passed. Accordingly, while the Syrian planned, Jehovah disappointed the most cunningly devised schemes by sending timely warning of them through His prophet. This also was in accordance with the prophet's mission. And so in our case also, whatever plans the enemies of God and of His people may make, we have this comfort, that they are known to our Prophet. Whether the attack be on the truthfulness and inspiration of the Scriptures, or consist in defiance or scorn of His Church, or be directed against the character and well-being of His people, the Lord can easily provide means of safety. He knoweth their thoughts afar off, and "He that sitteth in the heavens shall laugh; the Lord shall have them in derision."

Nor ought *we* to be "ignorant of his devices," who is Israel's great enemy. We have been "warned" "not to pass such a place." If after that we fall into the ambush, the guilt and loss must be on our own head. We know that "thither the Syrians are come down," and that our strength is not equal to theirs. A needless battle, however it may end, must in a sense be loss and defeat. If we expose ourselves to known temptation, we have no right to expect deliverance. It is not sufficient that these ought not to be temptations to us. They will cease to become such, when we have so far overcome as to avoid them. "Resist the devil," but flee from temptation. To flee from temptations is already to have gained the victory over them; knowingly to expose ourselves to them is already to have been overcome, for it implies to a certain extent the consent of the heart. Therefore, to go into known temptation is to go into sin. And sin lies not merely in the outward act, but also in the inward yielding. Let us beware of needlessly mixing with worldly society, or taking part in worldly schemes or pleasures. To run without necessity into outward danger would be folly, well deserving its appropriate punishment. Why should we be less careful, where the interest of our souls is concerned?

If the subject had not been so solemn, it might have been almost exciting to watch the attitude of two of the principal actors in this scene. On the one hand there was honest incapacity in the spiritual ignorance of Ben-hadad, and in his perplexity in accounting for his repeated failures; while, on the other, there was similar incapacity and ignorance, only mixed with religious conceit, on the part of the king of Israel, as he foiled the plans of his enemy. We feel that both men were out of place—Ben-hadad in warring against Israel; and Joram in overmatching Ben-hadad. The king of Syria had well calculated his chances. He "took counsel with his servants, saying, In such and such a place shall be my camp." And his camp *was* there. The operation had been well planned and was well executed. The camp of Ben-hadad was there, but not his prey. We will do this or that; we will buy and sell, or come and go! The plan is admirable, and the mode of executing it unexceptionable. One small element only has been omitted from the calculation—that God is in heaven. Not what men can, but what they may, shall they be able to accomplish. They may not be deficient either in skill, courage, or energy. But what of that? There is this saying of Holy Scripture: "Thou fool, this night thy soul shall be required of thee." Plans of worldly greatness, of power, or of wealth, for which men have sacrificed their all, will be overthrown before the breath of the Almighty! And, oh, how much may have been sacrificed to gain only disappointment! Perhaps the salvation of the soul; certainly usefulness, peace and joy on earth, and a blessed reward in heaven!

As for the king of Israel, so far as we can judge from the sequel (ver. 21), these deliverances seem only to have engendered in him a sense of confidence, as if all were right, and he a special favourite of heaven. Things often go wondrously well with worldly men; difficulties and dangers disappear. They think and speak as if they were the right men, always doing the right thing, always at the right time, and always in the right place; as if Providence itself followed in their steps. And, as Matthew Henry expresses it, the king would regard the warnings of his danger, but not those of his sin, just as many "will save themselves from death, but not from hell." They are willing to shape their course so far by the Word of God, but not far enough. No one likes to be regarded as an infidel, a blasphemer, or in open sin; most men in respectable positions attend church with more or less regularity, and conform to much that is good and praiseworthy. But, alas! the heart may all the while be as much estranged from Jehovah, as was that of the king of Israel.

Ben-hadad was sorely distressed by the unexpected reverses which he met. However cunningly the scheme was devised, however secretly executed, the same unvarying result followed each raid. Baffled in his every endeavour, only one explanation suggested itself. No doubt, blame attached to some one; there must be a traitor among his counsellors. But did blame attach to any one? Should not these constant defeats rather have been regarded as a call from God to desist from such undertakings? It is strange and sad, how often the dealings of God are misunderstood, or remain unrecognised. The means which men use are not in fault; God is against them. Something similar holds true in regard to the Gospel. If its appeals do not reach the heart, they will probably give offence to the hearer. The preacher is said to be too violent, too fanatical, too personal. Yet the fault lies not in the preaching, but in the hearing.

There is still another lesson to be learned. As it appeared to Ben-hadad, there was some traitor to tell his secrets. But it was not so; the prophet only did his God-appointed work. For, if an Elisha does not announce Syria's schemes and Israel's danger, he is of little use in the land. Similarly, we also preach not to dead, but to living men; not to the past, but to the present generation; not what suited former, but existing circumstances. We must be personal, not in the offensive sense of interfering in the concerns of others, or of intruding between God and their souls; but in that of being thoroughly in earnest in trying to bring them individually to Christ. A mere repetition of doctrinal statements, from the fall of Adam to the restitution of all things, will do no good. We must know and tell where the Syrians lie in ambush. And is it not sometimes as if a faithful preacher read our very thoughts, had listened to our conversation, or witnessed our last action? And yet it is only the Word of God, which has been applied by the Holy Spirit. David, in strongest language, condemned the crime which the prophet had parabolically described. But till the words came to his conscience: "Thou art the man," he failed to recognise his own sin in the parable. Then the indignant monarch became the humbled penitent. And thus must he who is familiar with only the phraseology of orthodoxy be brought to feel his guilt and need, if he would be saved. The object of the living ministry is not to introduce new, or to alter old truths, but to present them in ever new forms, adapted to the changing wants and circumstances of the times. Our mission, like that of Elisha, is to tell Israel of a present God, and to warn Israel of present danger. But He alone can give the grace "rightly to divide the Word of truth," and "to receive with meekness the engrafted Word."

There is almost a tone of emotion in the language which Ben-hadad addressed to his servants, for his heart "was sore troubled for this thing." But the appeal could only give pain to consciously innocent men. At last, one more bold, or more observant, than the others broke the silence. There was not among them a traitor; no, "none, my lord, O king: but Elisha, the prophet that is in Israel, telleth the king of Israel the words that thou speakest in thy bedchamber." It is exactly the conclusion which a spiritually unenlightened man would draw from the history of Naaman's cure. It expressed all his knowledge, and all his ignorance, of Divine things. Elisha the prophet was all-powerful; but it was only Elisha, not Elisha's God. So men still speak of the work of God. This preacher, or that man has, by his eloquence, his earnestness—his fanaticism, if you will—gained immense influence. But it is not God, it is not the truth, it is not the Holy Spirit. *He* is an able man; but there is not the Living God in it. The influence of the man accounts for all. Remove the man, and the result will cease. If the friend or relative who has been influenced, could only be withdrawn from such exciting sermons, or such proselytising company, he would be as before. But if the work has been Scriptural and of God, it is not so. If ever again the man be as before, he has never been other than before. Under any supposition, your labour is in vain. If it has been the work of man, you need not fear—it will pass away. But if it has been the work of God, it will *not* pass away, even though every preacher or associate were withdrawn. Leave it then to the test of Gamaliel, and avoid the folly of Ben-hadad and his counsellors.

The suggestion of this counsellor seems to have commanded the immediate assent of Ben-hadad. Nor are we left in suspense as to the device which was to put an end to the evil. Elisha was all-powerful: therefore Elisha must be seized and secured. It never seems to have occurred to this heathen council that Elisha was merely an instrument, and that the God of Elisha could raise up or employ others for the same work. This plan once agreed upon, they appear not to have anticipated any further difficulty, not even this obvious one, that, as before, the prophet might know what had passed in the king's council chamber. Their first object now was to ascertain where Elisha was; the next to render his escape impossible. We shall presently see by what means, and with what result they attempted to compass their purpose.

Elisha did not court secrecy, and it was easy to learn that for the time he was in Dothan. A remarkable place this, the history of which might have taught Ben-hadad the hopelessness of his attempt. Dothan was beautifully situated about twelve miles from Samaria. Northwards spread rich pasturelands; only a ridge of hills separated it from the great plain of Esdraelon. From its position, it must on that side have been the key to the passes of Esdraelon, and so, as guarding the entrance from the north, the defence not only of Ephraim, but of Palestine itself. On the crest of one of those hills the extensive ruins of Dothan are still pointed out, and at its southern declivity yet wells up a fine spring of living water. This may be one of the two wells from which Dothan, the "two wells," derived its name. From these hills Gideon of old had descended upon the host of Midian. Here Joseph had overtaken his brethren, and was cast into a dry well. And it was from that height that the sons of Jacob must have watched that Arab caravan, slowly winding from Jordan on its way to Egypt, to which they sold their brother, in the vain hope of binding the Word, and arresting the Hand, of God. And now once more, and on a like bootless errand, the soldiers of Syria hurried, under cover of night, across the plain of Esdraelon, and gathered around the ancient Dothan.

It would have fared ill with Dothan if its defence had only consisted in mountain fastness or in the strength of its walls. The Syrians had crept all round it; every gate and postern was watched; there was no escape for man or beast. What an array of power: "horses and chariots, and a great host." And all this to capture a single unarmed man! Surely this time the plans of Ben-hadad could not miscarry. Then, what great things might be expected from the capture of Elisha! Perhaps he might even be converted into a friend and ally; at least, help would be permanently withdrawn from Israel. All this time the inhabitants of Dothan were unconscious of their danger. How often is precious sleep sent to rock us to forgetfulness of the past! How often does the angel of sleep hold us in blessed ignorance of the dangers and difficulties of the morrow, and of the host of Syria all around Dothan! Through how many dangers have we thus been carried, which we did not know till they were past. The Lord waketh, and His Hand is outstretched, not only to guard and to bless, but also to restrain and avert the evil. "So *He giveth* His beloved sleep," and the fevered brain and aching heart are soothed in the shadow of His wings.

Morning dawned, and the sun rose over the hills of Samaria. In the cold grey light the servant of Elisha—as we infer from the text, another than Gehazi—had risen and gone forth. What a sight met his gaze! The rays of the morning sun were glittering on the spears, and reflected from the armour and the chariots of Syria. Whithersoever he looked, all around were armed men! Escape seemed impossible. Hastily turning, he rushed into the presence of the prophet to announce his terrible discovery. But it called forth neither fear nor excitement in the prophet. It seemed as if the sun had not shone on Syrian lance or chariot, and all his rays only gladsome fallen into the prophet's heart, or shone around him in heavenly glory. The perplexed cry of the servant was: "Alas, my master! how shall we do?" But to Elisha there was neither question nor perplexity about the matter; or if there was, only so far as the servant, not as he himself was concerned. And yet this identification with his master would prove the safety of the servant. Nay, all Dothan was safe, for the warfare was only against the "master;" and the "master" could not be hurt or injured. Every assault upon our Dothan also is really intended against "the Master;" and therefore not only "the prophet," but all the people in Dothan are safe. "Master, carest Thou not that we perish?" But could they perish, when the Lord was in the ship? Could the Master perish? "Alas, my master, how shall we do?" What of these assaults on the Church, on our lives, property, and honour—on our Dothan? This is our answer, The Master is identified with us! The battle is not against us; it is against Him. How strange that, in our unbelief, we so err and sin as to ask, with doubt and fear, how we shall do? How can we ever say, The Church is in danger, or the truth is in danger, or we are in danger? Dothan may be encompassed, but the Master is there, and the God of Elisha reigneth.

CHAPTER XX.

MORE THAN CONQUERORS.

"And Elisha prayed, and said, Lord, I pray thee, open his eyes, that he may see. And the Lord opened the eyes of the young man; and he saw: and, behold, the mountain was full of horses and chariots of fire round about Elisha. And when they came down to him, Elisha prayed unto the Lord, and said, Smite this people, I pray thee, with blindness. And he smote them with blindness according to the word of Elisha. And Elisha said unto them, This is not the way, neither is this the city: follow me, and I will bring you to the man whom ye seek. But he led them to Samaria. And it came to pass, when they were come into Samaria, that Elisha said, Lord, open the eyes of these men, that they may see. And the Lord opened their eyes, and they saw; and, behold, they were in the midst of Samaria. And the king of Israel said unto Elisha, when he saw them, My father, shall I smite them? shall I smite them? And he answered, Thou shalt not smite them: wouldest thou smite those whom thou hast taken captive with thy sword and with thy bow? set bread and water before them, that they may eat and drink, and go to their master. And he prepared great provision for them: and when they had eaten and drunk, he sent them away, and they went to their master. So the bands of Syria came no more into the land of Israel."—2 KINGS vi. 17-23.

THE question, "How shall we do?" is one so frequently wrung from sorrowing hearts, that it could not remain unanswered in the Bible. The Lord Jesus came to answer the questions of anxious hearts, and though they be of our weakness, yet even that weakness, when not allied with wilful unbelief, finds sympathy and help. For He has listened to the prayer, "Lord, I believe, help Thou mine unbelief." Often sorrow comes with such fearful suddenness, that it is difficult to realise anything other than that a terrible blow has fallen. Only yesterday we met, and parted so happy and joyous. Life seemed without a cloud. Now all is changed. A letter, a sentence, an accident, and the whole fabric which we had reared is utterly swept away. With what we have lost all seems lost. Life has nothing more for us. Is there no escape? "How shall we do?" To sink were to perish; and yet there seems no help for us anywhere. It is at such times that we ought joyously to cherish the conviction, that one comfort is still left. It consists in realising that Christ is identified with us. We are not alone in this Dothan; the Master is also there. No—it is not merely an idea; it is a fact. Nothing can befall us but through Him and with Him. And thus, even without further explanation, so soon as the burdened heart realises a present Christ, the question, "How shall we do?" answers itself. "Stand still and see the salvation of the Lord!"

These convictions ought alone to be sufficient for us; yet in our weakness God often condescends to us, and in compassion grants sight where faith should have been enough. "The Lord pitieth them that fear Him. For He knoweth our frame; He remembereth that we are dust." We should be satisfied to labour even without visible encouragement, to bear without visible deliverance, and to trust without visible token for good. But the Lord adapts Himself to our frame, and no temptation assails us greater than we are able to bear. With the temptation He also maketh a way to escape. He says, "Fear not;" but He never says it without at the same time pouring gladsome light into our hearts. On this occasion the prophet prayed, "Lord, I pray Thee, open his eyes, that he may see." And immediately the denser medium parted, like a misty curtain rent by the rays of the sun. What before had seemed empty air was peopled; on the height, up its sloping sides, far as he could see, every place was occupied by another army—"horses and chariots of fire"—the same host of which one of the outposts had taken Elijah to heaven in a whirlwind. Truly might Elisha say, "They that be with us are more than they that be with them."

And can we not still say the same? Heaven and hell are indeed in conflict. All unseen to us, the air is peopled with principalities, powers, and dominions. Of the contest we know little beyond the fact, that the Lord encompasseth His people. The ministry of His angels will only be fully understood when our eyes shall have been opened, and when we shall hold personal converse with them in another state of existence. This, however, we are assured, that His Name is above every name that can be named, whether in heaven or on earth. Without drawing sword or bow He conquers, leading captivity captive, and we, identified with Him, are more than conquerors, through Him Who has conquered.

One and only one sore battle was there in which the Divine Redeemer bled and died; and the conquest of redeeming love has been for ever achieved. Look around and mark it: all has been accomplished and provided. Both our present and our future safety are ensured. Though the Syrians should encompass us, the mountain is full of horses and of chariots of fire. Sin, sorrow, and death have been swallowed up in victory. When in distress, let us pray that our eyes may be opened. It only needs this to remove our fears, whether caused by temporal or spiritual dangers. If we saw more than what appears to the eye of sense; if our minds were spiritually enlightened to discern things as they really are, our apprehensions would speedily give place to assurance. Christ died for us, yea rather, He is risen again, and sitteth at the Right Hand of God. Spiritual enlightenment would at once remove all doubt by removing ignorance or misapprehension. When the women, deeming Him dead, mourned for the supposed removal of His body, and failed to recognise Him, His voice in a moment banished their sorrow. When we cannot see the Lord, and mourn over an absent Saviour, His word of grace recognised will change our sorrow into gladness. When, like the disciples on their way to Emmaus, we are perplexed, unable to understand the ways of the Lord, and feeling as if our hope were passing, like that sunlight at even, He will make Himself known to us in the breaking of bread. And when certain destruction seems to await us on the morrow, an Angel may waken us to liberty as he wakened Peter. So noiselessly do the chains drop, and the massive gates open and again close, so light are our footsteps that not one of the many sleepers around shall perceive it; that to ourselves it may appear like the vision of a dream, and yet we are free. But a little longer—and we shall be free! The prison-house, the chains, the guard and warders, the night and fear, all left behind—and golden sunlight on the hills around Zion! Nay, we are already free, for "they that be with us are more than they that be with them."

The vision of such help at hand immediately removed the fears of the young man. He was now content to follow the prophet even to meet the hosts of Syria. The joy of the Lord is our strength. If we have assurance of His Presence, we shall be prepared to encounter any foe or to undertake any labour. What we need is full conviction. Firmly convinced that our sins are really forgiven, we have boldness of access unto God. Fully believing that none shall pluck us out of His Hand, the spiritual contest is no longer uncertain, and need not be feared. Certain that the Lord will give that which is good, the issue of future events is no longer doubtful, and we banish alike care and anxiety.

The host of Syria met the two unarmed Israelites. But Elisha had prayed, and the same power which had opened the eyes of his servant, now closed those of his persecutors, or covered them with a film of delusion. The student of history knows how often this miracle has seemed repeated in times of public persecution, when they, who were sent to slay, were in some unexpected manner led in another direction, to the wondrous deliverance of those who appeared doomed to die. Most of us also, if observant, may have learned how often determined enemies, who had come to take our Dothan, have been smitten apparently with blindness, and taken their way to Samaria. Attacks upon Divine truth, measures which threatened the existence of the Church, or the spread of His Word, have thus been rendered harmless, and they, who went to capture our Elisha, have wakened to find themselves captives in the citadel of Israel.

"This is not the way, neither is this the city," Elisha could most truthfully say to the blinded host of Syria. They had not come to destroy Dothan but to take the prophet, and the way to Dothan no longer led to that result. "I will bring you to the man whom ye seek." But what a terrible discovery will it be when he is found. They shall meet him face to face, but in circumstances far different from what they had expected. There is yet another application of this. The hostile armies of Syria shall meet the Master, but, oh, how differently from what they had imagined—as Judge and Lord in the midst of His own city. Judicial blindness has fallen upon many. They imagine that Elisha may easily be captured. By their arguments they will compass and storm Dothan, and lead him away. For nearly nineteen centuries has host after host made the attempt. Every age has produced its new objectors and its fresh objections; and every host has been alike confident of success. They think that those who before them had gone to the attack, had not striven to beset every gate and postern. But they deceive themselves and are deceived. Every point of attack has been attempted and has failed. Now the authority of the Old Testament, then that of the New, has been called in question. At one time we have been confidently assured that the mission of Moses, at another that the mission of Jesus had been misunderstood. On the one hand we are told that Christianity is not new—only a reform of the old. On the other hand, it is declared to be demonstrated, and that by those stones beneath our feet, which once had almost burst into Hosannah to the Son of David, that neither the New nor the Old Testament can be true! Yet these very stones *shall* cry out, Hosannah, to shame our silent masters in Israel. Similar objections have been raised (indeed wondrously like them even in point of form as in the matter of fact), and the same vaunting has been made in every age. But by what formula do these men, who boast of destroying our hope, who will turn the current of the river of life, and arrest the attraction of the greater magnet, propose to explain the mysteries of our souls; or what remedy to substitute for the experience of renewed hearts? They have not succeeded with their own disciples; and they cannot satisfy the longing of the soul, or give peace to the weary. Smitten with blindness, they shall follow as captives the unarmed Elisha whom they have come to capture. The next generation will only remember their names to record their blindness, and that they awoke in the midst of Samaria.

The scene which now followed, as sketched in the sacred narrative, must have been one of the strangest ever witnessed. The Syrians, with Elisha as their new leader, left Dothan. They rapidly moved over the plain, till the battlements of Samaria came into view. Still they pressed onward, and the foremost, preceded by the prophet, entered the gate of the Israelitish capital. We can imagine with what feelings of wonder the guard at the gate would allow them to pass. It must have been that with uplifted hand and look of command Elisha had forbidden opposition. But what meant this strange occurrence? The Syrian host was not larger than could be safely admitted within the walls of Samaria. Had they come as friends or foes; and was the prophet their captive, or were they his captives? The heavy tramp of armed men, the clattering of horses' hoofs, and the noise of war-chariots in the streets of Samaria, must have brought every face to the lattice. It was a division of Syria's army, in every respect well appointed, but entering Samaria, as if they marched into Damascus! The city gates swung to after the last rider, and soldier and citizen hastened after the Syrians to the market-place. What new manifestation was Israel to witness? As leader of the strange host Elisha now paused. Once more he prayed, this time: "Lord, open the eyes of these men, that they may see." It was so. A look of indescribable surprise, and then of terror, must have passed over them as they recognised where they were. The boldest and bravest must have felt appalled on finding themselves thus suddenly and hopelessly in the power of their enemies.

To us also there may be an awakening as sudden as that described in this history—full of joy to some, full of unutterable terror to others. Sudden death is sudden glory to the children of God. One burst of light so bright, that all of earth fades in its glory; one mightier bound of life which, like the returning tide of strength in Samson, breaks down this temple; one louder blast which, like the trumpets of the priests, brings down the walls of the city; one mighty rush of joy, which carries before it the weak barriers—and all that we feared is past. Our feet touch the other shore; we have not had the pang of parting, and we have the joy of meeting; we have not had the pain of death, and we have the joy of life; we have not heard the voice of weeping, and we are greeted by the songs of angels; we fell asleep on earth, and we woke in heaven, in glory, with Christ, with all the saints. Many a welcome there awaits us—of relatives, of friends;

of angels, of men; of Christ, of God. All that is dim is behind; all that is bright is around. But blessed as is such dying, equally fearful is that of the unprepared and the impenitent. Another breath, and twofold death shall hold the soul. All that is terrible, in death and after death, is now eternally present. On one fleeting moment hangs an eternity of misery. Oh, that some mighty hand could wake the sleeper! To be so altogether unprepared for it, hurried from darkness to darkness; helpless, hopeless, without friend, without Saviour, without ray of light, or moment of rest, or breath of hope, to be driven from earth with all that it offers of beauty, of joy, and of mercy so suddenly, so unconsciously, and without a farewell: from such "sudden death, good Lord, deliver us!"

From his palace King Joram must have watched the wondrous scene enacted in Samaria. He now passed through the multitude, which, still awe-struck, surrounded the silent Syrians and the silent prophet. Elisha had not yet found words; he wondered and he worshipped. Not so King Joram. He came as if he had been a conqueror; as if he had come to the spoil. The solemn spirituality of the event had not even awed him. It was not the Hand of God which he recognised; it was only the results which he calculated. It was not the miracle, it was its possible benefit to himself which engrossed him. "My father, shall I smite? shall I smite?" as if repeating the words in very impatience. Elisha was now addressed as his "father." The national prophet of Israel had brought a captive host to his feet; religion had rendered its tribute to royalty, and so for once received his acknowledgment. An unspiritual man is always the same, and always in the way, in seasons both of joy and of sorrow. In success he would fain appropriate in his own unspiritual manner what he has not gained, and to which he has no claim. In adversity he desponds and laments: "Nay, but Jehovah has called these three kings together to slay them." Alike untaught under opposite circumstances, he remains hopelessly and obstinately unapprehending, whatever lessons God may show in His wondrous dealings. It is difficult to say, whether the carnal zeal òr the inanity of such men offers most difficulty. They intrude into the house of mourning, and they are present in times of joy. In both, their religious platitudes and their glib professions are alike incongruous. First depressed and then elated, their restlessness is in striking contrast to this description of Holy Writ: "They that trust in Jehovah shall be as Mount Zion, which cannot be removed, but standeth for ever. As the mountains are round about Jerusalem, so Jehovah is round about His people, from henceforth even for ever."

Smite them? But they were not Joram's captives; he had not conquered them with his sword and bow. They were the captives of the Lord. Or did the king of Israel really think that all this had been done only for his own personal advantage, honour, and glory? It seems a hard thing to say, and yet there are those who speak and act as if everything existed or happened exclusively for their own behoof. Even religious men may, through a narrow sectarianism, come to look at all things only as they will affect them and their little party or sect. A national event, a wave of revival, a great question, finds them only busy adding and subtracting, taking stock and making up a kind of balance-sheet of profit and loss to their own cause. It is said that the mountaineers, who for generations have looked from their heights into the far distance, obtain a keener sight and a wider range of vision than others. And opposite causes may, as we infer, lead to the contrary result. Is it not so in spiritual matters, and may not this in part account for the limited view so often taken by the party-man, and for his unreadiness to recognise the Hand of God, or His working in Providence? Let us beware lest, in our right and proper attachment to our own friends, we unfit ourselves for taking a wider range, and for discerning "the signs of the times."

Elisha rejected with indignation the proposal of the king. He had not come—God had not sent him—ungenerously to lead even enemies into a trap, and then to murder them in cold blood. On the contrary, "set bread and water before them, that they may eat and drink, and go to their master." The Lord had wrought this great miracle not to lure the blinded Syrians to the slaughter-house of King Joram, but to show before Israel and Syria His mighty power, how easily He could deliver, how vain were attempts against Him, how near He was to His people, how sure and safe they were, and how blessed it was to be His servant. But in the hour of success and prosperity it is often difficult to realise these things. Nothing mean or ungenerous should ever be done by the Christian; no undue advantage taken even of those whom we regard as the enemies of "the Master" and of Israel. One of the most painful occurrences connected with religious controversy, is the too often ungenerous, even unrighteous bearing of those who are engaged in it. They would smite whom they should feed. By introducing passions they degrade into personal questions what are the highest and holiest transactions, and convert the hour of devout worship into one of wretched animosity. All the more sad is such a state of matters, if we are on the right side of a question. Why recriminate or persecute? Set before them bread and water, and send them to their master. The cause of religion cannot gain by our bigotry. We are not to silence, but to convince men; we are not to exterminate, but to "overcome evil with good." "Vengeance is

Mine, saith the Lord"—and an awful thought it is. It is not by suppressing inquiry, but by meeting it with the meekness of wisdom; not by bandying hard names, but by seeking the spiritual welfare of others, that we shall promote the glory of God and the progress of His kingdom. To be very faithful, and yet very loving; very earnest, and yet very gentle; very consistent, and yet very charitable, is indeed a rare combination of graces. And a special beatitude is that to the men of true peace, not of compromises, to the peace-lovers, peace-bringers, peace-makers: they shall be called the children of God. Would that in our days the cry of Joram, "Shall I smite them?" were less frequently heard in the streets of Samaria, and the same kind of zeal less urgently displayed. Would that the leaders of our spiritual Israel had more of the spirit of Elisha—the rather that, after all, those whom a Joram might propose to smite are not Syrians and enemies, but brethren, heirs of God, fellow-heirs with Christ, and of the household of faith.

But Joram's policy was foolish as well as sinful. To have exterminated the Syrians would have brought speedy and fearful revenge. Nor would Jehovah have delivered from dangers so encountered. As it was, whatever Joram may have learned, or failed to learn, from the presence of the Syrians in his city, they at least had not been in vain with the prophet. Warfare, stern warfare was again to be waged between Ben-hadad and the king of Israel, but "the bands of Syria came no more into the land of Israel."

CHAPTER XXI.

FAMINE IN SAMARIA.

"And it came to pass after this, that Ben-hadad king of Syria gathered all his host, and went up, and besieged Samaria. And there was a great famine in Samaria: and, behold, they besieged it, until an ass's head was sold for fourscore pieces of silver, and the fourth part of a cab of dove's dung for five pieces of silver. And as the king of Israel was passing by upon the wall, there cried a woman unto him, saying, Help, my lord, O king. And he said, If the Lord do not help thee, whence shall I help thee? out of the barnfloor, or out of the winepress? And the king said unto her, What aileth thee? and she answered, This woman said unto me, Give thy son, that we may eat him to-day, and we will eat my son to-morrow. So we boiled my son, and did eat him: and I said unto her on the next day, Give thy son, that we may eat him: and she hath hid her son. And it came to pass, when the king heard the words of the woman, that he rent his clothes; and he passed by upon the wall, and the people looked, and, behold, he had sackcloth within upon his flesh. Then he said, God do so and more also to me, if the head of Elisha the son of Shaphat shall stand on him this day."—2 KINGS vi. 24-31.

TIME had passed since the Syrian soldiers had returned from their bootless expedition to Samaria, and told in Damascus the marvellous story of their capture. In its swift course, time wears deeper the channels which sorrow and experience have made. But the same swift course carries with it what has been carelessly flung from its banks. We love, the longer the more; we feel, the longer the deeper. But passing emotions are swept away, and leave not a mark. And so the impression made on Ben-hadad by the strange reception and dismissal of his troops at Samaria, was effaced, and only his enmity towards Israel or his restless ambition remained. Perhaps it was deemed unsafe henceforth to entrust to a single division the fate of a campaign; perhaps it was difficult to find volunteers in an undertaking which might meet with such resistance; perhaps Ben-hadad would gather up all his strength to a final and decisive trial. At any rate, "after this"—longer or shorter, we know not—"it came to pass that Ben-hadad, king of Syria, gathered all his host, and went up and besieged Samaria."

So the lesson had after all not been learned in Damascus! What was that lesson? It was that in the midst of apparent impossibilities, God could make a way of escape; that He could most easily turn aside seemingly certain destruction, not by striking down the uplifted arm, but by rendering the threatened blow aimless and harmless. In the supernatural blindness of the Syrian host, by which the prophet was saved and the heathen were put to shame, there was that which closely resembles the ordinary course of God's Providence. The blindness of the Syrians was indeed supernatural, but all the rest followed in its natural course. Similarly, when looking at it after the event, the plans and means employed by the enemies of religion seem sometimes as if they had been stricken with judicial blindness. And so in their natural course they miscarry. The next generation sees only the naturalness of the sequence; the overruling and restraining Hand of God at the first is not recognised. And, like Ben-hadad, they resume the warfare on a new and, as it seems to them, larger scale.

At most, then, the impression had been temporary and transient, as are those even of a religious character on men who are not under the influence of the Holy Spirit. They have their origin not in a change within, but in the pressure of circumstances without, and they gradually cease with that pressure. In dangerous sickness, or in affliction, religious feelings may be cherished and resolutions made, perhaps in all sincerity. But on restoration to health or comfort the latter state of such persons may become almost worse than the first. An impressive event does not always impress, nor an impression always improve. Many who, like Felix, indefinitely defer to a more convenient season their spiritual decision, have at one time or another, "trembled" at the Word of God, at the voice of conscience, or in view of some great "visitation." And yet it has not issued in their conversion to God. The fact suggests thoughts even more saddening. How much of what some people call their religion would be left, if all fear of death and hell were removed? But a religion whose sole motive is fear, not love, cannot be either spiritual or healthy. True, we are admonished to flee "for refuge" from "the wrath to come," but only to "lay hold upon the hope set before us." Perfect love passes beyond the stage of fear—it "casteth out fear." Such religion is cordial acquiescence in the Gospel of peace, on the part of renewed, humbled, grateful hearts; it is acceptance of Christ as Lord and Saviour by the inmost soul, and reception of the love of God in the gift of His dear Son; it is to lay ourselves open to the sunlight of that grace, which we have felt, and in which we have learned to rejoice, when we opened our hearts to its influences, that it may reach down to its deepest recesses, so that all which springs up there may spring and grow in its light and warmth.

But to return to our narrative. We read that there was once more war between Syria and Israel. It has been aptly remarked, that this will always be the case, even although Israel restores the captives of Syria. No lawful concession on our part can remove the abiding enmity between the "seed of the woman" and "seed of the serpent." It is the character of the great enemy of Christ to seek the destruction of His Kingdom; and his subjects, perhaps all unconsciously, follow his lead. Every extension of the Kingdom of our

Lord, even its continuance, implies defeat to "the prince of this world." Thus, all unseen, a warfare is really carried on. Then, let us at least learn the lesson that it is worse than useless, that it is foolish and sinful, to attempt compromises with the world. The cessation of its hostility can only be purchased by unfaithfulness to our Master. We shall be none the better for our *small* compromises—going so far, but refusing to go further. By such means we do not conciliate any one, but we wound our consciences. If the Gospel be really the truth of God, and if, as our consciences tell us, it means all that Evangelical teaching derives from it, let us embrace it cordially and unreservedly. If otherwise, let us cast it aside and cleave to the world. But these wretched compromises, the outcome of indecision, worldliness, and unbelief, involve sufficient to deprive us of all comfort and enjoyment in religion, but not to set us free from the enmity of the world, or the reproach of the cross.

The invasion of the land by Ben-hadad was apparently so sudden, or else it found Joram so unprepared, that even the mountain passes had been left undefended, which command the access to Samaria. The enemy advanced till he reached the gates of the capital. There also no preparation had been made, either temporally or spiritually, to meet the danger. Joram had not learned the lessons of the past any more than Ben-hadad. And so Samaria was in imminent danger. It was closely besieged by the whole army of Syria, under a bold and determined commander, while within its walls one held rule who was destitute of faith, one also wholly unfitted for any great emergency, a man of shifts and expedients. Besides, the city was ill garrisoned, and scarcely provisioned at all. To meet the threatening danger, it would have needed union among the people, and strong faith. But neither the one nor the other was to be found in Samaria. Indeed, Israel, as represented and ruled by Joram, had lost the meaning and purpose of its calling. We also need faith and united action as against the enemy. Otherwise, if the Lord in long-suffering send temporary deliverance, it will come, not through any Joram who may rule in Samaria, but through an Elisha, even though a price be set on his head.

In Samaria soon the horrors of famine were added to those of the siege. Pale hunger looked in at every window and lattice, and in its wake came pestilence and death. What days these were; what suffering was endured before it became publicly known; and what appalling knowledge of it did ultimately come! The calamity was all the more terrible, that absolutely not one ray of hope lighted up the gloom. The nation was divided into the followers of Joram and those of Jehovah. What hope could the pious in Israel entertain while a Joram was king, and the people had not repented of their idolatry, nor sought the Lord? And what confidence could they who looked not to God cherish, when the city was besieged by such an enemy, and the garrison and the people reduced to such straits? Whence was relief to come? As the pressure of hunger became more severe, the ordinary restraints, not only of social but of Jewish religious life, were cast aside. Men and women threw aside every consideration in their eagerness to provide any kind of food. Money had little value; it could scarcely procure the most repulsive kind of provisions, and in the common misery only a narrow line of demarcation separated the rich from the poor. An ass's head sold in the streets of Samaria, among eager competitors, for eighty pieces of silver, and a very small amount of the most wretched fuel for five pieces of silver. If even such meals could only be procured at such cost, what must the poor have suffered and done—

the men, the women, and the children that thronged the streets of Samaria!

As for those who feared the Lord, they would for the present have to suffer with the wicked, but not in the same manner. Nor could they cherish other hope than such as springs from the blessed conviction that the Lord will take care of His own. His promises concerning them could not fail. Amidst all adversity and danger, even were it such as beset Samaria, it is ours as Christians to realise, in the assurance of faith, that the very hairs on our head are numbered by Him Who feeds the birds of the air and clothes the lilies of the field. It is one of the grandest conceptions of inspired poetry, that in which David seems to see each morn, all creation gathering in presence of the Lord, and, so to speak, intently looking up till He openeth His hand and giveth to each his meat in due season, so satisfying the desire of every living thing. Verily, this mode of living is not by bread alone! And, when every other hope seems taken and all help fails; when, worst of all evils, a Joram reigns, and by his conduct and spirit seems to prevent the possibility of deliverance—if by faith we can rise to Him Who is the Living God, and by grace confess our sin and that of others with whom we are connected; if we can grasp the promises even while humbling ourselves, then may we still confidently look up and wait for Him. His promise will even then hold true, "Lo, I am with you alway (every day), even unto the end of the world."

Meanwhile in Samaria time passed in weary sameness. The sun set on the same haggard forms of men, on the same tottering figures of women, on the same pallid, wasted children, on whom he had risen. And still there was neither relief nor hope, but everywhere a dreary waste of misery and sound of woe. Dangers and trials like these break down the conventional barriers of ordinary life, and disclose the real condition of every man's heart. Stern want is an earnest questioner, and takes none but a truthful answer. On a bed of sickness, in the hour of sorrow, at the moment of danger, the real character of our principles appears. Never is man more selfish, or else more generous, than on such occasions. Principle is most stedfast and strong when put on its utmost trial; religion most lovely and winning, when its full influence is called forth. But what a terrible picture, when the "I must" of unrestrained selfishness asserts itself in all its ferocity, and, all considerations cast aside, passion appears in all its wildness!

It happened that on one of those weary days King Joram, his head bent, and with the look of a mourner, made his way to the city-wall to encourage the wan soldiers who kept watch there, when a sight terrible even in that city of terror startled and arrested him. A frantic woman rushed forward to intercept his progress. Either she had waited for the opportunity, or it was in sudden, frenzied impulse. It was not merely hunger and misery which glared out of those glazed eyes. There was something unearthly in her appearance, as if she had done with, or had forgotten, every restraint. Her piercing cry, "Help, my lord, O king," rang in Joram's heart, and woke its echoes. It shook and unnerved him. For a passing moment we seem to catch a glimpse of his real feelings, as when in the midst of darkness a flash of lightning suddenly shoots across the sky, for a moment making all most brightly, even painfully visible—the next, disappearing, leaves all in deeper gloom. Help thee! How shall I help thee? "If Jehovah do not help thee, whence shall I help thee? Out of the barn-floor, or out of the wine-press?" For once the king spoke truthfully. But he spoke in the bitterness of his spirit; not in repentant submission, but in angry, forced subjection to a higher power, which he could not resist. And still he blamed not himself, but Jehovah and His prophet; he felt the judgment, but he perceived not its cause. It is as if he said: The judgment is Jehovah's; if He do not help thee, how can I? There is also a tone of irony in his speech, as if, baffled and maddened, he knew not how to speak; and even when he tried to comfort, it was in a strain of bitterness and despair.

And the woman remained immovable, her wild eye fixed on the king. In some measure softened or frightened by this impersonation of despair, Joram inquired, "What aileth thee?" Then came the horrible tale. The imagination almost refuses to picture her, as, vehemently gesticulating, and with outburst of violent language, she poured forth the details of her unnatural bargain. The pangs of starvation seem for a time to have extinguished the commonest instincts of human nature. Probably she had not tasted food for several days, when she and her neighbour arranged the terms of their fiendish meal. "This woman said unto me, Give thy son, that we may eat him to-day, and we will eat my son to-morrow." She had done her part of the bargain—"so we boiled my son, and did eat him,"—and now the other refused to fulfil hers—"she hath hid her son." It is not merely that at hearing of such a story the heart sickens, but the horrible fact stood out that she could complain to the king, that the other had shrunk from doing that which now frenzied her—for, we take it, it was the recollection of the past more than her present wrong which glared from her eyes. It was that her neighbour had helped her in her crime, and then deserted her in it, as if her guilt would have become less if it had been shared by the other, or her misery lighter if another had felt the same weight! It was not merely that she could relate every circumstance, and tell how they had killed and boiled and eaten her son—for despair makes reckless, and what cared she, who had done such a deed, who knew it? but that she could appeal to the king for justice against one who, the temporary madness of hunger past, would refuse to commit the same deed, that seemed to have destroyed in her the common likeness of our human nature!

For a moment the king stood as rooted to the ground. Then, staggering under the weight of that tale, he stared wildly round, and with sudden impulse, seizing his royal robe, rent it in token of deepest mourning. The king passed on, and as the people looked on him, "behold, he had sackcloth within upon his flesh." Did King Joram then in secret wear sackcloth upon his flesh, and was he a penitent? What a small circumstance will often turn the current of popular feeling! What a little thing will in times of despair suffice to carry comfort and hope! The sight of King Joram in sackcloth almost blotted out the tale of horrors. For the moment it was a more joyous surprise to the people than tidings of approaching relief would have been. Yet, after all, what was it? Is sackcloth on the flesh indeed evidence of repentance in the heart? Would that it were so! Too often, alas, it is the reverse, and tells that the bitter sorrow within, of which it is the token, has only yielded its yet bitterer fruit of death. Let this not be misunderstood. In seasons of sorrow, in times of calamity, even a man destitute of religion wears his sackcloth. He becomes more grave and earnest; he attends more to the outward duties of religion; he feels more deeply; he gives up certain sins; he forms certain resolutions. Or, under the pressure of conscience, or in fear of death, he does certain penance, and feels anguish of spirit. But is this *repentance?* Tested by its character it is "sorrow," which "worketh death"—that is, which if carried to its utmost consequences would end in death. There is no element of life in it. Tested by its results, it passes away with the occasion, "as the morning cloud and as the early dew," and leaves the soul as before in its relation to God. Not so "godly sorrow." It also is sorrow; but it is godly. It worketh repentance, but such as needs not to be regretted, nor again repented of. Such repentance is life, and "to salvation." Have our sorrows been lasting and spiritual in their results; have they been unto eternal life and peace?

King Joram had speedily taken his resolution. "God do so and more also to me, if the head of Elisha, the son of Shaphat, shall stand on him this day." Joram, in sackcloth, calls down the curse of God, and proclaims a murderous purpose against His prophet! Surely a more striking lesson and louder warning could not be found of the insufficiency of merely outward humiliation. Yet such inconsistency, as sinfulness of conduct combined with outward religiousness, is by no means uncommon. All the more anxious and earnest should we be to have the springs of our inner life influenced by the grace of God. In such outbursts of passion as those of Joram, the real nature of a man involuntarily comes to light. His language was the same as that used by his mother Jezebel in reference to Elijah. The house of Ahab had learned nothing and forgotten nothing. Yet, at the time she so spake, Jezebel was a worshipper of Baal, while Joram wore sackcloth upon his flesh. But where was the real difference between them, and what practical good had his mourning effected in Joram? These are considerations which all should lay to heart, who, while wearing the outward mark of those who mourn in Zion, or outwardly religious, have not experienced an inward change through the influence of the Holy Spirit. Although wearing sackcloth,

Joram spake and acted like Jezebel. A man may be "not far from the Kingdom of God;" he may even be very near it, and yet not till he is within its boundaries is he safe.

The sentence of the king was to be executed—"to-day!" In their pride men may imagine they have it in their own power. Indeed, the messenger of Joram was immediately despatched upon his bloody errand. But it was easy for the Hand that had bound the eyes of the Syrians to stay the arm of a Joram. But how terrible for Israel, as well as sinful, if the king had been allowed to execute his purpose. The only hope of Samaria lay in the presence of Elisha. Thus the sin of men is ever also their folly. They destroy themselves while they rebel against God. May we have grace to act differently! In His mercy God is long-suffering. We may often have slighted His loving Presence, and delayed to answer His call. Yet He waiteth to be gracious. His purpose is really of love. He would bring us to Himself; He would make us His own. He would have us pass from desolateness to assured peace; from ruin to happiness; He would bring us to our gracious Redeemer; and whether He speak to us by His Word or in His Providence, we still hear in all the voice of our Blessed Lord, saying, "Come unto Me, all ye that labour and are heavy laden, and I will give you rest."

CHAPTER XXII.

UNBELIEF REPROVED.

"But Elisha sat in his house, and the elders sat with him; and the king sent a man from before him; but ere the messenger came to him, he said to the elders, See ye how this son of a murderer hath sent to take away mine head? look, when the messenger cometh, shut the door, and hold him fast at the door: is not the sound of his master's feet behind him? And while he yet talked with them, behold, the messenger came down unto him: and he said, Behold, this evil is of the Lord; what should I wait for the Lord any longer? Then Elisha said, Hear ye the word of the Lord; Thus saith the Lord, To-morrow about this time shall a measure of fine flour be sold for a shekel, and two measures of barley for a shekel, in the gate of Samaria. Then a lord on whose hand the king leaned answered the man of God, and said, Behold, if the Lord would make windows in heaven, might this thing be? And he said, Behold, thou shalt see it with thine eyes, but shalt not eat thereof."—
2 KINGS vi. 32, 33; vii. 1, 2.

WITHIN the besieged city was the temporary home of Elisha. For wherever there was danger or duty, there also was the prophet of God to be found. It was his mission to "endure hardship," to "bear contradiction," to be "in deaths often," if so he might serve his Master, and recall Israel to their God. Quiet resting-places like Shunem there were few in the life of a soldier whose lot was cast in times of war and confusion. The husbandman of Abel-Meholah must repress all softer feelings; he must forget the happy, peaceful retirement of his youth; he has put his hand to a plough that draws deeper furrows than those when he followed that yoke of oxen in the day that Elijah's mantle had been flung over his shoulders. And from that plough he must not look back, if he would cast in the precious seed, and see the golden harvest, and hear the Welcome Home of his Master in heaven. The house of Elisha in Samaria (saving perhaps in its lowliness) differed from the others around in no other respect than this, that it was a house of peace and calm, instead of the habitation of despondency and unrest. As Scripture so often, and sometimes so graphically, puts it to us —any home, however humble, any provision, however coarse, only let God's blessed peace by day gladden us with its sunshine, and by night rock us into quiet sleep. And angels guard such a dwelling; no real evil can come near it. We are not afraid of evil tidings; there are not evil tidings, only "good tidings of great joy," that God has loved us with an everlasting love, and with loving-kindness draws us unto Himself. A truly Christian home is the only happy home, where happiness ceases not with time, but grows into eternal joy; where even affliction worketh its peaceable fruits; where the Saviour's entrance has brought its "peace be with thee," a peace which has not turned back from us, nor will turn away from ours.

That quiet home in Samaria presented a strange contrast to the terrible scene just enacted on the city-wall, and its occupations to the resolution at which the king of Israel had just arrived. Here was Elisha, and with him were "the elders," no doubt entreating the Lord to stay His judgments, and to return in mercy to His land and people. A firmer stay and better defence this unarmed company than the soldiers who guarded the city; more hope and encouragement from their meeting than from the visit of King Joram to the city-wall. "Then they that feared the Lord spake often one to another: and the Lord hearkened, and heard it, and a book of remembrance was written before Him for them that feared the Lord, and that thought upon His name."

It was a blessed injunction laid upon the Hebrew exiles, to seek the peace of the places and of the people where they were scattered. And it is a blessed command to pray for kings and rulers, and for all who are in authority, to seek their good even when they compass our evil, to bless even when they curse. In some respects, indeed, we must share the evil which comes on the wicked around us; most assuredly our good comes upon them. And so we work on and pray on, well assured that the victory is ours, and that on the morrow light shall break through, and chase the darkness. Only in the chronicle unread on earth is it recorded, how and how often calamity has been averted from doomed cities and homes, and what untold blessings have been brought down by these humble assemblies of praying, believing men. Never let us despise such gatherings; never let us lightly esteem, nor seek to criticise or to calculate their results; but reverently put off our shoes, for the place of prayer is the place where God is, and is a holy place. It was in such assemblies, and no doubt to the lowliest in Jerusalem, that Anna first spake of the Saviour Who had been born in the city of David; it was in such an assembly that Elisha first announced the deliverance that was to be brought to Samaria.

Of a sudden the peaceful occupations of the hour were interrupted. The interruption came from Elisha himself. In vision he had seen King Joram despátching the messenger, and had heard the bloody commission given him. More than this, he had also seen how, so soon as the king's anger had exhausted itself in the proposed act of vengeance, it had given place to fear of the consequences, and how the vacillating Joram had quickly turned his steps to arrest the execution of his own sentence. Obstinacy and weakness, cruelty and cowardice, are generally conjoined. It is well, that those who would do evil so often lack the strength to see it executed. "The wicked flee when no man pursueth; but the righteous are bold as a lion." Not that the wicked are troubled by misgivings, but that they are haunted by thoughts of a "may-be" which they dare not encounter. King Joram was not penitent now, any more than he had been when he put sackcloth upon his flesh. Probably he would gladly have seen the prophet slain and out of his way, but he dreaded to do it himself. So, " Herod feared John, knowing that he was a just man and an holy, and observed him; and when he heard him, he did many things, and heard him gladly." Yet, as a man of his word and as a man of honour, Herod murdered the Baptist! And so many in our days alternate between attendance on faithful preaching and religiousness, and indulgence of self and sin. To-day in church with tears, to-morrow in the world with laughter; to-day depressed, to-morrow elated; to-day at Lenten fasts, to-morrow at the ball and the theatre—" double-minded," and therefore " unstable in all their ways."

The language in which Elisha expressed himself on this occasion might possibly have shocked polite ears. "See ye how this son of a murderer hath sent to take away mine head? Look—when the messenger cometh, shut the door. Is not the sound of his master's feet behind him?" There are circumstances in which the truth must be spoken plainly, even though it may seem offensively, in order to arouse men. It is a common objection to faithful preachers that they say offensive things, and say them offensively. This, however, be it remarked, is not unfrequently urged by those who are not shocked by seeing offensive deeds. What! would you rather look on with good breeding when men perish everlastingly? Would you refuse to shake a man violently, if he sleeps so heavily as not to hear any ordinary call that warns him of his danger? All needless offence to taste or education should, indeed, be earnestly avoided. For the pulpit is a place for earnest men, doing the most earnest work upon earth. It is not a place for self-exhibition nor vain-glory. But neither is it a place for lulling men to sleep. Our times need earnest men, and we will welcome them, whoever they be. Let us speak the truth of God; the salvation of souls depends upon it. Let us speak it as best we can; but let us also remember that our speaking is only a means towards an end, and that the object aimed at must be to induce men to turn to the Lord. Religious coarseness is most offensive; it argues that what is said cannot have been personally realised. But the foppish, affected pretence of being shocked by some expression used by an earnest man, is too often only the result of personal unconcern, or of dislike to the truth spoken.

If Elisha now offered a passive resistance by refusing admittance to Joram's messenger and detaining him, it was, no doubt, justified by the knowledge that "his master's feet" were "behind him." Blessed be God, in our land the question of the lawfulness of resisting or opposing constituted authority can only possess a speculative, not a practical, interest. Absolutely to deny it would be to condemn some of the most glorious events alike in our civil, and in our ecclesiastical history. The answer to the question depends in each case on the distinction between law and constituted authority, which is its minister; and further, on what is requisite in order to give to law its authoritative sanction, and to constitute it law; on the right relations between ruler and ruled; and, ultimately, on the fundamental principles which underlie society.

While Elisha "yet talked" with the elders, the king's "messenger came down unto him," closely followed by Joram himself. The narrative, from its pictorial character, becomes now exceedingly abrupt. The messenger is held at the door, and immediately afterwards the king himself (who may have come either to witness or to arrest the execution of his command) appears in the prophet's presence with these words—for they are the king's, and neither those of his messenger, nor of Elisha—" Behold, this evil is of Jehovah; what should I wait for Jehovah any longer?" This is a new phase in the feelings of Joram, or rather a new manifestation of the old feelings of unbelief, disappointment, and anger, which had prompted him to command the death of Elisha. He had long enough put it to the trial; he had endeavoured to propitiate the favour of Jehovah; he had put on the garb of a penitent, and worn sackcloth. All was of no avail; why should he wait any longer for Jehovah? What more could have been expected of him? and yet, "behold," the result.

It is impossible to regard this otherwise than as another evidence of the folly and self-delusion of Joram; and yet it is impossible not to pity him. True, "this evil" *was* "of the Lord;" but had Joram ever really waited for the Lord? He had recognised His power, and he could scarcely have failed to do so. But had he also recognised His purpose—the meaning of God's dealing in reference to the past, and its object in reference to the future? Under heavy affliction we all recognise God and His power, which cannot be resisted. But do we understand His purpose of love, and listen to His voice in it? Yet, when a child of sorrow, through his fast-falling tears, cannot see deliverance or hope; when he feels like a traveller who has long struggled on his difficult journey against blinding snowdrift and cutting wind, till, at last, when night overtakes him, he gives up further toil in very despair, and flings himself down to die—who could refuse him pity or sympathy? All the more, that we know that refuge and rest are within reach, but unknown and unheeded by him who strays further and further from the shelter. What shall we say to such? We will speak to them of Jesus, the Good Shepherd, Who in such a night as that, goes forth to seek His wanderers; of Him Who once changed a winter's night into one of heavenly brightness and of angelic song, "Glory to God in the highest, peace on earth, and good will toward men." We will not speak to them, for the present at least, of their past. We will speak to them of the morrow, with its glad tidings of plenty to come from the Hand of the Lord, of relief, and of safety; and we will pray that the wondrous message of God's loving-kindness may lead them to begin what they had never done before: to "wait for the Lord" "more than they that watch for the morning," and to "hope in the Lord."

It needed heavenly wisdom on this occasion to answer Joram. For what could the prophet say, and with what preparation to his hearers should he announce the coming deliverance? Best of all, as we now see it, without any preparation, simply telling it, just as we simply announce the Gospel to all who are shut up in Samaria. God never fails in His promise of direction to His servants, and the more urgent their need, the more ample His supply of present grace to guide them. "It shall be given you in that same hour—not too late, but also not too early—what ye shall speak." And this not merely for their own comfort, but because, in such circumstances, they speak and act specially as His representatives. As if to encourage us in our weakness, so many instances of this are on record that we dare not doubt, should the hour of public testimony or even of martyrdom come. Whatever our present fears, we shall "out of weakness be made strong."

And so Elisha, on this occasion also, rose to the full dignity of his position. Instead of replying to Joram's interrogation, he calmly proclaimed a very miracle of miracles. He was not there to argue with the king, but to preach

Jehovah; and this he did in language which must have startled even the most believing among his hearers. "To-morrow, about this time, shall a measure of fine flour be sold for a shekel, and two measures of barley for a shekel, in the gate of Samaria." In Samaria, where at present "an ass's head was sold for eighty pieces of silver"! Of all apparent impossibilities, this must have seemed the strangest that could be announced. Even in times of greatest prosperity such prices would have been unusually low. But whence was the supply to come? Even granting that the besieging army were immediately withdrawn, and that every gate were thrown open; that swift messengers summoned help from all the neighbourhood, so that during the next twenty-four hours supplies would pour into the city with the utmost rapidity possible—in the nature of things, how could such a prediction be fulfilled?

Many things, viewed abstractly, seem impossible, which nevertheless are matters of fact. It seems impossible that the dead should arise and live again, and we are tempted in our folly to ask, "With what body shall they be raised?" It seems impossible that the Son of God should have become incarnate, and taken upon Himself "the form of a servant." It seems impossible that, through simple faith in a Crucified and Risen Redeemer, a man should be freed from guilt and sin, have peace and joy, and become wholly changed in mind, heart, and life. Yet all this is so. It seems impossible that a Zacchæus should have gone forth as chief of the publicans to "see Jesus;" and, from that brief interview, returned to give the half of his goods to the poor, and to restore fourfold what he had taken by false accusations. And when we look back into the past, it seems impossible that sinners such as we should have been made the objects of Divine favour, and the subjects of His grace. The change is so great and so strange, that sometimes we still doubt its possibility. Yet, blessed be God, what is impossible with men is possible with God!

Elisha had returned to the king the best answer he could have given. In opposition to what Joram could or would do, he had told what Jehovah both could and would do on the morrow. Such a rejoinder was not only apt in the circumstances, it was needful for the prophet himself. There are seasons when the servants of God, forsaken by men, and not encouraged by any token of success or sympathy, have no other consolation than that of falling back upon their Divine commission. Not unfrequently the only support left us is the assurance, that the Word which we preach is indeed the Word of the Living God. Any doubt on that point would make us unutterably miserable, for in this lies our only felt comfort. It is then that evidence of the reality of our message, personal assurance of the glad tidings of marvellous heavenly deliverance from imminent death, is so precious to our own souls. We need such joy in the Lord to sustain us in our work; and never do we preach the Gospel of Christ with more boldness and fervour, than when, cut off from earthly support, or surrounded by outward difficulties, we ourselves feel cast upon it; and from its Divine character derive our encouragement in the work. And so Elisha himself may perhaps have needed such a message, thus abruptly given, quite as much as any of his hearers.

The king had listened to it in utter bewilderment; even "the elders" of Israel must have wondered. One only in this assembly heard it all unmoved. The chosen counsellor of Joram, "the lord on whose hand the king leaned," seems to have been a man of much stronger character than his master. He was out-and-out of the world, a courtier, from whose heart constant contact with the world had driven what little feeling he might naturally have possessed. Nothing is so hardening, or rather so destructive, to all genuine feeling of the heart as intimate converse with the world. The more we know of the world the less we like it, or indeed anything else. This is one of the miseries connected with wealth and position, that our enjoyment of what they offer is endangered by its very possession. Only very rich and well-watered soil will preserve its verdure under the constant glare of a fierce sun. It needs a very fresh heart, or rather one kept fresh by the springs of Divine grace, to preserve faith or affection of any kind under the strong light of a knowledge of the world.

The courtier was too well bred to contradict Elisha directly. It would have sounded irreligious, and it would have been of no use. He did not even openly sneer. But there is a cutting harshness, a dryness and coldness about his tone which seems to freeze one's very life-blood. "Behold, if Jehovah would make windows in heaven, might this thing be?" It is always heartless and cruel to make sport of the religious hopes of others. A scoffer must be a bad man. But in this instance there is something peculiarly offensive in the irony of his suggestion. By what means is this abundance to be brought about? By natural or by supernatural agency? It is impossible by natural means, and therefore we must look for windows in the sky, out of which this plenty may flow. And yet it was just by *natural* means that God would send all this supply. The mode of effecting His purpose was very similar to that so lately pursued in bringing the Syrian host into the midst of Samaria. Supposing, from whatever cause, a panic to arise in the camp of the enemy, their sudden flight would naturally lead to the result foretold. There was nothing strange after that in the fact that fine flour and barley would be sold at such a price in the gate of Samaria. Yet who could have foreseen such a panic? But

God might in many other ways have effected the same result. He often pours corn into famishing Samaria without raining it from heaven. A result which, viewed by itself, would seem miraculous, is often brought about in what seems the natural course of events.

Let us mark that in this lies the mystery of His Providence. When we ask of God health for the sick, bread for the hungry, deliverance for those in danger, we ask in each case for that which is a miracle; and yet as He brings it about it is not a miracle. A ship passes by and picks up the shipwrecked sailor; unexpected succour comes to the needy. All this, by natural means and in the natural course, brings about what really is a supernatural result. And therefore we pray. Pestilence stalks through the land. The direction and suggestion of those around is, to observe the sanitary laws on which the comparative safety of a district depends. And this is so far right, for we may not disobey God's law in Nature any more than that in His Word, and we will not presume to ask Him for help where we have disregarded His directions. But this is not all, nor nearly all. We will pray as well as work, and pray all the better that we have worked well. We will use what means we can; they are scanty enough. The result depends on His blessing. Men say, on a concurrence of circumstances, and that, if we only knew all, we should clearly perceive how, in the natural course, such concurrence must have led to the happy result for which Christians give thanks to God, as if the help had come straight out of heaven! Be it so. If we had known the "concurrence,"* we would have understood it, though at

---

* It is very remarkable that in the parable of the Good Samaritan, the expression which our Authorized Version renders "chance" really means "concurrence" ($συγκυρία$) : "And by a concurrence (viz. of circumstances) there came down," etc. (St. Luke x. 31).

present we do not know it, nor are likely to know it better in the future. But who caused this "running together" of the circumstances, who brought them together? And so long as our philosophy is unable to bring them together, or even to understand the concurrence, we will continue to trust in, and to pray to the God Who can, and Who will control all things. This is our philosophy of prayer; our theology of it is derived from the promises of the Bible; and our joy in it flows from manifold experience of the working of our God in the past.

The reply of the prophet to the lordly courtier solemnly appeals to us all. "Behold, thou shalt see it with thine eyes, but shalt not eat thereof." The unbelieving and the scoffer will indeed, in that great day of marvellous revelation, see it all, yet not enjoy it. In measure they already see without partaking in the peace, the joy, and the provision of God's saved people. But the warning comes home to Christians also. How often do they, by their unbelief, deprive themselves of rich blessings? We have not, because we ask not. We complain of darkness, coldness, and inefficiency, when we might have all things and abound. We have recourse to many devices, instead of fleeing to the One sure Refuge.

> Blind unbelief is sure to err,
>   And scan His work in vain;
> God is His own interpreter,
>   And He will make it plain!

Oh, that in all our dangers and difficulties, in all our thinking, and in our every undertaking, we took our stand firmly upon the Word of God, and believingly pleaded His promises! Then would all things be possible to us, and

> Our cheerful song would oftener be,
>   "Hear what the Lord has done for me."

CHAPTER XXIII.

STRANGE TIDINGS.

"And there were four leprous men at the entering in of the gate: and they said one to another, Why sit we here until we die? If we say, We will enter into the city, then the famine is in the city, and we shall die there: and if we sit still here, we die also. Now therefore come, and let us fall unto the host of the Syrians: if they save us alive, we shall live; and if they kill us, we shall but die. And they rose up in the twilight, to go unto the camp of the Syrians: and when they were come to the uttermost part of the camp of Syria, behold, there was no man there. For the Lord had made the host of the Syrians to hear a noise of chariots, and a noise of horses, even the noise of a great host: and they said one to another, Lo, the king of Israel hath hired against us the kings of the Hittites, and the kings of the Egyptians, to come upon us. Wherefore they arose and fled in the twilight, and left their tents, and their horses, and their asses, even the camp as it was, and fled for their life. And when these lepers came to the uttermost part of the camp, they went into one tent, and did eat and drink, and carried thence silver, and gold, and raiment, and went and hid it; and came again, and entered into another tent, and carried thence also, and went and hid it. Then they said one to another, We do not well: this day is a day of good tidings, and we hold our peace: if we tarry till the morning light, some mischief will come upon us: now therefore come, that we may go and tell the king's household."—2 KINGS vii. 3-9.

THE hours crept on wearily in Samaria, perhaps more wearily than before; for strange tidings had spread through the city. Men had hastily come in and told it in their homes, and then as hastily gone again to gather further news, or to speak of it to their neighbours and friends. The people moved about the streets and market-place with that indefinite restlessness which betokens some great general expectation. They discussed not a party-question, nor one between the prophet and the king. It was a matter which only too deeply concerned every inhabitant of the doomed city. Had the interview between Joram and Elisha taken place before even fewer witnesses, not an hour would have elapsed before its results were repeated in every house in Samaria. How that interview itself terminated we know not, and care not; probably the people also cared little for it. It may have been suddenly broken up, and each man have gone whither his feelings towards Jehovah led him—some to believe, some to pray, some to cavil, some to doubt, some to wait; but every man to tell of what he had heard. Thus, on that day, in the streets of Samaria, every one must have preached the Gospel of Jehovah, truly or of pretence. It was a universal proclamation of the wonders of the Lord, such as only found its counterpart in Jerusalem on the day of Pentecost under the Apostolic announcement, and will again find it on that other Pentecost, when what has been whispered in secret shall be proclaimed on the house-tops.

What a day of excitement! These tidings coming so soon after the other, after that horrible tale about the two mothers, and after the woman's frenzied complaint! There must have been in Samaria not a few who had known that mother, known the dead child, remembered the day, and perhaps recalled some circumstances connected with the tragedy. The story had quickly spread; its horrors might well send a thrill through every heart, and cause each household to feel its own a twofold load of misery. And now this announcement of the prophet, with all its incredible hope, with the report of what "the lord" had answered, and the prophet had rejoined! To judge from his bearing and from the after-history, my lord was not a popular favourite in Samaria; yet every man instinctively felt that, as so often, unbelief had rational probabilities on its side. On the other hand, the judgment upon the courtier had been so calmly and authoritatively pronounced, that the waverers once more wavered. Meanwhile, as the hours slowly passed, no visible change of any kind appeared. Mothers tried to quiet their children over their scanty evening repast by telling what, as a matter of hope, was fading out of their own hearts. The daylight was slowly creeping out, the darkness was slowly creeping in, and yet no sign of hope, nor relief! The twilight, so sudden and brief in the East, had given place to evening, and evening had fallen dark around the city. A weary guard came to relieve a weary guard, and the night closed in. Few would know other than fitful and broken slumbers that night, startled by each sound, only to find themselves starting at their own dreams.

Yet, most of this weary time, Samaria was truly and really free. The besieging army was no longer around its walls. Danger, famine, and want were all past. Yet Samaria knew it not, and watched, mourned, and suffered, as if all its misery were unremoved. How often is it so with us! We misunderstand the great fundamental fact of the Gospel. While attending to the command to believe, we forget, or fail to realise, in Whom we are to believe. We are to believe God; we are to believe the message of His love; we are to believe the offer of His mercy; we are to believe in a Redeemer Who died for us, and rose for us, and for us sitteth at the Right Hand of God. Samaria is free. God *is* reconciled: Christ *has* made an end of sin, and *has* brought in everlasting righteousness. These are facts, whether we believe them or not, whether we accept or reject them. "God is in Christ, reconciling the world unto Himself." Our faith is not to move Him to come near to us in Christ, nor to become reconciled. Christ *has* made reconciliation; and it is there, whether, like the Samaritans, we are ignorant of our deliverance, or not. There is the fountain; there is the bread; there is the Saviour. Having, as sinners, felt our need of such provision, faith has simply to realise it as made for us, and to lay hold on this provision as announced to us in the Gospel. Faith does not procure anything for us; faith sees that all *has been* procured for us by our Blessed Saviour. It simply accepts what He has given; and therefore we may expect instantaneous conversion, since all that is requisite is to credit God's testimony concerning the finished and accepted work of His dear Son, our Lord and Saviour Jesus Christ.

It was almost symbolical of its condition that Samaria should, as it were, have hung out such a dark escutcheon as the four lepers "at the entering in of the gate." Apostate from God as the majority of the people were, the Levitical law which banished the leper outside the city was still observed in its literality, even at a time like this. And so, between the heathen enemies and perishing Israel, banished by the law, were those who represented death under the law. Jewish tradition has it, that these four lepers were Gehazi and his three sons. If so, it would have been a marked retribution that he, who sold himself for two talents of silver and two changes of garments, should now perish outside the gates of Samaria in face of the Syrians. Certainly these lepers spoke and acted as Gehazi might have been expected to have done in the circumstances. Yet probably, according to our notions of the fitness of things, Gehazi and his three sons, or similar personages, would have been the last to whom the fulfilment of Elisha's prediction should have been committed. But God often chooses what to us would seem the most unlikely instruments; instruments as unconscious of their work as the tools in the workman's hands, that so the work may be seen to be of Him, and the glory all His. Thus the weak things of the world have been made to confound the things which are mighty, "and base things of the world, and things which are despised, hath God chosen." Not that the means are inappropriate to their purpose, but that they require the Divine power to make them adequate. The living voice is the most appropriate means for making known the Gospel; but who would have chosen such preachers and such preaching? The most suitable means for providing plenty in Samaria, was to drive the Syrians from their well-stored camp. But who would have chosen four famishing, thievish lepers to communicate this benefit to Samaria?

Yet lepers may also be used, and used for much good. Let no one say: I am an outcast, I cannot do anything for God or for man. You can. That mysterious bond which connects man with man, gives to each power and influence over the other. When listening to the story of a humble labourer or missionary—what this man or that woman said and did—you sometimes feel as if to attach importance to all this, and make it the subject of serious consideration, were like self-delusion or elaborate trifling. It is not so; for the springs of life rise deep and still. All this speaking and doing, however humble, is not of doubtful importance. These are the many-coloured threads, which, woven together, make up the web of our social life. Every man, woman, and child is of importance; for they all have immortal souls, with unlimited capacity for good or for evil. If there is nothing without its use in God's wide world, not the tiny insect, that proudly marches with its gold-dotted coat of mail, nor on the upland moor the unheeded floweret, with its exquisite little petals, all bound together in one, and each delicately hued by heaven's own pencil, shall not man, immortal man, *any* man, be capable of use, and of conscious use, or of service? To live would be dreary indeed, if it did not also mean to serve; for it is this possibility of service which constitutes the Godlike in our nature. God does not separate the rich and the poor; before Him there are neither rich nor poor, only the loving and the unloving, the serving and the non-serving. It needs not wealth of money, of intellect, of knowledge, or of influence—only wealth of love, gotten from His own eternal treasury of love. "Inasmuch as ye have done it unto one of the least of these My brethren, ye have done it unto Me." And the Lord may and does use all as instruments in His working. One condition only has to be fulfilled —that *He* shall have all the glory. Willingly or unwillingly, so far as we are concerned; willingly to our honour, unwillingly to our shame, but certainly He will have all the glory.

So those four lepers were between Samaria and the camp— as many among us are between famine and plenty. In the extremity of their need, they began to reason, like the prodigal son in the parable. Such reasoning with ourselves in our great need has the advantage of being honest and truthful, and therefore it is generally just and trustworthy. "Why sit we here until we die?" Why, indeed? Anything but quietly to sit down and to perish! Here is their alternative. "If we say, We will enter into the city, then the famine is in the city, and we shall die there: and if we sit still here, we die also." Most correctly reasoned. Either way certain destruction awaited them. So we say to those who have become sensible of their guilt and need. If you attempt to go into the doomed city, even if you were to succeed, you would perish. If you remain where you are, you will equally perish. What then? "Now, therefore, come, and let us fall unto the host of the Syrians: if they save us alive, we shall live; and if they kill us, we shall but die." Truly, the children of this world are wiser in their generation than the children of light. The sinner, awakened and afraid, often reasons thus: The Gospel, indeed, bids all come to Christ; and the work of Christ is sufficient to procure acceptance with God to the most guilty. But may *I* come? shall I, who have so sinned against light and truth, not be rejected? How shall I come, or how may I know whether I have really gone to the Saviour, and am pardoned? But this is to mix truth with error. Even upon the supposition made: If we were to continue in our present condition, we must certainly perish, while on the other hand, we fear, that if we apply to Christ, we might fail. Still, we may succeed and be saved. Thus we have the certainty of death, as against the possibility of life. Which, then, will it be wise to choose? But is the supposition correct? On what part of the Word of God can such fears be founded, or by what experience, of our own or of others, can it be supported? Is not the opposite of such a suggestion the fact? There is not a truth more clearly or repeatedly stated in Scripture, nor more fully borne out by the records of the past, than that of God's absolute willingness to receive *all* that come unto Him. David and Saul of Tarsus; Hezekiah and Peter; the adulterous woman and the Magdalene, with countless thousands in heaven and upon earth, are there to attest it. But have *we* ever made trial of it? Why not; and why not *now?* "The Spirit and the Bride say, Come. And let him that heareth say, Come; and let him that is athirst come. And whosoever will, let him take the water of life freely."

The brief twilight was fading out as the four lepers "rose up to go unto the camp of the Syrians." Stealthily, and not without often halting, they proceeded, for darkness might insure greater safety, or secure the possibility of flight. At last they reached the place where pickets and outposts might have been expected. Everywhere absolute silence prevailed, and they passed on unchallenged. Had they not been seen, or were the Syrians so confident as to neglect the ordinary precautions of war? or was it intended to allow them to go on till retreat was impossible? But there was not time for reflection now; they had chosen their part. So they passed still on. The camp had evidently been occupied, for they heard the neighing of horses, and the watchfires were burning. The four lepers crept along the rows of white tents. No sound, nor sign of life. What deep sleep held the Syrians! They would listen at one tent and at another, but no sound of man was heard. They came "to the uttermost part of the camp of Syria," but "behold, there was no man there." This state of uncertainty could no longer be endured. So one cautiously looked into what seemed an officer's tent. It was empty. But on the rude camp table might be still the untouched evening meal, just as if waiting for the arrival of the guests. For a while the lepers waited and listened. Then they went in, "and did eat and drink," their sense of security increasing as they found themselves undisturbed. The rich repast finished, they went out again to listen. Still no sound betokened the approach of men. So they carried out of that tent all that it contained of "silver, and gold, and raiment, and went and hid it" in some place of security beyond the camp. Then they "came again, and entered into another tent, and carried thence also, and went and hid it."

By this time, and the first cravings of greed sufficiently appeased for them to think, the lepers must have been convinced that, unaccountable as it might seem, the camp of the Syrians was in reality deserted. Indeed, at that very time the once proud host, scattered and broken up in the darkness, was hastily fleeing towards Jordan, nor resting till its waters were interposed between them and their supposed pursuers. The reason of that panic was natural, its origin supernatural, though no doubt also brought about by natural means. In the twilight the lepers had risen up to go unto the camp of the Syrians. In the same twilight confusion and terror were settling upon that camp of the Syrians. As the shadows of forms and objects were lengthening out into one great shadow all around, it seemed, first to one, and then to another, then to many, and then to all, as if they heard strange noises here and there, toward the flank, in front and in rear. What could it be? It was not the rushing of wind, nor was it the falling of rain, nor was it the bursting of waters. To their excited imagination, as every moment they heard it more distinctly, it seemed to approach nearer and still nearer. Evidently it came from those hills in the immediate vicinity, on which the dark shadows had already settled. It was in vain to peer into that darkness, whatever it might conceal. And still the mysterious sounds from the two opposite directions in front and rear continued, and seemed to grow as they listened. The boldest, who had at first laughed his comrades to scorn, now heard this inexplicable something, and the most unconcerned admitted that it was no ordinary noise. Whether one suggested it, or whether the question put at a hastily summoned council of war had been overheard, it spread, as flames over the dry grass, from end to end of the camp. On this side, over these hills, "the kings of the Hittites," and on that side, over those hills, "the kings of the Egyptians" are coming! "The king of Israel hath hired" them; hence the long and patient resistance of Samaria!

Their indefinite fears now took definite shape. The sounds which they heard were "the noise of chariots, and the noise of horses, even the noise of a great host." A sudden panic seized the Syrians, who, in the fast gathering darkness, expected to meet suddenly and unpreparedly a threefold attack, probably at fearful odds. From this side would descend the Hittites, from that the Egyptians, and there lay dark and frowning Samaria. Only one way of escape seemed open:

along that plain and towards Jordan. If they could only flee unperceived, so as to elude their assailants, and gain time! So they "left their tents, and their horses, and their asses, even the camp as it was, and fled for their life." An army well appointed, and which, under other circumstances, would not have feared to encounter an enemy, fled, pursued by no man, only by their own fears! What if, after that panic had unmanned and scattered them, an enemy had dashed amongst the fugitives? There is none so bold who may not tremble and flee if pursued by his own thoughts. The fearful sound may have no farther reality, at least not that which had been attributed to it; yet it is sufficient to make the most unconcerned rise up and flee into the night. What if then met by a real pursuer? What if terror and attempted flight were followed by judgment and vengeance, and long unheeded guilt and speedy destruction to overtake the fugitive?

But of this strange event the four lepers were ignorant. They only knew that the camp remained as it had been, and that the Syrians had deserted it. Here was all the abundance which had been stored up for a perhaps protracted siege. It was all without owner now. When the Lord God sendeth deliverance to His people, He will do so in a marvellous manner. It needs neither the Hittites, nor the Egyptians, nor even Israel. They shall hear a sound, where yet there is no sound; they shall not be discomfited, but they shall flee. And they will leave all behind them—horses, asses, gold, silver, changes of raiment, provisions. They will leave it behind for Israel. The enemies prepare weapons, and lay up stores against us. Thus in our days their wisdom and might, their learning and researches are mostly all enlisted against the cause and truth of God. What of that? They will flee, and when they flee, all will belong to Israel. All their discoveries, all their achievements and treasures, will be found not to be opposed, but to contribute to the cause of our God. Therefore, being so persuaded, we are in no way afraid of the result, if only the word of prophecy be with us.

But these four lepers now began to be conscious of yet another fact, which, alas, seems more difficult of apprehension to many in our days. "Then they said one to another, We do not well: this day is a day of good tidings, and we hold our peace: if we tarry till the morning light, some mischief will come upon us: now therefore come, that we may go and tell the king's household." Sound, patriotic, and even religious, though somewhat tardy, reasoning, which might well come from the lips of a Gehazi! As with so many in the world, the first impulse had been that of selfishness and sensuality: eat and drink; the next, that of possession: take it, carry it thence, and hide it, to lie there concealed, or to be added to the other two talents, which were the price paid for his leprosy. And what then—after these two impulses have been satisfied, or at least, their cravings appeased? Then, fear of the mischief which may come upon them, if they tarry till the morning light; a religiousness sprung not from love, though they bring "good tidings," but from fear of the consequences on the morrow!

There is yet another, and a very solemn, lesson here to all who are truly the servants of the Lord Jesus Christ. This day *is* a day of glad tidings. Do we then hold our peace? How do we, who realise this blessedness, make it known to others, both directly and indirectly, by speech, by deed, by life, and by service? What are we saying and doing for the Lord Jesus, Who loved us, and died for us? Or shall we "tarry till the morning light;" and will not, in that case, "some mischief come upon us," when the Master asketh of each an account of his opportunities and of his work?

CHAPTER XXIV.

BREAD ENOUGH AND TO SPARE.

"So they came and called unto the porter of the city: and they told them, saying, We came to the camp of the Syrians, and, behold, there was no man there, neither voice of man, but horses tied, and asses tied, and the tents as they were. And he called the porters; and they told it to the king's house within. And the king arose in the night, and said unto his servants, I will now show you what the Syrians have done to us. They know that we be hungry; therefore are they gone out of the camp to hide themselves in the field, saying, When they come out of the city, we shall catch them alive, and get into the city. And one of his servants answered and said, Let some take, I pray thee, five of the horses that remain, which are left in the city (behold, they are as all the multitude of Israel that are left in it: behold, I say, they are even as all the multitude of the Israelites that are consumed:) and let us send and see. They took therefore two chariot horses; and the king sent after the host of the Syrians, saying, Go and see. And they went after them unto Jordan: and, lo, all the way was full of garments and vessels, which the Syrians had cast away in their haste. And the messengers returned, and told the king. And the people went out, and spoiled the tents of the Syrians. So a measure of fine flour was sold for a shekel, and two measures of barley for a shekel, according to the word of the Lord. And the king appointed the lord on whose hand he leaned to have the charge of the gate: and the people trode upon him in the gate, and he died, as the man of God had said, who spake when the king came down to him. And it came to pass as the man of God had spoken to the king, saying, Two measures of barley for a shekel, and a measure of fine flour for a shekel, shall be to-morrow about this time in the gate of Samaria: and that lord answered the man of God, and said, Now, behold, if the Lord should make windows in heaven, might such a thing be? And he said, Behold, thou shalt see it with thine eyes, but shalt not eat thereof. And so it fell out unto him: for the people trode upon him in the gate, and he died."—2 KINGS vii. 10-20.

THERE are times when that which otherwise might only seem strange, is felt to be exceedingly painful. The glaring incongruity, the manifest folly implied in the pursuit of certain objects becomes inexpressibly sad, when the dignity of an immortal soul or its eternal interests are at stake. Foppery and love of amusements in old age; the clutch of money by a hand stiffening in death; the race of ambition which, whether won or lost, is sure to end in disaster—these, and many similar scenes, enacted every day, are sufficient to make serious men weep for their fellows. Passion is always unreasonable, but when it overshadows a life, its all-controlling power can only evoke wonderment, almost indignation. Yet it would not be difficult to find parallels in daily life to these lepers, who not only ate and drank to the full, but carried away "silver and gold and raiment," unconscious of the painful contrast between their condition and the objects which they so carefully secreted.

The night had far advanced before the lepers reached the gate of Samaria. Tardily repairing a grievous neglect, they now combined with their fear of consequences an amount of religious self-complacency, incredible, if it were not of such common occurrence. They chid themselves, yet almost in a tone of self-laudation and very gently, for not doing before what they now only did, partly because they had already got all they wanted, and partly from fear. But, truly, it cannot be too often repeated that "we do not well," if in this "day of good tidings" "we hold our peace." Every Christian has not only work to do, but a special work is assigned to him by the appointment of God, and another cannot do it for him. It is as if a commander ranged a line for battle. Each soldier holds his post and must do his work, and, in a certain sense, the failure of one is the breaking up of the whole line. Without presumption, we may say that God leaves His people in this world, not merely to fulfil in them His own purpose of sanctification and grace, but to employ them in His own service. If in ordinary life it is regarded as wrong, when put in a position of trust, to discharge its obligations "indirectly," or by proxy, can such services to the cause of God be acceptable in His sight?

But here also it may be said, that the root of the evil lies in unbelief. Alas, many, if they avowed the truth, would confess that they never have had a "day of good tidings," not merely pleasant at the time, but which left no sorrow behind, and never caused a regret that they had been heard. There is not an unalloyed pleasure on earth apart from true religion. God has given us much that is good and pleasant; but the fairest flower withers, and the brightest sun sets. Besides, all is so tempered that we never can find below what always and fully satisfies the heart. But there are "good tidings;" so good, that they will make the oldest heart grow fresh and young; so good, that they will carry a gladness that shall outlast time itself; so good, that God Himself spake them, angels sang them, and men were content to die for them. They are the tidings of God's love to us in Christ Jesus our Saviour. When these come home to us, individually, as sent to us by God the Father, realised for us by God the Son, and applied to us by God the Spirit, we bless the Lord "Jesus Christ and God, even our Father, Which hath loved us, and hath given us everlasting consolation and good hope through grace," and we pray that He may still "comfort our hearts, and establish us in every good word and work."

It was far on in the night, when the commander in charge of the principal entrance to the city heard voices without, demanding speech of him. He could scarcely have been prepared for the communication which the lepers now made. Late as it was, such tidings brooked no delay, and he hastily despatched some of the guard to carry them to the king's palace. The hurried steps of the soldiers through the silent streets of Samaria must have brought many a watcher to the lattice. "What is it?" And, perhaps, before the guard had returned from the palace to their post, it was known through the greater part of the city that the Syrian camp was said to be deserted, and that tidings to this effect had been carried to the king.

While the period of brief rest was thus giving place to a new and even more intense excitement than had been witnessed during the previous day, a most humiliating scene was enacting in the palace. If ungodly men bear themselves ill in sorrow, they bear themselves still worse in joy, and, worst, when the issue is doubtful. In the multitude of devices and shifts, in the balancing of chances and possibilities, there is such utter absence of any firm purpose or lofty thought, as to make only this plain: that nothing is plain. They are confident where they should fear, and they see difficulties where none exist. Only in this they are consistent, to take a mean, low, contracted, selfish view of all things. Joram had been roused from his sleep to hear the wondrous tidings. It was not long before his more intimate advisers had gathered in his chamber. One of the first suggestions which, in the circumstances, we might have expected, would have been of Elisha and his prediction. But not a word of this was whispered. So far as appears, no allusion was made to it by any, least of all by the king. He did not see Jehovah in it, nor even hoped to do so. His mind only reflected himself. It was the same man who had insisted that Jehovah had called the three kings together to kill them; who had rent his clothes, declaring that Ben-hadad had sent Naaman in order to pick a quarrel with him; who had rushed among the bewildered Syrians in the market-place, proposing to smite them. "Let favour be showed to the wicked, yet will he not learn righteousness: in the land of uprightness will he deal unjustly, and will not behold the majesty of the Lord."

It is always so. Outward circumstances will make no

difference, while the heart remains closed against the Voice of the Lord. Sorrow or joy, judgment or deliverance, find a Jehoram as he had been before. It is not in them to work a change; the soul must be affected by His grace, before men give heed to His dealings. Here is the outcome of all that King Jehoram had learned from the events of yesterday, or, indeed, from what he had seen and heard during all his previous life: "I will now show you what the Syrians have done unto us. They know that we be hungry; therefore are they gone out of the camp to hide themselves in the field, saying, When they come out of the city we shall catch them alive, and get into the city." And this is all that he remembers of God, of Elisha, of the promises, and of the gracious purpose of mercy! Such sordid, contracted, foolish calculations, out of which God is kept, even though He has spoken in His Word and Providence, form the sum total of what many have learned during a long life, and carry with them to their graves.

Had the opinion of the king prevailed, Samaria would have remained a doomed, famine-stricken city. Would no one, then, make trial, or suggest another alternative? Would all sit still and perish, while there was bread enough and to spare? The application of these questions to many in our days needs not further illustration. But there is another lesson, important for us all to learn. Many of our cares and difficulties are, like those of King Jehoram, imaginary; they spring from unbelief and distrust. We do not rise to the height of God's promises, and therefore we remain on the level of our own thoughts. One factor has been omitted from all such calculations—the promises of God. What of the morrow? But then, who knows whether to us there will be a morrow; or, if there is, where it may find the Syrians? A mountain-road looks more steep before than after we have commenced the ascent. And, besides, faith can remove mountains. These are truths to be treasured up against the hour of need. For it is, indeed, most difficult to realise, not that there is a God in heaven, but that, in the fullest sense of the expression, He is the Living God.

In that midnight council there was one who, if he failed in strength of anticipating faith, was at least so far taught as to be humbled, and to take a right view of the present state of Israel. His language reads like that of one chastened and softened, and who therefore considered the end of things. His words were sad, but they embodied the only remnant of hope: "Let some take, I pray thee, five of the horses that remain, which are left in the city (behold they are as all the multitude of Israel that are left in it, and as all the multitude of Israel that are consumed),* and let us send and see." It can make but little difference to send five horsemen on even a forlorn hope. Whatever may betide them, it cannot be worse than what has already befallen many in Israel, and what will shortly befall many more. If this was the logic of despair, it was at least sound reasoning. And why shall we not make similar experiment? We complain of doubts, of darkness, of want of peace. Why not go forth, and see for ourselves? Why encompass ourselves with imaginary difficulties in going, when to stay is to surround ourselves with real and certain sorrow?

And so God had once more at the right time the right instrumentality in readiness. The appeal to the common sense of the council, supported as it was by bitter experience, prevailed where the Word of God had been unavailing. The king despatched on this errand two war-chariots, probably in order that if one were attacked, the other might make its way

* This is the correct rendering of the passage, and the alteration, though very slight, shows the proper meaning of the words.

back to the city. Only the fleetest and strongest horses were used for such purpose in warfare; only the stoutest and bravest soldiers manned these chariots. No doubt abundantly refreshed for their difficult task from the scanty provisions still left, they prepared to sally forth. Grey morning was already breaking, and in its cold light objects attained distinctness. By this time the streets must have been thronged with citizens, pale with eagerness and excitement. How many voices would cheer the charioteers as they swiftly sped; how many eyes follow them from the ramparts, as they rapidly moved through the zigzag of Syrian tents that dotted the plain beneath. The city-gate had opened and closed again. Certainly no outposts had arrested the chariots; and now they were lost to view. That fresh morning air must have felt so different from the stifling atmosphere of the city, and alike charioteer and horse would enjoy their new-found liberty! How they must have bent forward, and bounded onward! Through the camp of Syria, and farther, still farther along that road—it was not necessary to ask which, for the Syrians had marked it. Strewed along the way lay what had been cast aside as useless weapons; garments thrown off to make the flight easier, and vessels carried from the camp, but not carried further in the struggle for life; while perhaps here and there were forms that had drooped and fallen never to rise, or footsore, worn men, fugitives seeking shelter. Onward and still onward, over the undulating plain; onward, till the rays of the sun were reflected in golden light from the fords of Jordan! And still everywhere the same scene of defeat and confusion! What a picture this of the road of life, strewed with the wreck of hopes, pursuits, and occupations, when those who have hastened along its course have passed to the other side of Jordan. What a picture this also, when in that other morning light the swift messengers of the King shall pass to the boundary-line of Jordan, and back again, along a highway marked by what had once been cherished, by what had been attempted to be taken along in the flight, but ultimately cast aside as utterly useless. Lost, lost—all lost; and this is what remains on the soil of Israel of Syria's proud host!

The charioteers drew rein. They turned their horses' heads, and even more swiftly passed back along the course which they had come. The sun was standing high in the heavens, when first the turrets, then the ramparts, then the houses of Samaria came again in view. Eyes even more eager than theirs must have descried them in the far distance. On the highest watchtower stood the watchman. A spot in the distance; it moves—no, two spots! They neared; yes, they were the king's two chariots. Welcome, messengers of liberty and of peace! The gates swung open and closed again upon the two chariots. The horses were covered with foam, and the men wearied with labour and excitement; but it was all true: the Syrians had fled beyond Jordan, and Samaria was free! And now who will hold this swaying populace? They will burst through every barrier, like a pent-up stream. Woe to him who stands in their way! Fling all the gates wide open. Men, women, and children, go out, hasten out. They feast, they spoil; they take of all they see, till they are weary of the taking; they revel, they are drunk in their madness of joy; they are unrestrained and unrestrainable.

Who will hold this swaying populace? I will: I Jehoram, I their king! But what of Elisha all this time? To all appearance, neither he nor his God were remembered by the king or by the majority of the people. And yet the Word of the Lord had been but partially fulfilled! What was not recognised in His dispensation of mercy must be felt in that of His judgments. The excitement and turmoil in Samaria rendered advisable some extraordinary measures for preserving order. The king would appoint one to the temporary command of the city, on whose coolness and determination he could place implicit reliance. Who so fit for that office as "the lord on whose hand he leaned"? From what we remember of him in the interview between Jehoram and Elisha, he certainly possessed all the needed qualifications; only that his power of ruling would be derived from an unbending, proud will, and not based upon that winning kindness and known high principle which can alone secure respect and obedience in times of public excitement. The confidential adviser of the king may have been obeyed, but neither his character nor his demeanour, as known to us from this history, would make him popular. And so he was the most unsuitable man on that day "to have the charge of the gate."

But what sudden madness could have seized the king to appoint this lord, or the lord to accept such a charge, with the prediction of Elisha as yet only half fulfilled! Fuller evidence could scarcely have been given, how utterly and hopelessly insensible Jehoram was to the dealings of God. Accordingly, this was the last warning and message from God which Jehoram ever received. It was the last time also that he encountered Elisha. Henceforth, only judgment was to be executed; for the time of long-suffering and patience, with its many visitations of mercy, had passed. The doom pronounced upon the house of Ahab was to be no longer delayed. Jehoram, "often reproved," still hardening his heart, was nigh unto destruction. What solemn lesson this to us, who are still within sound of God's voice, and within reach of God's provision!

As for the lord of Samaria, he took command of the city-gate, utterly unconscious of what so soon would befall him.

Heedless of the warning, he rushed to his own destruction. Did he ever look up to heaven, remembering his taunting jeer about the windows which might there be opened? Did he see—not a window opened, but a window closed in the heavens above him? Was no friendly voice raised in warning? Probably the details of yesterday's interview with Elisha had already faded from his mind; for the ungodly for a time forget their sins, even when swift vengeance is about to overtake them. Thus too many go on unconcerned, who would tremble could they behold the unseen finger lifted in warning, or recall the unheeded voice, " Cut it down, why cumbereth it the ground?"

The sun had not yet declined in the sky when the new governor of Samaria stood in the gate. In vain did he try to command order. His voice was not heard in the noise and tumult of those who passed out and came in, and in the creaking of the heavily laden carts which carried the spoil into Samaria. In the gate of Samaria, and facing the multitude, now gathered also the fortunate owners of the spoil to dispose of their merchandise. Trade had long been neglected, except in those melancholy bargains in which wealth tried to obtain the most wretched supplies for its wants. Now, every vehicle had been put in requisition, and the horses and asses of the Syrians had helped to draw all this plenty into Samaria. There gathered the sellers and buyers, chatting, shouting, bargaining, joking in the unbounded licence of such a recoil from despair to exultation. There, literally, and perhaps unconscious of fulfilling the prediction, were they offering for sale " a measure of fine flour for a shekel"! "two measures of barley for a shekel"! A very Babel of voices and confusion! But what were they to do with all this abundance; and who would venture to stop or to order them from the spot? His commands not heeded, the governor threw himself among them to enforce respect and obedience by his presence. Vain attempt! The multitude still passed to and fro, regardless of lord or king. Was it in anger and purposely, or was it by accident that they bore him down? His voice was stifled in the noise of those who offered their flour and barley for sale. Hundreds of feet passing and repassing "trode upon him in the gate." When at last he was rescued, all that remained of the proud lord was a mangled corpse.

And so, both in blessing and in judgment, "it fell out," "according to the word of Jehovah."

CHAPTER XXV.

FAITH AND ITS RECOMPENSE.

"Then spake Elisha unto the woman, whose son he had restored to life, saying, Arise, and go thou and thine household, and sojourn wheresoever thou canst sojourn : for the Lord hath called for a famine ; and it shall also come upon the land seven years. And the woman arose, and did after the saying of the man of God: and she went with her household, and sojourned in the land of the Philistines seven years. And it came to pass at the seven years' end, that the woman returned out of the land of the Philistines: and she went forth to cry unto the king for her house and for her land. And the king talked with Gehazi the servant of the man of God, saying, Tell me, I pray thee, all the great things that Elisha hath done. And it came to pass, as he was telling the king how he had restored a dead body to life, that, behold, the woman, whose son he had restored to life, cried to the king for her house and for her land. And Gehazi said, My lord, O king, this is the woman, and this is her son, whom Elisha restored to life. And when the king asked the woman, she told him. So the king appointed unto her a certain officer, saying, Restore all that was hers, and all the fruits of the field since the day that she left the land, even until now."—2 KINGS viii. 1-6.

WAR and famine had passed from the land. But the wounds inflicted upon the unhappy people were not healed when they had ceased to bleed. Altogether the reign of King Jehoram lasted only twelve years. Of these, not less than seven were a period of famine ; how many more passed in war between Israel and Syria, we can only guess from the Scripture narrative. What households must have been desolated during that time, what wretchedness and misery inflicted ! The track of the invading army lay along the most fertile districts, and right into the heart of the country. The scanty remnant which the long drought might have left would be trampled down and swept away by the chariots and horsemen of Syria. That track must have been marked by the ruins of once peaceful villages laid in ashes by the flame of war, their once happy inhabitants driven forth to swell the great crowd of woe—and all this on account of the unrepented national sins, embodied, so to speak, in the person of Jehoram! Surely, the cries of widows and orphans had been coming up into the ears of the Lord God of Sabaoth, and swift judgment would soon overtake the house of Ahab.

Great changes had taken place in the land. The traveller would scarcely have recognised districts once so familiar to him. Blackened ruins where hamlets and farmsteads had been; a broken roof or terrace where once a happy family had gathered at even; charred doors, and swinging remnants of lattices, to mark what had been homes of comfort and of modest wealth. Shunem also was sadly altered since the prophet had last visited it. The "great house" was still there; but it stood empty, or else was tenanted by strangers, who had no claim to its possession. And the family to whom it belonged, where were they—the husband, who in his quiet ways so reminds us of Isaac, that noble-hearted, great woman, and the God-given, God-restored child? They were all gone these many years. Affliction, long and terrible, had visited that household. For God's people are not exempt from the trials which befall others. Though originally caused by sin, and continuing so long as sin continues, they are in the present dispensation as certainly part of God's law in Providence, as storms are part of His law in Nature. The difference between the pious and the ungodly lies in the tenderness and mercy with which affliction is tempered, and in the blessed results which afterwards flow from it. Snow and rain and tempest must come, for we live in a cold clime. But the good gardener has sheltered the tender plant; he tends and nurtures it, and when gladsome spring again woos all into life, the tender plant will burst into fresher and brighter beauty than it had ever worn before.

And the first token of mercy in this chapter of the Shunammite's history, was the message which Elisha brought her. A famine was to desolate the land, the same which had taken Elisha to Gilgal among the sons of the prophets (iv. 38). So far as we know, it came unannounced, except to the woman in Shunem. In the midst of all his work and trials, Elisha had found time to go and warn his friend of the impending calamity. No doubt, God had sent him. Even the manner in which we are told that "Elisha spake unto the woman, whose son he had restored to life," teaches us a most precious lesson. "Arise, and go thou and thine household, and sojourn wheresoever thou canst sojourn: for the Lord hath called for a famine." She is not the "great woman" now, but she who had received great mercy. And the experience of mercy received in the past is pledge of mercies to be received in the future. For God is faithful, and will not forsake His own. A prayer heard in the past is pledge of prayers to be heard in the future. Each blessing we receive is but one link; a link fastened on to other links, the whole forming that chain of sovereign love by which Christ binds a soul unto Himself. His love has two poles—*from eternity to eternity*, and all that lies between them is ours in the covenant of grace.

Never could the Shunammite have stood in greater need of direction. For, as we infer from the silence of the narrative about her husband, she no longer enjoyed his support and protection. The greatest calamity that can befall a woman had befallen her—she was a widow. And now another trial, next in poignancy only to her great sorrow, had come upon her. She had been directed to leave Shunem, and with her household to "go and sojourn wheresoever" she *could* sojourn. To one of her spirit, and with her remembrances, the pang of such a parting must have been sharp indeed. We recall her figure, as in the guest-chamber she had declined Elisha's offer of court patronage, with the proud, or rather dignified, assertion, "I dwell among my own people." If there was one thing dear to her, it was home and family; if there was one thing of which she felt proud, it was her nationality and independence. All this was now swept away; a thing of the past, not to be looked back upon, if her heart was not utterly to fail.

Truly trials come to us in what is dearest, in what we feel most deeply and keenly. Else they would not be *trials*—would not try our faith, and hope, and patience; nor would they be to our sanctification, to make us holier, more entirely God's, to bring and to keep us nearer to Him than we had been. So the wise physician in very pity and kindness applies the remedy to the wound. And the Shunammite must begin life anew; she must take her orphan boy by the hand, and leave her great house, and Shunem, and the land of Israel itself. She must go among strangers, she does not know whither—"sojourn wheresoever" she *can* sojourn, wheresoever God will provide for her a sheltering roof and "daily bread." But the God Who has sent her the message of warning will not forsake her; just as the God Who forewarns us, that if we were without affliction, "whereof all are partakers," we would be bastards, will not forsake us after He has, in His afflictive Providence, owned us as "children."

The very depth and greatness of her trial, however, would help the Shunammite in bearing it. That under God she was now so entirely cast upon her own resources, upon her womanly tact and prudence, upon her strong heart and her great love for her child, would engage her mind, and divert the current of her thoughts from unavailing regrets. She had much to do, and she must do it all herself; she must provide for herself and for her boy; she must decide, she must act. And in very mercy it is often so in our trials. We must brace ourselves to bear such a weight; the tree must be planted firm and deep to stand the storm. If it was the best and most merciful thing for the Shunammite that she had to choose for herself, it was also in accordance with the ordinary course of God's dealings. Our conviction that God will overrule all for the best, that He will support us under trials, and finally deliver us from them, must not engender in us listlessness. We must rouse ourselves, and think of the best means, and act up to our best judgment— and that all the more that we are assured God will bless the means, and help us by the way. None will fight so well as he who is sure of the victor's crown; none will bear and work so well as he that knows deliverance is at hand.

And in her trials she had twofold consolation. For had not the Lord Himself sent to forewarn her? This bitter parting and going had been directed by Himself. It is unspeakable comfort in trial to feel that it comes to us *directly* from God Himself. If only we can realise that this is the Hand of the Lord, it will not be so difficult to add, "Let Him do to me as seemeth good unto Him." Then again the prophet had used to her a peculiar mode of expression. He had said, "Jehovah hath called for a famine." This famine, then, was God-summoned, one of His many messengers come to fulfil His pleasure. If so, it could not ultimately bode ill to His own people. In this also there is great consolation. "Is there evil in a city, and the Lord hath not done it?" Even the real evil, of course not sin, but trial and judgment, in a district, city, or family, is of the Lord, "called for" by Him, sent by Him—one of His veiled angels, whose "working," when put "all together," will be found for "good to them that love God, to them who are the called according to His purpose."

Perhaps the sublimest act in the life of the Shunammite was when in simple faith she obeyed the prophet's direction. For as yet there was plenty in the land, nor any indication of approaching famine, except in the message of Elisha. To yield such absolute obedience in what involved such trial and renunciation of all her own, simply on the ground of the prophetic word, was no ordinary "victory over the world." It was to give up "certainty for uncertainty," and to act directly contrary to all that prudence or worldly wisdom would have suggested. It was like the faith of the sons of the prophets who sat down to the poisonous mess, after Elisha had cast meal into it. But must not ours be, in measure, a similar faith: simple trust in the Word of our Master, when, without further evidence than it, we forsake all things that we may follow Him? And is not that life the happiest in which, like Abraham, we are willing to go, "not knowing whither," so that we go at His bidding? This characteristic of obedience is, indeed, the most marked spiritual feature in the faith of the Old Testament saints. They were *children*, and as such reverent and obedient. Prophet and people, they had simply to obey; the one to say what he was told, the other to do what they were told—and on the same ground, that Jehovah, their covenant-God, was the Living and the True God.

So simple, indeed, had been her faith that, in parting, the Shunammite had made no legal provision to secure her property. She was perfectly sure that the God Who had sent her away would bring her back, and restore to her, or to her child, the inheritance of their fathers. Seven long and weary years, probably of want and difficulty, had passed over them in the land of the Philistines. At the close of the appointed period, punctually to a day, she returned to the land of Israel. We can imagine what her feelings must have been as she neared the well-known scenes of her earlier happiness. All her trials were soon to end; she would again be in Shunem. What then must have been her dismay, when, on arriving, she found her possessions in the occupancy of others, who refused to relinquish their hold of them? And was this what she had waited and hoped for? Disappointment, and again disappointment, only more bitter and hopeless than any that had yet blighted her expectations!

Disappointment and ever disappointment, the world would say, and perhaps some Christians, "in their haste," be tempted to re-echo! And why all this? Every step she had hitherto taken had been in accordance with the will of God. And so, we add, the "will of God" was being "perfected" in her "sanctification." In the land of the Philistines, she had not been of them. Not a moment longer had she remained there than was absolutely necessary. And let us not linger with the world longer than is really needful. We are not to go out of the world, but even while in it let us not be of it, nor tarry amid its associations and pursuits from choice rather than from necessity. We must not remain in it more than the seven years of famine. And what a happy sight, when a whole household, like that of the Shunammite, sets out together to return to the land of Israel!

But even so, trial and disappointment may await us. The great enemy will whisper in our ear: What profit is there in serving the Lord, where is now His promise; and would it not have been wiser and better to have followed the other direction? The neighbours of the Shunammite had, during the seven years of want, perhaps not undergone more privations than she, and they were now in undisturbed possession of their lands, while she was a homeless outcast upon the world. Yet not so; she was an outcast upon God, and richly would He provide for her. Surely, we argue, the love of God to her must have been very great, when He dealt so closely with her. First, she had passed through a long period of silent endurance, till her heart's desire had been granted. Then came the removal of her child; then the death of her husband; then her departure from Shunem; then years of poverty and trial; and now the loss of property and position. What a thorough weaning of all her affections from that which is seen, and what lessons of trustfulness and of dependence on that which is unseen! Whatever she had and loved, she had first to give up, that again she might receive it from the Lord, and hold it of Him and in Him. And so in the case of all His people. When we are told not to love the world, neither the things that are in the world, nor to set our affections on things that are below, we are not directed to renounce natural and right feeling. We are only instructed how to hold these things, as receiving them from God, and enjoying them in God—and so to be ready to relinquish or to have them, still looking up to God. This is to enjoy earthly good without trembling for its loss, and to bear its loss without foregoing its enjoyment. We are neither to be indifferent to earthly blessings, nor to be dependent on them for our happiness. But we are to trust our Father, alike when He gives and when He withholds, and still to rejoice in Him. And this is one object in the progress of our sanctification, where every dealing has its special and definite object, and where we should seek to have by grace the understanding of each trial and the attainment of its every purpose.

In the circumstances, only one course remained to the Shunammite. Her last hope of redress lay in an appeal to the king. Yet how unpromising was such a suit! The whole organisation of the Jewish state, political and religious, was one of directness, if the expression may be used. Judgment depended in most cases upon the justice of the judge, rather than upon the explicitness of the law, just as religion depended rather on direct intercourse with God, than on that full and clear expression of truth which is granted us by the Holy Spirit under the New Testament. Little could at any time have been expected from a Jehoram. Possibly he or one of his subordinates had confiscated or disposed of the Shunammite's property during her long absence. Still, she was in the path of duty when "she went forth to cry unto the king for her house and for her land." It was quite consistent with her former conduct. With the same brave heart, and in the same spirit of Jewish independence in which she had declined court-favours, as dwelling among her own people, she now appealed directly to her king for redress.

And here we observe once more the same mârvellous concurrence of natural circumstances which throughout this history has so frequently led to miraculous deliverance. Only in this case it appeared more distinctly in what men would term the ordinary course of Providence. *It so happened*, or rather God had so arranged it, that the Shunammite and her son arrived in Samaria at a very peculiar period. Such circumstances had never before occurred, and would never again occur during the reign of Jehoram. As we infer from the narrative, Samaria had just been delivered from its imminent danger. The Shunammite may have come the very day, or at least very soon after that event. The mind of the king was still full of it, and, taking it in connection with the judgment executed upon the "lord" to whom he had entrusted the command of the gate, the whole had made a deep impression upon Jehoram. After his own fashion, he began to be religious—that is, he became, for the time, not a worshipper of Jehovah, but an admirer of Elisha.

Alas, to this also there is a parallel in our days! How often does increased earnestness on the part of the religious world amount only to admiration of a favourite preacher, not to conversion unto God! Under such influence a Jehoram may seem to act justly and liberally, but the heart has remained unchanged; and when the temporary excitement is removed, Jehoram is still found cleaving to the sins of Ahab. "By their fruits ye shall know them." Are our principles dependent on our admiration of the men who advocate them? Has our religion its ebb and flow with the favourite preacher; or would we hold the same views and principles, no matter who advocated or who opposed them, and cherish the same religion, though not surrounded by the halo of the loved presence? Popular idols have their day—in too many instances, a very short day. But true religion is the conviction, the spiritual life and outcome of a renewed heart; and principles are neither mere logical sequences, nor yet the cant sayings of a party, but the hallowed expression of spiritual life.

It is most instructive to watch these two who are now introduced on the scene together: Jehoram and Gehazi—so unlike, and yet so like each other, most of all in their religion, which is a mixture of the truest worldliness and of the greatest respect for *results*, provided they are palpable. The picture is so life-like, that we instantly recognise every feature. These two together, immediately after the relief of Samaria, especially if (as already stated) Gehazi and his sons had been the lepers who brought tidings of the flight of the Syrians; and the king who wishes to hear not about Jehovah, but about Elisha, conversing with the leper! "Tell me, I pray thee, all the great things that Elisha hath done." It was characteristic of Jehoram to put such a question while, but a short time previously, he had sworn the death of Elisha.

And it was characteristic of Gehazi to dilate on such a topic, even while he and his bore in their bodies the perpetual mark of their unbelief and hardness of heart.

And thus it came that Gehazi was expatiating on all the marvellous results achieved, when, just as he had reached that part of his narrative about restoring "a dead body to life," the Shunammite herself, with her restored child, so unexpectedly appeared to present her suit to the king. What a wonderful coincidence, or rather what a gracious arrangement in Providence! A week earlier, or a week later, and how different might the result of her petition have been. But to come just as Gehazi was telling her story was indeed a most marked, though, if God's people were reviewing the story of their lives, by no means a singular disposition of events. Sorrow, want, and care must have greatly altered the appearance of the Shunammite since Gehazi had last seen her in "the great house." Her son, too, had grown from a child into a manly youth. But, with his quick eyes, Gehazi at once recognised them, though the Shunammite had failed to know in the leper the prophet's servant. "My lord, O king, this is the woman, and this is her son, whom Elisha restored to life." The monarch, startled by the coincidence, demanded of his petitioner particulars of the wondrous tale. So, instead of begging, she had only to tell the wondrous works of the Lord. When she came to her personal wrongs and wants, it was quite natural that Jehoram should, on the impulse of the moment, order justice to be done unto her. She was to receive not only her own, but "all the fruits of the field since the day that she left the land, even until now," and a special "officer" was "appointed" to see the royal command duly executed.

The sun was still shining down upon the streets of Samaria. The king and the leper were still standing together, talking "of the great things that Elisha had done." But the Shunammite and her son were hastening back, with hearts too full for utterance "of the great things" which Jehovah had done. Now, at the end of her story, but not before that, all had been made clear; the meaning of all God's dealings was plain. Not only were her land and "the great house," with its ever dear memories restored; but more than that—far more than she could ever have expected. Her faith had its recompense, and "all things" had indeed "worked together for good." She had lost nothing—no, nothing—not even those scanty fruits which had been consumed by strangers during the seven years of her absence.

And so it *shall be*. In the great day of recognition, when faith shall have had its full trial, and patience finished her perfect work; when we go home to our own sunny Shunem, for which these many years we have longed, and when we enter "the great house," it will be found that "all things" have "worked together for good." Then, though long forgotten by us, nothing shall have been forgotten by Him— nothing, absolutely nothing shall have been lost—not even the scanty fruits of those seven years of famine, which we thought for ever gone from us, devoured by strangers. All, all will be restored by the King. Bread cast upon the waters these many days gone by; a cup of cold water given in the name of a disciple; every word, every deed, every look of love—all is safely garnered, and will be restored, to our wondering and humbled gratitude. What recognitions then, and what a recognition! And then to enter into the joy of our Lord, and to be for ever with the Lord! Such is the end of the story of grace—such the final return. Who would not wish to begin that story of grace *now*, and to look forward to its completion, though it were by trials, yet "not many days hence"?

CHAPTER XXVI.

ELISHA AT DAMASCUS.

And Elisha came to Damascus; and Ben-hadad the king of Syria was sick; and it was told him, saying, The man of God is come hither. And the king said unto Hazael, Take a present in thine hand, and go, meet the man of God, and inquire of the Lord by him, saying, Shall I recover of this disease? So Hazael went to meet him, and took a present with him, even of every good thing of Damascus, forty camels' burden, and came and stood before him, and said, Thy son Ben-hadad king of Syria hath sent me to thee, saying, Shall I recover of this disease? And Elisha said unto him, Go, say unto him, Thou mayest certainly recover: howbeit the Lord hath shewed me that he shall surely die. And he settled his countenance stedfastly, until he was ashamed: and the man of God wept. And Hazael said, Why weepeth my lord? And he answered, Because I know the evil that thou wilt do unto the children of Israel: their strongholds wilt thou set on fire, and their young men wilt thou slay with the sword, and wilt dash their children, and rip up their women with child. And Hazael said, But what, is thy servant a dog, that he should do this great thing? And Elisha answered, The Lord hath shewed me that thou shalt be king over Syria. So he departed from Elisha, and came to his master; who said to him, What said Elisha to thee? And he answered, He told me that thou shouldest surely recover. And it came to pass on the morrow, that he took a thick cloth, and dipped it in water, and spread it on his face, so that he died: and Hazael reigned in his stead."—2 KINGS viii. 7-15.

IF times of judgment are solemn, seasons of deliverance are perhaps even more solemn. When judgments are abroad, the inhabitants of the land may learn wisdom. But mercy not only passes unheeded; it may be, that, instead of leading to repentance, " Jeshurun waxed fat and kicked." Accordingly, in times of judgment, the hope may still be cherished, "Before I was afflicted I went astray, but now have I kept Thy word;" while in seasons of calm and peace this danger seems ever present, "Ephraim is joined to his idols, let him alone." Most solemn of all is a season of sudden calm following upon one of judgment. For, when God has first called attention to His Word by afflictive providences, and these have not had their spiritual effect; and then sought to draw us by such singular interpositions, as made it appear that it was His Hand, and yet we have not given heed, a solemn pause often ensues. It is the last pause, that of preparation for judgment. Like stillness in an atmosphere charged with electric clouds, it precedes a tempest, soon to burst in angry thunder, and with destroying lightning.

There was a lull in the storm which all the years of Jehoram's reign had, with rare interruptions, swept over the land. Samaria had been in the greatest straits, and scenes only to be re-enacted in the last terrible siege of Jerusalem had struck terror in every heart; yet the only impression produced had been impassioned and murderous enmity against the messenger of the Lord. Again, Samaria had been miraculously delivered from its besiegers; peace and unwonted plenty had been poured into her lap. Yet, the only result of it had been talk between Jehoram and leprous Gehazi about "all the great things" which Elisha had done! But no further "great things" had Elisha to do for Israel; indeed, nothing more at all in Israel till his dying day. Not only Jehoram but Israel were to be left alone; soon to be cut down, as cumbering the ground. What a solemn history this in its lessons to us all! Looking back upon the past, God has dealt with us by afflictions. Have we improved under them; and have we been directed to the Lord, Whose spiritual warnings they convey, and Whose judgments they prefigured? Again we have been delivered; but in the heaven-sent deliverance have we recognised His voice, still, small, gentle, of pity, of mercy, and of salvation? Or has it all been in vain, so far as *we* are concerned? In the lull of the storm, let us pause to consider how the past has been spent, and what preparation is making against that inevitable future, which no longer will be one of trial, but of final decision.

And yet matters had never before looked so hopeful for Israel. The long famine was past; the war was ended. More than this, in his palace at Damascus the great enemy of Israel, Ben-hadad, lay sick—as was currently reported, dangerously ill. Yet in all this seeming calm an unfulfilled prophecy still hung as a dark cloud over the land. The prophecy was not heeded by most, perhaps not even known to them. What mattered it? Events in Samaria had shown that they heeded not even warnings of the morrow. And so in these days also we are surrounded by many and loud warnings as regards the morrow. If they are left unheeded, what matters it that the more distant word of prophecy, concerning the fast approaching end of all things, is unknown or made the subject of ridicule? This mocking unbelief is itself a sign of the times, and a commencing fulfilment of the prophecy. "When the Son of Man cometh, shall He find faith on the earth?" "Where is the promise of His coming? for since the fathers fell asleep, all things continue as they were from the beginning of the creation." Yes, truly, as they were from the beginning of the creation! For, in their wilful ignorance, they forget that as, in those olden times, a flood of judgment swept "the world that then was," so a flood of fire is "kept in store"—mayhap deep down in the vaults of the earth, or in the embrace of some sun—"against the day of judgment and perdition of ungodly men."

Similarly, in those days, after the relief of Samaria, and when golden sunshine again flooded the land, might any who had known of that dread transaction by the cave on Mount Horeb (1 Kings xix. 15) have asked: Where is it? "All things continue as they were." For as yet the cloud of judgment had been hid from view, still clinging, as it were, to the rocky sides of Mount Horeb. A threefold answer had Jehovah there given to the doubts of Elijah. His work should be established in Elisha; His word in the judgments which were to burst upon Israel through Hazael; and His vengeance would be executed upon the house of Ahab by means of Jehu. All these three persons, however different their work, were to be God's instruments; as it were, "anointed," set apart, for their work. But each in doing his work would act, not from any impulse nor necessity from without, but strictly in accordance with his own nature and disposition; and yet, in so acting, fulfil that to which he was "anointed." In becoming a prophet, Elisha acted in accordance with his inmost spiritual experience and nature, as appeared in his conduct when called by Elijah. The cruelties perpetrated against Israel by Hazael were the natural outcome of a man who could so deliberately plan the murder of his master. And conduct more accordant with the character of Jehu, as we see it in every recorded act of his life, could scarcely be imagined than his bearing toward the house and the followers of Ahab. In the mercy of God, Elijah only lived to take his part in one of the threefold predictions, by which Jehovah would vindicate his authority. He set apart Elisha, and then ascended into glory. This limitation of Elijah's work was in mercy, not only to the prophet but to Israel. For before Hazael would become the rod of His Hand against Israel, and before Jehu would execute vengeance on the house of Ahab, He would, in His long-suffering, interpose the mission of Elisha, if peradventure tardy repentance might arrest the slowly upraised arm of judgment. So slow is our God in executing vengeance, so patient, so merciful. What precious encouragement this in returning to Him; what solemn warning in resisting the word of His grace!

Once more Elisha found himself "on the way to the wilderness of Damascus." He was to take up the thread of Elijah's work, exactly where it had been broken off when the mantle of the old prophet had first been flung around his shoulders (1 Kings xix. 15, 16). So far as any spiritual good to the king or to Israel as a nation was concerned, the work of Elisha, from his calling to that moment, seemed to have been in vain. Individuals had been saved, sanctified, blessed; the authority of God had been vindicated; but the summer was gone, the harvest was ended, and yet Israel was not saved. So Elisha once more stood where Elijah had been; and with saddened heart took up the broken thread of his work. Never, even in his life of trial and sorrow, had Elisha undertaken a more mournful commission.

But why was the prophet sent on such an errand? Surely, it was not to unchain the tiger, who would so soon lay waste his beloved land and people, but to establish it before Syria and before Israel, that this judgment was of the Lord; and that he should set forth this truth, to his own and to all generations, that in what a Hazael did, in accordance with his own character, there was an "anointing" and appointing on the part of Jehovah. And here also, to the unspeakable comfort of God's people in troublous times, applies the question, "Is there evil in a city, and the Lord hath not done it?" Verily, no—for "the Lord reigneth."

"And Elisha came towards Damascus;* and Ben-hadad,

* The rendering of our authorised version, "Elisha came to Damascus," is incorrect, and ill accords with the statement (ver. 9), that "Hazael went to meet him," "and took with him forty camels' burden."

the king of Syria, was sick; and it was told him, saying, The man of God is come hither." The vicinity of such a visitor could not remain long unknown. Elisha was now regarded, even in Syria, as "the man of God." Oh, to live in such directness of confession and consistency of conduct as to be everywhere known by a similar designation! Let us ask ourselves: What is most marked about us; of what will men, in their daily intercourse with us, have most occasion to take notice, as constantly appearing in our dealings with them, under all circumstances, and at all times? Will it be: a strict man, a person prone to anger, a proud man, a man who knows how to look after his own interests; or will it be : a rich man, an ambitious man, a learned man, a clever man, an amusing man; or will it be: a good man, "a man of God"? However much we may seek to shut our minds against the fact, mostly all of us carry the great characteristics of our history quite on the outside, intelligible to all who have knowledge of such matters, just like those great mansions all shrouded in silence that hang out the armorial bearings of their dead. By what will we be chiefly known and remembered in this generation and in the next, in this world and the other? Will it be as inheriting all the beatitudes, as good and holy men, who love and do the work of God? Let us ask ourselves questions such as these, when we commence the lifework of laying up for ourselves treasures, that we may decide of what kind they shall be. Let us ask them of ourselves, ever and again, as we pause to take breath in the busy hours of our lifework, that we may see what in the past is worth preserving, and what in the future worth pursuing. The very thought of a "man of God" brings blessing and comfort; his very person and life are a call to God and to peace. His very presence seems to make a roof-tree more sheltering, a home brighter, a district safer, a neighbourhood better—nay, the path of life itself less rugged and lonely. And why should we not all be known as men of God, as temples of the Holy Ghost, as disciples of Jesus, as children of "our Father Which is in heaven"?

Tidings of Elisha's proximity had reached the palace; had been carried into the king's sick chamber. Far other now were his feelings in reference to the prophet than when he had sent his soldiers to bring him alive or dead from Dothan. For Ben-hadad was sick; and the feelings of a man on religious subjects when sick unto death are other than those of a man in the enjoyment of health and vigour—that is, if his feelings have not been under the controlling power of Divine grace. To the most careless, when about to enter the eternal world, there is a reality about eternal things never felt before. And yet, though our pity is moved as we see the strong man bowed, and hear him speaking in such softened tones, his inquiry is essentially that of an irreligious man, and its object that of a heart which is not spiritually affected. "Take a present in thine hand, and go meet the man of God, and inquire of Jehovah by him, saying, Shall I recover of this disease?" So this, summed up in Scriptural truthfulness, is really all: "Shall I recover?" Truly, a fit subject for inquiry at the close of such a life!

And yet, like so many others, whose hearts are uninfluenced by higher motives, Ben-hadad had unconsciously surrounded himself with that which made the attainment of his dearest object impossible. Men wish happiness, prosperity, recovery, and yet they banish from their presence a Naaman, and summon to it a Hazael. They intrust their all to that which will lead to their ruin, and they make *him* their counsellor who will deceive and destroy them. A life like that of Ben-hadad is only too surely followed by a deathbed inquiry such as his. God forbid that we should deny the possibility of deathbed repentances; but we say it even more energetically: God forbid that we should trust ourselves to them. What is likely to be the uppermost thought after such a life? Is there not too often, even in the prayers which falter from blanched lips, more of the "Shall I recover?" prompted by fear, than of the language of spiritual repentance: "Lord, I believe, help Thou mine unbelief."

But none of these solemn considerations moved the king's trusted messenger and friend. Altogether, Hazael is perhaps one of the most repulsive characters presented in Scripture. When he undertook his master's commission, he had already deliberately resolved upon his murder. At the same time, he took measures to deceive, and if possible to gain Elisha. His whole conduct bore the worst traits of the Oriental character. Even the procession of forty loaded camels bringing a "present of every good thing in Damascus" was a piece of hypocrisy. It is not for a moment to be thought that he would have been guilty of the folly of offering to a solitary traveller provisions and luxuries, which we may calculate as having amounted in the aggregate to about thirty thousand pounds weight. It was probably an Eastern display when a few camels' burdens were thus distributed over so many. The attitude and language of Hazael were characterised by mock humility and hypocritical earnestness. He "came and stood before him, and said, Thy son Benhadad, king of Syria, hath sent me to thee, saying, Shall I recover of this disease?" Did Hazael wish to conciliate the dreaded prophet, or were his measures taken with the view of misleading the people of Damascus as to his designs? But he failed to impose on Elisha. The reply, which at once unmasked him, was, "Go and say unto him (that is, as thou hadst intended), Thou shalt surely recover: howbeit Jehovah hath showed me that he shall surely die." *

It fills the heart with unutterable sadness to feel helpless in presence of death; to know that a man may certainly recover, and yet to see that he shall surely die. When we look upon a world, for which the means of recovery have been provided; when, in preaching the Gospel of Christ, we realise what issues depend upon the decision of men; when we stand by a deathbed, trying to pour into ears too long closed against it the gracious message of Christ's work finished for us, feelings of sadness and responsibility at times almost overwhelm us. Which of these men, women, and children whom we daily meet, with whom we hold such pleasant, easy, familiar intercourse, who are now so joyous, happy, and unconcerned, shall be ultimately lost? It is not a harsh, only a true saying, for both they and we must perish if we are without Christ. It is not harsh, for the means of recovery are within reach of all: they may "certainly recover." What shall we say or do to induce them to banish Hazael from their side? Blessed be God that, knowing that the work of conversion is the Lord's, we can retire from such unpromising efforts to the stronghold of prayer.

And yet even a Hazael had his repentance! "And he (Elisha) settled his countenance stedfastly, until he (Hazael)

---

* Our Authorised version renders it, "Thou mayest certainly recover," in the sense that there was nothing mortal in his disease, and that under ordinary circumstances he might have recovered. This view, though adopted by most Rabbinical and modern interpreters, is incompatible with the original, which can only be rendered as in the text, the mode of expression being precisely the same as that afterwards translated, "he shall surely die." The meaning is: I know it all, go and tell him as thou hast planned, "Thou shalt surely recover," but God hath shown me alike thy murderous plan and its execution.

was ashamed." Elisha could not leave an immortal soul to go to its ruin without at least attempting its rescue. He fixed his gaze stedfastly upon the bold, bad man, till Hazael felt that his inmost thoughts had been read, and quailed under the look. An unwonted blush passed over the murderer's face. There is not a conscience so seared which at some time or other has not been roused to fear, even if not to repentance. But the pangs of conscience, as they are of the most acute, so also are they of the most transient kind. No faculty in man more easily awakened, none more readily lulled to sleep, than conscience. While most we feel them, we are on the eve of losing its impressions. They are like an echo, mostly heard when we are silent and listen. The next moment, and its voice has died away. Therefore, and even on this ground, the danger of trusting our moral and spiritual guidance to a monitor so uncertain, is great. Besides, while we examine each act separately, we fail to discern the character of our lives as a whole. It is as when we look down into the deep blue sea, or up into the deep blue sky. Examined separately, each particle of that water, or of that air, seems colourless. Only when viewed in its totality do we become aware of its shadings. So is life. Each action separately may have its excuse, its reasonable motive, its colourless aspect. Only when viewing a life in its totality, in its relation to God, do we come to know its real character. Hence the importance of a "single eye," whose stedfast undivided gaze is ever directed towards God, and views all things as in His light.

Not even Hazael seemed to realise his future of wickedness. "The man of God wept"—as Jesus wept when "He beheld the city." Too eager to divert the current of thoughts which for a moment had moved him, Hazael inquired the reason of his tears. Even when told the story of his future cruelty in all its literality, and divested from the dazzling glare which ambition or passion would cast around such a picture, it failed to influence the Syrian. For a moment he had not yielded to, but heard the voice of conscience. Only for a moment. He now saw before him but the one object of his life—felt only the one master-passion that ruled him. The tale of horrors recalled his purpose; it was a means to his end. He was not startled, merely afraid that he might not succeed in compassing it. "But what is thy servant the dog, that he should do such a great thing?"* And Elisha answered, "Jehovah hath showed me thee as king over Syria." † Hazael was silent. So the fates were in his favour; and yet he was ill at ease. "So he departed from Elisha."

The rest is soon told—all the rest of a long and prosperous life; all the rest of the commencement of a terrible reign. Ben-hadad listened and was deceived. The next day there was solemn proclamation throughout Damascus. King Ben-hadad lay dead in his palace. No trace of the murder, no track of the murderer, save where the recording angel had marked it. "And Hazael reigned in his stead."

* The above is a correct rendering of the passage. The Authorised version would seem to indicate an abhorrence on the part of Hazael, which is neither in accordance with his character, nor expressed in the original.

† This is the correct rendering, and shows that Elisha in no way encouraged his murderous design; on the contrary, rather warned him of it. We may add that the murder was committed by means of a "coverlet," literally, a thick *woven* cover, dipped in water, by which Ben-hadad was choked.

CHAPTER XXVII.

JUDGMENT COMMENCED.

"And he (Ahaziah, king of Judah) went with Joram the son of Ahab to the war against Hazael king of Syria in Ramoth-gilead; and the Syrians wounded Joram. And King Joram went back to be healed in Jezreel of the wounds which the Syrians had given him at Ramah, when he fought against Hazael king of Syria. And Ahaziah the son of Jehoram king of Judah went down to see Joram the son of Ahab in Jezreel, because he was sick. And Elisha the prophet called one of the children of the prophets, and said unto him, Gird up thy loins, and take this box of oil in thine hand, and go to Ramoth-gilead: and when thou comest thither, look out there Jehu the son of Jehoshaphat the son of Nimshi, and go in, and make him arise up from among his brethren, and carry him to an inner chamber; then take the box of oil, and pour it on his head, and say, Thus saith the Lord, I have anointed thee king over Israel. Then open the door, and flee, and tarry not. So the young man, even the young man the prophet, went to Ramoth-gilead. And when he came, behold, the captains of the host were sitting; and he said, I have an errand to thee, O captain. And Jehu said, Unto which of all us? And he said, To thee, O captain. And he arose, and went into the house; and he poured the oil on his head, and said unto him, Thus saith the Lord God of Israel, I have anointed thee king over the people of the Lord, even over Israel. And thou shalt smite the house of Ahab thy master, that I may avenge the blood of my servants the prophets, and the blood of all the servants of the Lord, at the hand of Jezebel. For the whole house of Ahab shall perish: and I will cut off from Ahab him that pisseth against the wall, and him that is shut up and left in Israel: and I will make the house of Ahab like the house of Jeroboam the son of Nebat, and like the house of Baasha the son of Ahijah: and the dogs shall eat Jezebel in the portion of Jezreel, and there shall be none to bury her. And he opened the door, and fled. Then Jehu came forth to the servants of his lord: and one said unto him, Is all well? wherefore came this mad fellow to thee? And he said unto them, Ye know the man, and his communication. And they said, It is false; tell us now. And he said, Thus and thus spake he to me, saying, Thus saith the Lord, I have anointed thee king over Israel. Then they hasted, and took every man his garment, and put it under him on the top of the stairs, and blew with trumpets, saying, Jehu is king. So Jehu the son of Jehoshaphat the son of Nimshi conspired against Joram. (Now Joram had kept Ramoth-gilead, he and all Israel, because of Hazael king of Syria. But King Joram was returned to be healed in Jezreel of the wounds which the Syrians had given him, when he fought with Hazael king of Syria.) And Jehu said, If it be your minds, then let none go forth nor escape out of the city to go to tell it in Jezreel."—2 KINGS viii. 28, 29; ix. 1-15.

JUDGMENT was rushing on its course, swift, yet so noiseless, that not one of the many whom it would soon overwhelm knew its approach; least of all Joram, king of Israel. He was still prosperous, indeed more prosperous than ever. King Jehoshaphat had been succeeded on the throne of Judah by his eldest son, Jehoram, a namesake of the king of Israel. Close bonds connected the two royal houses; for the king of Judah had married Athaliah, the daughter ot Ahab and Jezebel (and grand-daughter of Omri), and the two Jehorams were brothers-in-law. The same policy prevailed in Judah as in Israel, for Jehoram "walked in the way of the kings of Israel, like as did the house of Ahab." But his troubled reign came to a speedy and terrible close. He died of internal "sore diseases," unloved and unregretted. As Scripture expresses it, he "departed without being desired." "His people made no burning for him," and though "they buried him in the city of David," they did not venture to lay him "in the sepulchres of the kings."

Thus trouble was fast coming upon Judah also. Jehoram was succeeded by his youngest son, Ahaziah, who reigned only one year. What his rule would have been, sufficiently appears from the fact that he was under the absolute sway of his mother. His life is characteristically summed up in this, that "he walked in the way of the house of Ahab, and did evil in the sight of the Lord, as did the house of Ahab." In fact, Ahab and Jezebel might now have been said to reign in Judah as well as in Israel. Yet what Ahab could never obtain, Joram possessed. It will be remembered that King Ahab had died from a wound received in the battle of Ramoth-Gilead (1 Kings xxii.). At that time, Ben-hadad held the chief city of Gilead, and to rescue this stronghold from the Syrians that ill-fated expedition had been undertaken by Ahab and Jehoshaphat. But now Ramoth-Gilead was in the possession of Israel (2 Kings ix. 2, 14, 15); and when the warlike Hazael contended for it

JUDGMENT COMMENCED.

with Joram, he was defeated, and obliged to retreat. The king of Israel had been slightly wounded in the engagement—only slightly wounded; and the victor went to be healed at the summer-palace of Jezreel, where, at this time, the Queen-mother Jezebel and the whole court were. Festivities succeeded each other, for Israel was victorious: Ramoth-Gilead was in their possession, though still threatened by the Syrians; and King Ahaziah had come down to visit his ally and friend Joram at Jezreel.

Ramoth-Gilead, Ahab's son, Jezebel, and Jezreel—what coincidences! Only coincidences, men would have said; yet, where the carcase was, thither the eagles, with dark, flapping wings, and hoarse cry, were fast gathering. Strange coincidences these, sufficient to make even the least superstitious in Jezreel uneasy, if he remembered them. But who would remember them at that time? Not Joram, not proud Jezebel, not the guard that had ridden behind Ahab on the day when he was so sternly encountered by Elijah, and when the words of defiance had died on the lips of the monarch; not the forsworn elders of Jezreel, always venial, even to murder; not "the men of Belial" in Jezreel; not the dogs that had licked the blood of Ahab, as one washed out the dead man's chariot; nor the dogs who were still sniffing at the greensward on that spot close by, where, as people said, unyielding Naboth had been stoned, and lay buried. Yet there were many in Jezreel who might have recalled the terrible crime connected with that new portion of the palace-garden and offices in the king's favourite summer residence. They were then in the year 884 before our present reckoning.* Just

---

* Amidst the somewhat perplexing chronology of this period (to which, in this place, no further reference can be made), the year 884 before Christ has by almost universal consent been fixed upon as that of Joram's death, and as the commencement of Jehu's reign.

thirty-six years before that, Ahab had ascended the throne, and only seventeen years ago the patrimony of Naboth had been wrested from him with his life. A very short time in which to forget alike such events and the threatening of such judgments!

But the word of the Lord could not tarry. Swiftly, and unconsciously to themselves, all the actors in the last scene were brought to their places. And so shall it be in the days preceding "the end." Many events predicted in connection with it, may seem at present improbable of occurrence, perhaps even incompatible. But the difficulties surrounding the predictions of Christ's Second Coming are by no means so great as those which must have perplexed our fathers, when trying to combine the prophetic signs of His First Coming. Such, indeed, were they, that after His coming our Lord, on one occasion, silenced His questioners by propounding only one, and that among the least of these difficulties: "If David, then, call Him Lord, how is He his son?" And we know how terribly the mystery of His death, when they had fondly hoped that He would have delivered Israel, weighed as a heavy burden on the hearts of His disciples. Yet it now appears all clear to us; and each prophecy of His First Coming, however seemingly incompatible with the other, or improbable of fulfilment, has become literally true. So shall it be, in due time, with regard to the predictions of His return and reign. So shall it also be at the last with each of us, when those apparently incongruous events and leadings, unintelligible while viewed separately, shall have become plain and connected, and our life's story be finally and fully told.

King Joram had never been popular, nor had his reign been ever really prosperous. The constant wars with Syria must have severely taxed a people which had suffered so long from famine. Whether in peace or in war, his every act had proved a failure. Least of all was he fitted to cope with an opponent such as Hazael of Syria. Temporarily Israel might indeed hold Ramoth-Gilead; but was not the army of Joram even now beset, and constantly threatened? And where was the king himself? Not with his army, as Hazael, but in the luxurious retreat of Jezreel, to which he had retired on little better than the pretext of being healed of a wound; for never did it disable him when inclination or fear demanded his presence. Though the people had apostatised from the service of the Lord, they could not but remember that their king had been head and front in their offending. If there was any truth in the prophetic word—and who that had seen Elijah, or heard Elisha, could doubt it—the king was the sole cause of all their misfortunes. Since that accursed house of Ahab had gained possession of a throne to which they could assert no claim, the ancient laws, the ancient worship, and the ancient customs of Israel, had all been discarded, and only trouble and disaster had attended their rule. So might many reason in Israel, even among those who were not religious. Dangerous mutterings these; a dangerous spirit of disaffection; dangerous materials to which to apply the torch—and that torch lay ready to be kindled.

Behind the battlements of Ramoth in Gilead was the flower of the Jewish army, picked men, inured to war. In the absence of the king, the garrison was commanded by the bravest and most experienced of his captains. Jehu, the son of Nimshi, had almost from boyhood followed war as a man does his loved pursuit. He must have been still young when he first attained a post of distinction in the army. For, seventeen years before this he was already of the King's body-guard, and had ridden with his friend and comrade, Bidkar, close behind King Ahab on that memorable day, when he encountered

Elijah. The message of awful threatening which he had then heard, Jehu could never forget, not even amidst the excitement and turmoil of his campaigning. Every word of it was indelibly graven upon his mind. And now Jehu had attained the highest post which could be held under a monarch so jealous as Joram, who apparently would not appoint a chief captain of the host, even while he himself was incapable of commanding. This also may have contributed to that general disorganisation and discontent, which, as will soon appear, was extensively prevailing.

In the large hall at Ramoth all the captains of the host were gathered, either in military council, or, as is more probable, carousing. That, in their unrestrained communications, much dissatisfaction had been expressed with King Joram, and with the state of matters in Israel, we may infer from the readiness with which they so soon afterwards proclaimed a revolution. It might almost seem, as if this very thing had formed the topic of their conversation, and as if the event which immediately followed had been its practical conclusion.

Suddenly their converse was interrupted by an unexpected arrival. With the freedom which in the East characterises intercourse, unannounced, one stood before them whom, from his peculiar appearance and perhaps dress, they at once recognised as "one of the children of the prophets." For in Old Testament times, and especially in the case of the prophets, even their outward bearing was designed to teach. Immediate silence ensued, and every eye was fixed on the figure within the door. How often is a feast startled by a sudden messenger from the Most High. O, never to be where we cannot receive such message! It is not for us to live where we may not die.

The young man, instructed in his duty, gave not the company time to recover. Abruptly he said, "I have an errand to thee, O captain." In rank there was, through the jealousy of Joram, no distinction between them. But Jehu, who, by tacit consent, commanded among these commanders, replied, in name of the others, "Unto which of all of us?" And the young man, to whom this was sufficient evidence that he addressed Jehu himself, said: "To thee, O captain."

At a sign from the young man, Jehu left the table and followed his strange companion. Not one of those captains but would for the moment have obeyed the young prophet. Thus one of the objects in view had already been attained by the very brusqueness of his strange deportment. The company was startled and awed. Whence had he come; what message did he bear; and why this secrecy? In one of the inner chambers, out of sight and hearing of all, the young man paused, and, without further speech, took from his breast the box of sacred oil, and poured its contents over the head of Jehu. Then, with rapid but distinct utterance, he repeated the very words of the curse which had, in Jehu's hearing, once fallen upon the head of Ahab. Only this was new, that Jehu was anointed king, and appointed instrument of the Divine judgment. Not only in truth and righteousness, but in mercy to himself, it was also thus early explained to Jehu, that the Lord would "avenge," "at the hand of Jezebel," "the blood of His servants the prophets, and the blood of all the servants of Jehovah." And so the cause of God was to be vindicated, and in the blood of the murderers was their public sin to be washed out. For God never forgets His messengers nor any of His people, and though not only seventeen years but seventeen centuries may have elapsed, the curse which has all along silently followed shall at last burst in storm of judgment.

No sooner had the young prophet spoken the words of his

commission, than "he opened the door and fled." His footsteps were heard across the corridor, down the broad flight of stairs, across the square, and far in the distance. He fled, as a man who speeds for his life. Soon the city-gates and battlements were behind him; he had gained the open country, and was free. Yet before he could return to him that had sent him, the result of his errand would be known in Jezreel, travel on to Samaria, and soon be repeated in every home of Israel and Judah. For it would be a day of blood and of disaster, ere that sun would set in the west.

The prophet of mercy had sent the young man on this terrible errand. In great kindness, the Lord had spared His servant the grief of personally executing such a commission. And well had the youth done his work. He had been enjoined secrecy; for this, as every commission, must come personally and individually to him who is to do the work. Every one must take upon himself the duty incumbent upon him. Nor must the prophet tarry. He has no explanations to make; he has brought a command. Far less must he stay that Jehu may make use of him, by putting him in the chariot beside him, as soon afterwards, in similar circumstances, he did to Jehonadab, the son of Rechab (chap. x. 15). For of all dangers to which religion can be exposed, one of the greatest is that it be made subservient to worldly purposes. This will be attempted both in private and in public. Every Jehu will endeavour to have a prophet in his chariot. Worldly men will try to make use of our religion for promoting their own objects. To "make merchandise" of what is highest and holiest; to use it in order to advance worldly interests, or plans, is the most odious kind of hypocrisy. In this let us be "wise as serpents," and beware of allowing religion to serve as an ally to the meanest selfishness. Similarly, it becomes us, in these days of party-strife and contention, to be on our guard against identifying religion with one or another political movement or party. As Christian men, we are bound to take a Christian view of all questions which concern the public welfare. As Christian ministers, we may even "have an errand" on some particular occasion. But having delivered it, "let us open the door and flee." As ministers of the Lord Jesus, or as His servants, we have no business to identify spiritual religion with one or another party in the state, nor to ride beside Jehu when he enters Jezreel.

For a few moments Jehu stood alone in the inner chamber; then, yet irresolute how to act, he returned to his companions. The pale face and confused mien sufficiently indicated, that even Jehu's well-known resoluteness and daring had not been proof against what he had heard. "Is all well? wherefore came this mad fellow to thee?" were questions which greeted him from all parts of the room. Had he come to divulge some plot in Jezreel, some secret plan of the Syrians against Ramoth-Gilead, or had he only, by his "madness," startled their comrade? Such are the two thoughts which the world still associates with a religious movement. Is there any real danger; or is it only the fanaticism of this preacher? The word "mad" rises most readily to the lips of Jewish captains in the days of Joram, to those of a Festus and an Agrippa, and to those of the men of our own days. Passing strange, that during these well-nigh thirty centuries, the world has not got beyond this explanation of religion and of religious men. Yet there was nothing mad either about the man or his behaviour.

But Jehu had not yet taken his final resolve. Accordingly, he met the questioning of his comrades with an evasive reply. Did he mean that they had themselves suborned the man, and prompted his communication, in order to carry out their own views? Or was it wholly an evasion, implying, what need to ask about the communications or the bearing of such a person?* Jehu was not a religious man, nor did he act from religious motives on this or any other occasion. The message of the prophet was in his mind subject to the calculation of chances. Would he be likely to succeed in his attempt, and would the army support him? The answer of the captains set his mind immediately at rest. Evidently the prophet had not brought tidings about the Syrians; for these Jehu would unhesitatingly have communicated to the council of war. His message must therefore have been connected with Israel and its king—with the subject of their late conversation. They would not brook delay nor evasion. Eagerly they crowded around Jehu. "It is false! Tell us now!"

With the quick instinct of a practised military commander, Jehu understood it all, and with characteristic vigour and decision at once possessed himself of the situation. In briefest terms he told them the substance of what he had heard. It is strange how much more easily men are influenced in the mass than individually. Is it that the sense of danger and responsibility seems to decrease when it is shared by the many, or that spreading sympathy represses the influence of calculating thought? These captains, who, if spoken to privately and individually, might have hesitated and objected, now rose *en masse*, and "hasted, and took every man his garment, and put it under him on the top of the stairs, and blew with trumpets, saying, Jehu is king!" A right royal carpet this of generals' upper garments on that balcony that overlooked the great square! The blast of the trumpets summoned the soldiery. It is a military revolution; Jehu is

---

* The original will bear both interpretations.

proclaimed king! Again the trumpets sounded louder and longer than before; but their blast reached not to Jezreel.

At the suggestion of Jehu the city-gates were immediately closed and guarded. None was allowed to go forth from Ramoth, nor to carry tidings to Jezreel. Once only the gates opened; it was to allow Jehu and his followers to pass in their war-chariots and with their horsemen. And "he driveth furiously." But swifter far than the wheels of his chariot, though all unheard and unseen, travelled the vengeance of the Lord, the God of Israel.

CHAPTER XXVIII.

JEHU AND JEHONADAB.

"And when he was departed thence, he lighted on Jehonadab the son of Rechab coming to meet him: and he saluted him, and said to him, Is thine heart right, as my heart is with thy heart? And Jehonadab answered, It is. If it be, give me thine hand. And he gave him his hand; and he took him up to him into the chariot. And he said, Come with me, and see my zeal for the Lord. So they made him ride in his chariot."—2 KINGS x. 15, 16.

BATHED in the golden sunlight lay fair Jezreel, the royal city of Ahab. So calm, so peaceful, and so beautiful, it seemed like an enchanted scene. From distant Carmel in the west the eye could discern its battlements, with the great watch-tower springing out from the midst of them, and farther on in the west the swelling mountain-pass, and near it, nestling among trees and vineyards, the white houses of lovely En-gannim, "the spring of the gardens." Then, to the east, far as the eye could reach, lay the deep Jordan valley. For with its back, as it were, planted towards Carmel and its range, facing the threefold opening of the Jordan valley, chiefly the one which cleft wide against it, Jezreel stood like a royal stag at bay, keenly looking over to the west, whence alone its enemies might come. Down its rocky foundations, which on one side rose sheer up a hundred feet from their base, it frowned defiance into the Jordan valley. There stood its high watch-tower—there, last remnant of its greatness, it stands to this day—close beside that large window which commanded the magnificent view, the great window of royal Jezebel's apartments; close beside the great gate also, which at the same time was principal entrance to the city and to the royal residence, for these battlements formed part of the king's palace. Right in front of that gate spread an open space, and beyond it the road sloped down towards the Jordan valley. By the side of it, still following along the way, undulated the royal domains, pleasure-grounds and gardens, till where, at about a mile's distance, bubbles and rushes from under a limestone cavern, out of the crevices of the rocks, a most beautiful spring, that gradually expands into a broad sheet of water forty or fifty feet wide.

We take our stand here to look around; then down into that crystal-like pool, teeming with fishes that glide along its sunny surface, or plunge into its pebbly depth to rise again in graceful circles. This is the boundary of what were Naboth's possessions, and as we look back towards Jezreel, these were his fields and his vineyards; and there, where we stand, he and his were stoned to death; in this pool Ahab's bloody chariot had been washed; and here nightly did the vilest of the people hold their orgies. Yet a memorable spot this! For, here at the spring of "Harod" or "trembling" had Gideon encamped before his attack on the camp of Midian, and here the valour and faith of his soldiers had been tested (Judges vii.); here also had royal Saul lain with his army before the fatal battle of Gilboa (1 Sam. xxix). And now another and yet more terrible fulfilment of prediction was soon and for ever to mark the place.

Up from Ramoth in Gilead and along that Jordan valley a small party of chariots and horsemen hurried with utmost speed. It was Jehu and his chosen companions. If ever, that day his driving was furious. It has already been stated, that Jehu was not a religious man, in the spiritual sense of the term. He was simply a soldier, bold, resolute, defiant, who would carry out his purpose to the utmost. He had no desire of building up the house of Jehovah, nor of serving Him. He had accepted the commission of destroying the house of Ahab and all his followers, and this he would unflinchingly discharge. Beyond that he knew nothing, and cared for nothing, save the establishment of himself on the throne, and the future safety of his line. It is always far more easy to destroy than to build. A Jehu may cut off, root and branch, the worship of Baal; but it needs a spiritual man to promote and establish in its place the service of Jehovah. The sword of Jehu could not effect this; nay, it would not have been unsheathed in such a cause. Connected with every great religious movement there are those who help it by destroying the old, which is doomed to judgment. And these also have their work and commission, to which they are "anointed." The *negative*, or what is false and wrong, is easily discerned; the *positive*, or what is right and good, is only apprehended by grace. God has always a Jehu in readiness; but, blessed be His Name, He can also raise up an Ezra and a Nehemiah.

And now in the far distance, full in the slanting western sunlight, the faintest outline of Jezreel came into view. Soon also the practised eye of the watchman on the tower espied the company. As his deep, sonorous voice proclaimed it, Joram directed a horseman to be sent forward to inquire whether they brought tidings of peace or of war. The messenger reached the company, but to his question Jehu, not slackening rein, deigned no other answer than to direct him to the rear. In vain the watchman strained his eye for the return of the horseman. He had seen him join the company, but he had not left it again. This also the watchman, as in duty bound, reported. A second messenger was despatched, but with the same result, similarly announced by the faithful watchman. And now as the company came nearer, though their faces could not yet be descried, there was something peculiar about the foremost chariot. So rapidly it moved, there was no mistaking it, none in the land so urged on his war-chariot. "The driving is like the driving of Jehu the son of Nimshi."

As yet, in his ease and unconcern, not a shadow of suspicion, not a breath of fear, had fallen on the king of Israel. Like all who are near sudden destruction, when most he should have feared he was most unconcerned. Two messengers of peace had gone, not to return in peace. So is it, alas, with too many in our own days. Again and again have the faithful watchmen warned them of the impending danger, with no other result than the unconcerned, cursory inquiry: Is it peace? The thought of impending ruin never enters till it is too late. Not even that two messengers had gone without bringing back a reply roused suspicion, nor yet the approach of Jehu. Probably the general had come to announce in person another victory over the Syrians, or the conclusion of peace. So might Joram have reasoned. By his command two chariots were quickly made ready, and the two kings went out to be the first to receive good tidings. Through that gate, down the undulating plain, right in view of the large window in Jezebel's royal apartment, now where the old palace grounds end, now where the new "garden of herbs" begins, passed the royal chariots. There, just in "the portion of Naboth the Jezreelite," they met Jehu and his company. Strange coincidence! But what was this? Joram had quickly turned his chariot; he fell; his chariot was surrounded; a bloody corpse lifted across the road by armed men, and rudely flung into "the garden of herbs." And lo, there, Ahaziah fled toward the west, up the steep ascent towards En-gannim, although in vain, for he would soon be overtaken by these horsemen in full gallop, and never again would he see the City of David.

All this had Jezebel witnessed from the casement of her window: how the arrow sped from Jehu's strong bow, and passing through the heart of her son, trembling, and dyed in his gore, stuck in his chariot; how her grandson Ahaziah had vainly fled up that hill, pursued by the horsemen. She had not heard the words of Jehu, who had fastened on her the guilt of this, and of much more blood; she had not seen how he pointed his friend Bidkar to the spot where the bloody corpse of Joram lay in the frightful distortions of such a death, just " in the portion of the field of Naboth the Jezreelite," nor known that he reminded his companion in arms of what they both had heard on that day when they "rode together after Ahab." Yet she understood it all, and prepared for it all. Even if she had not, there were those around only too eager to explain it. The cavalcade had resumed its slower progress when she left the window. A few minutes more, and she returned to it, and now with her own hand flung wide open the lattice. She would die a Queen. So she put the Eastern adornment round her eyes, arrayed herself in her queenly head-dress, and gazed down, not without scorn, upon the approaching cavalcade.

As Jehu reached the gate, right under her window, he was startled by a voice above him taunting him in tones of bitterest irony. It was Jezebel. The call, "Who is on my side? who?" was quickly answered by eunuchs at this and that window. Another moment, and the proud Queen was dashed headlong from her window, and her blood bespattered wall and horses. Over her body, and into Jezreel, was the conqueror's course. So perished Jezebel. There is something terribly grand about her last moments. They seem like the rocky peaks of those dark mountains, untrodden by man, which frown up to heaven amid a wilderness of glaciers, and shake from their rugged sides the covering of snow, as if impatient of being wrapped in the folds of a mantle, even if it were of death. What capabilities for good had not this stern, strong woman possessed, yet all turned to evil, all lost! And what misdirected energies, what misapplied talents, what wasted lives, what terrible loss, both for time and eternity, in so many around us! And is this all that has been left of Jezebel—cast from her window by some hireling eunuchs, and trampled under foot by the horses of Jehu?

In the palace of Jezreel there was feasting. The conqueror "did eat and drink." The sterner mood had passed, and thoughts of the future were crowding in upon the victor. His commission must be fully discharged, and Ahab, with all his adherents, destroyed. But with this came other thoughts, less bloody and more ambitious. Jehu was now king, and kingly authority must be respected, save where such respect might interfere with the safety of his own throne. It had been well to show contempt for the descendants of Ahab, for this contempt vindicated the revolution. But queenly Jezebel had been every inch a queen; not a usurper, but the daughter of a king. Let Joram's bones bleach in the field; but let "this cursed woman" be seen after and buried. It is here, if we mistake not, that we are at the turning-point in the life of Jehu, where thoughts of self and of personal ambition spring up to overshadow all, and to bear a terrible harvest. It is here, at the very threshold of his reign, that its curse commences. The same ambition that explains his tardy regard for the dead "king's daughter" also explains his cunning and cruelty towards the relatives and friends of Ahab, and towards "the brethren of Ahaziah." They were the mingled motives of a determined, unscrupulous man, who combined with the execution of his higher commission the most ambitious and selfish thoughts. And so, while he "destroyed Baal out of Israel," he "departed not from the sins of Jeroboam the son of Nebat;" and while he received the reward for executing his commission, yet "in those days Jehovah began to cut Israel short, and Hazael smote them in all the coasts of Israel."

At last the work of vengeance was completed, at least so far as concerned the house of Ahab. Jehu prepared to enter Samaria for the first time, and in triumph. But though all resistance was trampled out, how would he be received in the royal city of Israel? He had only one plea for his presence as king: the sentence of Jehovah. Disguise it as you may, it was the plea of religion. But as yet no religious man of prominence had declared in his favour; nor, while such were his ways, while he mingled personal ambition with punitive justice, were they likely publicly to homologate his acts. Elisha never met him, so far as appears from the narrative—never, from the day of his entry into Jezreel to that of his death. It was now, just after he returned from "the pit of the shearing-house," into which he had cast the two and forty bodies of "the brethren of Ahaziah," that Jehu met Jehonadab the son of Rechab. Thus late in this marvellous history another actor comes on the scene, that we may be instructed and warned from his conduct and experience. It almost seems as if the type of every movement and danger in religion were to be introduced, that the Church in all ages may learn lessons of piety and wisdom.

Jehonadab, the son of Rechab, was no doubt a servant of Jehovah—an earnest, a sternly earnest man. In his veins flowed the fierce Arab blood, for he was a son of the wilderness. Yet none more Israelitish than the tribe to which he belonged. Along with the children of Judah, those of the

Kenite, Moses' father-in-law, had entered the land of promise, and among them they dwelt (Judges i. 16). Yet not exclusively among them, for we find some also in the extreme north of the land. There Jael, the wife of Heber, the Kenite, had executed fierce Arab vengeance—though in a righteous cause—upon Sisera (Judges iv. 10-24). The stern Arab, Jehonadab, was well known to all in Israel. In his retirement he had heard what Jehu had done, and he was now hastening "to meet him."

At sight of Jehonadab Jehu drew rein. The monarch and the zealot "saluted" and "blessed" each other.* Knowing the mingled character of his own motives, Jehu was at first disposed to distrust the sincerity of Jehonadab's allegiance. But the simple-minded, uncompromising son of the desert was little versed in reading men's thoughts. What he said he meant, and would carry in dreadful earnest to its fullest consequences. The compact, a most unequal and incongruous one, was soon made. They grasped each other's hands, and Jehu lifted Jehonadab into his own chariot. There, as he stood beside him, he whispered into his ears, "Come with me, and see my zeal for Jehovah." Alas, it was *not* zeal for Jehovah. Would that he had never ridden beside Jehu! Two more unlike in their inmost purposes could scarcely have been found in Israel, and yet they were allied for the time.

But why will a Jehonadab ever come up into the chariot of a Jehu? Such associations can never bode good to the cause, nor to the people of God. Jehu may have his own work, which he pursues as best he can. But it has nothing

* The latter is the correct rendering of the original. The Hebrew text implies that Jehu "blessed" Jehonadab; but according to Josephus and the LXX., Jehonadab first blessed Jehu. Probably both the one and the other may have actually occurred.

in common with the zeal of Jehonadab, which, however mistaken perhaps in some of its manifestations, is earnest and sincere for Jehovah. An obvious danger to be avoided, is to let our religion flow in the channels of a zeal, which after all is rather the outcome of natural character than of the renewed heart. A man may be truly Christian; he may mean to do what is truly Christian; and yet he may do it in a truly unchristian manner. He may hold the truth, and speak the truth—but not in love. He may hold Scriptural views, but pour them forth in the bitterness and severity of a harsh natural character. He may teach others, or educate the young, or deal with youthful converts, and do so from the most pure Christian motives, yet in a manner wholly incongruous, harshly pushing the diseased with horns, and driving on the weak. This is not as our Blessed Lord spake and acted. The new wine must be kept also in new bottles; and not only to forgive, but even to "be pitiful" and "courteous" in so doing, becomes the pardoned debtor towards his fellow-servant. No wonder that work carried on in a wrong spirit miscarries; that children are often alienated, that men and women learn zeal rather than love, and that all in the end leads to no higher or better results, than those which Jehonadab witnessed when in company with Jehu.

There is yet another lesson at which, indeed, we have already hinted. Let us avoid the terrible mistake of Jehonadab in joining his religion to that of Jehu. The two have nothing in common. The only object of Jehu could be to make use of Jehonadab; and Jehonadab will return from him saddened in heart. Let us not imagine that we can cultivate personal religion in company with a Jehu; nor yet desire to witness his "zeal for Jehovah." The temptations to it will be many and strong. It is something for a Jehonadab to ride by the side of a Jehu—and to see the public vindication of principles by those in authority and power. But our principles need not, and they cannot, be so vindicated. God can use a Jehu, we cannot. He can arrest, we cannot cope with him. Our principles are not so asserted, and only our carnal zeal, though in a good cause, can be gratified. Never let us identify ourselves in a religious cause with men in whose spirituality we have not the fullest confidence. They may defend the truth which we cherish, but we must learn not to say "a confederacy, a confederacy," even where many around are glad to hail it. "Be ye not unequally yoked together with unbelievers, for what fellowship hath righteousness with unrighteousness?" It is wrong to argue that we may avail ourselves of the help of any one. Only to a very limited extent—certainly not so as to identify ourselves with them in a religious cause. God employs every instrumentality, and all will praise Him—"dragons and all deeps; fire and hail; snow and vapours; stormy wind fulfilling His word." God uses all as His instruments, but we may not have them as our associates, least of all in His work.

What Jehonadab, the son of Rechab, saw on that day in Samaria, when the vast temple of Baal was filled in every corner, and how it had been brought about, need not be repeated in this place. "But Jehu took no heed to walk in the law of Jehovah, God of Israel, with all his heart: for he departed not from the sins of Jeroboam, which made Israel to sin." And when at last the zealous Arab turned him from Samaria, to leave its deceptions and disappointments behind him, and again to tread more lightly a soil unpolluted by hypocrisy and bloodshed, it must have been with saddened heart and sorrowing, yet with stern determination that neither he nor his descendants should ever again be joined in such alliances. And may it not perhaps have been in perpetual memorial of this, and in perpetual warning of it, that the Kenites, who had hitherto "dwelt at Jabez" (1 Chron. ii. 55), received it in perpetual law from Jonadab, the son of Rechab (Jer. xxxv. 6, 7), to "drink no wine," not to mingle in social fellowship, neither to "build house, nor sow seed, nor plant vineyard, nor have any;" but all their days to "dwell in tents," that they might "live many days in the land," yet always as "strangers" therein?

CHAPTER XXIX.

THE LAST INTERVIEW.

> "Now Elisha was fallen sick of his sickness whereof he died. And Joash the king of Israel came down unto him, and wept over his face, and said, O my father, my father, the chariot of Israel, and the horsemen thereof. And Elisha said unto him, Take bow and arrows. And he took unto him bow and arrows. And he said to the king of Israel, Put thine hand upon the bow. And he put his hand upon it: and Elisha put his hands upon the king's hands. And he said, Open the window eastward. And he opened it. Then Elisha said, Shoot. And he shot. And he said, The arrow of the Lord's deliverance, and the arrow of deliverance from Syria: for thou shalt smite the Syrians in Aphek, till thou have consumed them. And he said, Take the arrows. And he took them. And he said unto the king of Israel, Smite upon the ground. And he smote thrice, and stayed. And the man of God was wroth with him, and said, Thou shouldest have smitten five or six times; then hadst thou smitten Syria till thou hadst consumed it: whereas now thou shalt smite Syria but thrice."—2 KINGS xiii. 14-19.

A LONG time had elapsed since the events recorded in the last chapter. Jehu had reigned over Israel twenty and eight years. During his rule, Hazael of Syria possessed himself of the portion of Israel which lay to the east of the Jordan (x. 33). Jehu was succeeded by Jehoahaz, his son, whose reign lasted seventeen years. More troublous times were they than even those which had preceded. Ben-hadad, the son of Hazael, now also held a considerable portion of the territory west of the Jordan (xiv. 25), and so reduced was Israel, that of his whole army King Jehoahaz had left him only "fifty horsemen, ten chariots, and ten thousand footmen" (xiii. 7). Yet one unvarying characteristic marked the reign of the two kings of Israel. They both "did that which was evil in the sight of Jehovah, and followed the sins of Jeroboam." At last the increasing calamities which befell his reign, led Jehoahaz to "beseech Jehovah." In mercy and compassion to His people, and in remembrance of His covenant with the fathers, the Lord hearkened, and delayed his final judgments. He "gave Israel a saviour" in the person of Joash, the son of Jehoahaz, who three times defeated Ben-hadad, and re-took the cities west of the Jordan, which his father had lost (2 Kings xiii. 22-25). Thus the Lord, in His goodness, is easily entreated, even of those who have long sinned against Him, and in long-suffering delays to execute punishment.

But for at least these forty-five years, from the accession of Jehu to that of Joash, the history of Elisha presents a blank. His ministry to Israel as a nation had ceased, and even his more private ministrations during that long period remain unnoticed and unknown. And if an Elisha was content for well nigh half a century to labour in obscurity, why should we despond, when outward tokens of success and visible results are denied us? It is a good work in which we are engaged; it is the work of the Lord. We labour in hope, we sow in faith; the Lord will have the reaping, and safely garner it all. Paul, Apollos, and Cephas are only ministers, only servants. The Kingdom is His, and to Him Who is the King will we raise our hearts and hopes.

So this half-century of ministry had absolutely nothing in it worth recording for the Church on earth, till the time of Elisha's sickness and death. Yet such a life could not close without some final testimony to its power and great object. If not otherwise, God may own us on our death-beds. The testimony of a life shall be sealed in death. Little do they know, who wonder at the afflictions of God's people, what precious lessons have been learned, what mighty sermons have been preached in sick rooms and on death-beds. The letting down through the roof of the bed which bore the poor paralytic, laying him at the feet of Jesus, was itself a testimony more powerful than many a long life.

A reverent awe creeps over us, as we enter the sick-chamber of the old prophet. Here lies, with laboured breath, with feeble arm, and heavy hand, the man who once restored the dead to life, and so often poured forth words of fire which had kindled all Israel! There is something sacred, even to natural feeling, in the sick-chamber and at the dying bed; life and death contending over the prostrate form, time and eternity meeting. He who lies there is soon not to be of us. The light of another world, bursting through the mists of earth, will soon disclose to him the meaning of all the mysteries around. And to stand by the dying bed of a faithful minister, of an honoured servant of the Lord—how solemn, yet how saddening! The experience of the past will not fail him in the future; what he has spoken and done he shall hear and enjoy; and much more than that, more than heart can conceive, or has ever entered the thoughts of man. Yet we shall hear that voice no more on earth, nor see the play of sacred emotions on the loved face, nor be guided by his counsel, nor helped by his example, nor cheered by his presence. All that once we knew so strong, is now so weak; but even in such weakness God's strength is made perfect.

Not like Elijah with fiery chariot and horsemen, was he to be removed, who had the double portion of his spirit. After long and weary toil, he must pass weary and alone through the valley of the shadow of death. No miracle here for Elisha; no visible sign for the onlookers. But the same God "takes" both unto Himself. With both also, the last thoughts on earth clustered around their life-work. Elijah's latest act was one of faith and power, when he divided the waters of Jordan. Elisha's also shall be one of faith and power, when his trembling hands shall give strength and bring blessing ere they stiffen in death. Yet, after all, it was not Elisha but Elisha's God; and the deliverance was in answer to the prayers of Jehoahaz, although by the instrumentality of the prophet. And so it ever is. The blessing comes from God, comes in answer to prayer, though, it may be, by the instrumentality of His servants.

A visitor, more noble even than Naaman, had arrived at the humble abode of the dying prophet. It was Joash, the youthful king of Israel. And what had brought him there, who also " did that which was evil in the sight of Jehovah," nor " departed from all the sins of Jeroboam " ? No sooner was he admitted into the sick-chamber, and had fastened his gaze upon Elisha, than he bent over him and burst into passionate grief. " O, my father, my father, the chariot of Israel, and the horsemen thereof ! " The tears and the words of Joash were not those of hypocrisy. The young king was thoroughly in earnest, alike in his grief and in his concern. All the more, that he knew not the God of Israel, and trusted not in Him, would he dread the removal of one whom he regarded as a "father" that could give counsel and help, who to his mind seemed really " the chariot of Israel, and the horsemen thereof." So the son, who has most neglected the guidance of his father, most feels and mourns his loss; so we most mourn the lost blessings which we have left unheeded while within our reach ; so shall some look back in helpless anguish on that mercy which has for ever receded from their grasp. Strange, that mostly we only realise our blessings when for ever we have lost them—except, where grace has opened the heart, that grace may pour into the empty recesses its richest treasures, and when with life it has given the enjoyment of that life, and of all else besides.

" The chariot of Israel, and the horsemen thereof ! " Once more Elisha now stood in imagination by the banks of Jordan ; once more he saw that vision of Jehovah ; once more, floating on the breeze, came down to him the prophet's mantle ! It was a blessed remembrance for a dying prophet ;

it was a blessed light to shine in the dark valley; a blessed hope also with which to quit earth and its labours. Yes—
"the chariot of Israel, and the horsemen thereof!" Jehovah liveth and reigneth still, and for ever. But far different was its meaning to the young idolatrous king, who, never having seen the fiery vision, identified that chariot and those horsemen with the person of Elisha, and now wept at the approaching departure of Israel's help. It was not so. The dying Elisha would show him that it was not so. By this vision would he strengthen himself; in one last act would he sum up his whole life of faith, and with his latest breath, repeat his first confession of faith. And so shall Joash, if possible, be taught. So shall the power of the Lord be magnified. So shall the prayer of Jehoahaz be answered. So shall the compassion of the Lord towards Israel be shown. So shall the faith of the dying Elisha be owned. Such and much more is the wondrous concurrence of objects attained when God's purpose is carried out in the course of His Providence.

While thus Joash had employed what in reality was to him a phrase without proper meaning, it had struck a chord in the heart of Elisha which must have wakened memories the most blessed and suitable to his wants. So sometimes a word spoken even by ungodly men has served to awaken sinners, and to bring comfort to believers. But let us beware how we use religious phrases without realising their meaning. Few sins so harden the heart as hypocrisy; and among the causes which impoverish the soul, we place in the foremost rank the indiscriminate use of religious phraseology. How often, in speaking to the conscience, are we met and silenced by religious platitudes. Again, some people seem to regard it as needful to have religious conversation, not, indeed, from love nor yet under the pressure of a full heart, but from religious conventionality, or as what is little better than religious gossip. A practice more hurtful or impoverishing to the soul can scarcely be imagined. We ought indeed to be always in the spirit; but there is serious danger of making that which is holy profane, and that which is full of richest meaning trite by its indiscriminate use. Let our conversation never outrun our present experience; nor let us drain the last drop of oil from our lamps. Revival of religion had better be sought in converse with God than in talk with man.

It is most comforting to mark, how in infinite condescension the Lord meets the first appearance of repentance on the part of men. We are too prone to cherish harsh thoughts, or to limit the Almighty. Never was there a genuine desire, however weak, never a prayer, however faltering, never a tear of anxiety, nor an upraised look, but grace went forth to meet it. The Ear of the Lord is ever open to every cry. Even though it were not yet truly Evangelical repentance, if there be any tendency heavenward, there is that on the part of God which meets and encourages it. If only men continued to wait upon the Lord, how many buds, killed by the storm, would have opened into blossom and ripened into precious fruit! Who knows but that first inward cry may be the voice of the Spirit? Who knows but that the tears of a Joash over the dying prophet may in due time give place to joy in the Living God? For, all tendency to what is good is of the Holy Spirit, though, alas, all do not seek nor receive His special grace.

Elisha had not witnessed unmoved the sorrow of the king. He now directed him to make ready the bow. Joash obeyed, and the prophet laying his hand upon that of the monarch, thereby consecrated to God the work about to be done. And now it must be successful, even though the arrow shot through the opened lattice eastwards, towards Syria, seemed to rush only into empty air. This also is the meaning of our consecration to the ministry, even our solemn appointment by God to do His work through those so appointed themselves, and the solemn consecration of that work unto God. It is, so to speak, the historical Church, reaching up to Jesus Christ, in the persons of His representatives, and in the name of God giving solemn commission, consecrating an individual to the service of God, and repeating over him the historical blessing, which here and ever has its fullest meaning : " Lo, I am with you alway, even unto the end of the world." And then, if we are not only outwardly, but inwardly and spiritually also, rightly called, we must open the window, and though we seem to speed the arrow only into mid-air, it flies eastwards, towards Syria, and it is "the arrow of Jehovah's deliverance, and the arrow of deliverance from Syria."

Joash had obeyed; and once more came the prophet's command to test whether the young king had really learned to believe. " Take the arrows ; " and the king took them. " Smite upon the ground." The direction seemed mysterious. What could be the object of taking arrows from the quiver and shooting them out of the window towards the ground? Besides, the circumstances were now different from what they had been. When first the king had been directed to shoot, it had been towards the east, and Elisha had first laid his hand in blessing upon those of Joash. Now that this visible help was withdrawn, the king hesitated. In fact, the views of Joash were similar to those of Naaman, when he expected healing only if the prophet came out, and calling upon the name of Jehovah would strike his hand over the place. So long as the hand of Elisha was upon those of the king, he would unhesitatingly draw the bow. But as Naaman, before his heart was influenced by Divine grace, turned away from the simple direction of faith, and from personal contact with the Lord, so Joash on this occasion. Among us also, too many depend for their religion on the presence of an Elisha. So long as they are in the company of religious men, or under their influence, they continue stedfast. But no sooner is this visible support withdrawn, and they called upon to go forth for themselves, in simple faith and dependence upon the Lord, than their artificial religion gives way. It would be a painfully interesting inquiry, how many of those who now make fair profession of religion would continue stedfast under other and adverse circumstances, when restraining or hallowing influences were withdrawn, and when, deprived of such outward help, a man must by grace learn himself to draw the bow at the command of the Lord. And are not even Christians too often dependent upon man? Many pious practices would be neglected or discontinued under adverse circumstances. And may not this also be among the reasons for the early withdrawal of eminent servants of the Lord, and for other afflictive providences, that so our faith and hope may be placed in Him alone? For all true religion is derived from God Himself, and depends for its nurture and manifestation upon His grace. This holds ever true: "Flesh and blood hath not revealed it unto thee, but My Father Which is in heaven."

Thus it came that Joash, neither feeling the prophet's hand upon his, nor understanding the object of shooting towards the ground, yielded a reluctant assent. Thrice he took an arrow from the quiver, and thrice he drew the bow. Then seeing no result from it, "he stayed," although the quiver was not empty. But by this unbelief "he stayed" the blessing also. And this is still too often the case. We know that prayer is always answered; that faith can never be disappointed. At the command of God we go forward; we pray, we act. We shoot the arrow once, twice, thrice! Always it is seemingly directed only to the ground. And then we "stay:" we become faint, we grow weary in our asking. We do not trust ourselves fully to what we believe; we do not quite commit ourselves to it; we go so far, but not all the way. We shoot not every arrow in our quiver, but only a few, and so by our unbelief the blessing is stayed. Yet even thus the Lord gives according to our faith. Thrice shall Syria be smitten. Had it only been otherwise, had we " smitten five or six times," we had smitten Syria till we had consumed it. Perfect success would then have attended our work; a perfect blessing descended upon our childlike trustfulness and obedience.

But in that solemn hour of death and parting Elisha was not guilty of weak compromise. Once more he had sought to bring deliverance to the kings of Israel, and in dying to teach them how to live. Once more he had failed. "And the man of God was wroth" with Joash. How different from the weak and unmeaning compromises of which even good men are too often guilty! Oh, that we could ever keep before us, in dealing with others, on the one hand, the love and pity of Jesus, but on the other also the dread day of realities, and the account which each must give of his opportunities for service, and of the use he has made them!

The old prophet departed in peace. The long and toilsome journey was over. His last, as his first act, had been one of testimony for God; his last, as his first mission, one of mercy towards Israel. Angels bore him upwards. Yet, as though to prove that the Lord God of Elisha still liveth, while clouds and darkness thickened round the history of Israel, it *was* according to the word of Jehovah. "And Jehoash, the son of Jehoahaz, took again out of the hand of Ben-hadad, the son of Hazael, the cities, which he had taken out of the hand of Jehoahaz, his father, by war. Three times did Joash beat him, and recovered the cities of Israel."

CHAPTER XXX.

"HE, BEING DEAD, YET SPEAKETH."

"And Elisha died, and they buried him. And the bands of the Moabites invaded the land at the coming in of the year. And it came to pass, as they were burying a man, that, behold, they spied a band of men; and they cast the man into the sepulchre of Elisha: and when the man was let down, and touched the bones of Elisha, he revived, and stood up on his feet."—2 KINGS xiii. 20, 21.

WHO that in life has ever spoken to his fellow-men, by word or by deed, is silent in death, and after death? For good or for evil, he still speaketh. In a sense, even that part of our life which has been spent on earth is immortal, like the soul which gave to that life its character. At least, it endureth so long as anything upon earth endureth. Nothing around us ever perisheth, it only lives in other forms; the flower, the leaf, the dust—all are imperishable. No movement ever wholly dies out. Every life, even the humblest, has its influences; some known, most unseen, and perhaps unfelt, but all real and lasting. And so we continue to live upon earth, and to speak, long after we have ceased to live, and our lips have been sealed in death. What solemn import does this give to every action, that its influence must for ever continue, not only so far as we, but so far as others also are concerned. In blessing or in cursing, in brightness or in guilt, for God or for Satan, even the lowliest life endureth. The sin and shame, or else the purity and faith, of the past, sow their seed in the present, and our earth ripens its harvest, to be reaped at last by the heavenly mowers. And so, while for the present we may "rest," each shall "stand in his *lot at the end of the days.*"

That which Elisha had spoken, both living and dying, he yet spake "being dead." It was: that the Lord God of Israel reigneth, that He is the Living and the True God. This was the meaning of his first exclamation, when entering on the prophetic office; this was the object of his mission, and the bearing of all his prophetic deeds; and this was the lesson of his last interview with Joash. The prophet might depart; the God of the prophet remained. Whether the prophet were present or absent, the power and grace which he represented would continue. And when, as we are told in this narrative, a dead body, hastily thrown upon the bones of Elisha, was restored to life by the contact, it would remind all men of what Elisha had said and done, and of Elisha's God; and so he, being dead, yet spake.

It is strange, how ofttimes the end of our lives resembles their beginning. Thoughts of childhood, and of first opening purpose, gather around us with the shadows of evening, and when we stammer our last farewell to life, we often speak it in the long-forgotten language which first we had learned. It almost seems as if the curving lines were to bend into a circle, and thus beginning and end to meet. The first public act of Elisha was in connection with Moab, and at the last these sons of the desert again came as witnesses around his grave. From the first, Elisha was a type of the Lord Jesus Christ, as Elijah had been of His precursor, and at the last he appears to foreshadow, in his grave, the power of that empty tomb in which Jesus had lain, and the reality of that life and resurrection which have sprung from it. And so this miracle of deed, seemingly the last wrought in Israel, stood out as a finger-post, pointing forward, through many centuries, to Him Who was to come, and to that greatest miracle of deed, in which all former miracles were to be summed up and fulfilled.

Elisha had died, and, as tradition informs us, been buried with great demonstrations of reverence. For, in all centuries men have loved to build the sepulchres of the prophets, whose living word they, as well as the men of the former generation, rejected. It seems not only an act of justice to the dead, but to mark our own advance on those who had failed to understand departed worth, thus gratifying both to our self-consciousness and to our self-righteousness. As if in the higher sense these men had departed, and as if our resistance to their testimony gave not the lie to the hypocrisy of our pretensions! Thus some of the historical philosophers of our days profess to have made discovery of "the mission" of the Reformers, of the great and earnest men of old, of a Wesley or a Whitfield—some higher mission to which these men, if they were upon earth, would certainly feel themselves strangers—while they still obstinately reject that which had been their conscious object in life. Would the Apostles be more readily listened to, if they reappeared on the spot to which the tradition of their last resting-place attracts thousands of ignorant worshippers? Would their words be heard where their letters are not even allowed to be read? Or would Wesley and Whitfield be received in the simplicity of their Evangelical faith, and with the burning ardour of their earnestness, by many of those who deplore the coldness which drove them from the sacred edifices to the fields and the wayside? Truth is ever the same, and the most satisfactory test of our appreciation of that which was in the past lies in our reception of that which is offered in the present.

They had probably placed the honoured remains of Elisha in the niche of some rock-hewn vault, not coffining them in, as our practice is, to make the narrow bed a narrower prison, but laying them as in rest on a bier, and rolling a large stone before the entrance, or closing a door upon it. Winter had passed, and many feet had entered and left that grave-yard. And now a fresh green mantled it again, and unplanted flowers, sown by an unseen Hand, were springing. They are ever the sweetest tokens of remembrance—not of man's, but of God's remembrance of the earth, quite as symbolical as those thistles and thorns which mark its curse. Yet they were days of sore calamity to Israel. For although the Syrians were reduced, the land now lay open to other enemies. As the narrative bears, marauding bands of Moabites, wild Arabs from their desert homes across Jordan, swooped like birds of prey over the land, and swept before them every green thing and every living thing. Their terror had fallen upon the unarmed, unresisting people, who at their approach precipitately fled, preferring to leave their all rather than encounter such enemies.

It was spring-time; as always, a spring-time of sorrow as well as of joy. They carried one to his last resting-place. Sadly the procession moved to the grave-yard; the same where Elisha lay. How many sorrowing hearts in that assembly which would refuse to be comforted! Yet how near is sometimes deliverance, travelling on swift wing, when least it is expected. A rude disturbance threatened to put an end to the last sacred rites of affection and friendship. The rays of the sun were revealing what in the distance might seem a fast-moving cloud. But these rays were soon reflected from the poised lances of a troop of Moabites, rapidly bearing down upon the company of mourners. There was no time for deliberation; present danger banished thoughts of past sorrow. The great stone was rolled away from the nearest vault; and the body hastily laid in the niche, upon bones already there deposited. Then, both they who had come to bury and they who mourned, fled from the Moabites. No one remained to look into the tomb where they had laid the dead man. If they had stayed but a few moments, not even the fear of Moab would have driven them from the spot. For it had been the vault of Elisha, and oh, wonder of wonders, "when the man was let down, and touched the bones of Elisha, he revived, and stood up on his feet." The Moabites had come and were gone; the man, restored to life, yet bearing the vestments of death, had returned from the grave-yard; and, having been dead, yet spake of Elisha, of Elisha's God, of the Resurrection and of the Life; spake to the men of his generation; to those who lived and died after him; speaks to us, and will speak till He cometh, Who is the Resurrection and the Life. Truly a miracle this, the greatest as the last connected with the history of Elisha.

And what are the final lessons of this event, and, with it, of the whole history of Elisha, of which it may be regarded as the appropriate conclusion?

1. It was a Divine acknowledgment of, and a testimony to, Elisha's past life. If Elijah had been owned in dying, Elisha was yet more publicly acknowledged after his death. God put His seal to that life, and publicly showed before Moab and before Israel that it had been a true life. Nothing in it was to be lost. Even after death the lessons of that life were to continue. And nothing in a true, Christian, spiritual life shall be lost. God will give testimony to it. Though contradicted, opposed, and disregarded by men, such lives are treasured by the Lord. "And they shall be Mine, saith the Lord of hosts, in the day when I make up My jewels." How wonderful, that all our lives, who are sinners, may become such; how precious is sovereign grace that first makes, and then owns them as His; that first gives, and then

crowns its own gift. And how noble such lives, which never end in the blessing which they bring. What higher ambition than to desire, what greater joy than to possess, such life! Who would bed himself in the dust that could rise to heaven; who would live to self, the meanest, most sordid, and most wretched life, that could live in God; who would bring death to others, that might bear life to all around?

2. What passed in the vault of Elisha was also a Divine confirmation of his teaching. God leaves not Himself without a witness. Often, in the past history of the Church, have the dead bodies of His saints borne witness to Him, that He is indeed the Living and the True God. Stronger testimony to the truth and reality of Christ's Resurrection could not have been given than that of the early martyrs. A more emphatic confirmation of the doctrines of the Gospel cannot be afforded than by those who, in all ages, have suffered for them, and by those who, in our own days, are ready to endure affliction, persecution, scorn, and the loss of all things for the sake of Jesus. And the Lord has owned the teaching of His dead saints. From their graves living men have come forth. Their words and themselves were holy seed that has sprung unto life eternal. Not every one is called to be a preacher by word. But we all may, and ought to be, preachers by deed. A life that teaches how to live, and how to die, yet so as not to die, is a useful, noble life. All the more, if it has been spent in circumstances untoward, and where such teaching has been difficult. And God will give testimony to all such teaching. Who knows how, in the secret working of men's hearts, the conscience may have been reproved, or doubts removed, or encouragement felt, or example taken from the lessons of grace, so embodied in a life? And long after the turf has grown green over our graves may some dead soul, brought into contact with us, spring into new life,

and so God give testimony to what our words and our life had spoken, "that there is no God in all the earth, but in Israel."

3. For, if our life have any object, our teaching any meaning, it is to point to Jesus our Blessed Saviour. That was what we had learned and lived ourselves; and that is what we would teach and show forth to others. He is the Way, the Truth, and the Life; in Him is all. There the Father reveals Himself; there we have access to the Father; there we are adopted as His children. Christ is the sum of all we would know, feel, say, and do. It was Elisha's special honour to be a type of Christ, and another lesson which we learn from the last miracle in his history is in confirmation of this fact. Viewed as an individual, Elisha was a man subject to the same infirmities, liable to the same death as his contemporaries. Viewed as "the Master," unarmed he was mightier than the hosts of Syria, defenceless stronger than they, able to help in all difficulties, to bring relief in every affliction, and to triumph over all opposition, nay, even to break the bands of death. So the man Elisha "died and was buried," and his bones lay blanching in that vault. But as he was a type of Christ in life, so was he also in death. As by the grave of Elisha Moab and Israel met, and the dead man brought into contact with him lived anew, so around the tomb of Jesus, under His Cross gather Jew and Gentile, and whatever dead soul is brought into contact with Him lives. The death of Christ is our life, and to all ages this type brings before men the great reality, how in His dying He purchased our life, how personal contact with the death of Christ is needful, and how, "buried with Him," we shall rise with Him to newness of life.

Lastly, it taught all Israel, and was evidence to them, that death itself had not permanent sway, but would be swallowed up in victory, and so it became a prophetic representation of the Resurrection. Under the Old Testament such a lesson was specially necessary, for it was a preparatory dispensation, in which clear teaching on such a subject would have been inappropriate, as indeed it would have proved unintelligible. But here all men saw clearly in prophetic vision that death was not a conqueror but conquered; that its grasp was not so tight but it might be loosened, nor its sway so absolute but it might be cast off. When the dead man touched the bones of Elisha, he revived and stood upon his feet. So life had not been annihilated, only removed to another sphere; so this man's body was capable of being restored to life! And all this by contact with "the Master." And thus would the people learn that God was not the God of the dead, but of the living; that life to the dead would spring from the grave of Him Whose type Elisha was; that He would be the Resurrection and the Life, in Whom all types would be realised, and by Whom all prophecies would be fulfilled.

Above all, it would stand forth as the miracle of miracles, the highest point which Israel had attained, and from which farthest view might be got into the distant, glorious future. The last and the greatest miracle, the last and the fullest type of mercy in the history of Israel, it remained alone through succeeding centuries, until its meaning was fully explained by the Resurrection of Christ from the dead. Yet even before that, was it to Israel a constant testimony for God, for the Saviour, for the power of faith, for the victory over death. To us also it declares the same truths; and as we look upon it in times which so closely resemble those of Elisha, and the vision of the tomb in which the prophet lay seems blended with that of the empty tomb in which the Lord lay—comparing and contrasting these two tombs of the type and the Antitype, of the servant and the Master, of the man of God and the God-man, of the prophet and the Saviour—it stands out before us also as a waymark in the history of the Covenant, on which the inscription points us forward to that glorious future, when all of joyous Christian hope shall be so richly fulfilled. Then "Thy dead men shall live; together with my dead body shall they arise. Awake and sing, ye that dwell in dust: for thy dew is as the dew of herbs, and the earth shall cast out the dead."

And so to us also, and to all ages, till He cometh, in this last and greatest miracle:

"He, being dead, yet speaketh."

www.ingramcontent.com/pod-product-compliance
Lightning Source LLC
Chambersburg PA
CBHW071230230426
43668CB00011B/1373